Chantry Westwell

Maidens
OR MONSTERS?

Tales of Amazons, Goddesses, Queens & Temptresses in Medieval Manuscripts

University of Washington Press
Seattle

Dedication

To my family

Published in North America by
University of Washington Press
uwapress.uw.edu

Published in the UK by
The British Library

Illustrations from the British Library collections except for
the following: p. 195 and p. 321 Bibliothèque nationale de
France; p. 295 Musée Condé, Chantilly/Bridgeman Images

Cataloging in Publication Data
A catalog record for this publication is available from the
Library of Congress

ISBN 9780295753546

Design and typesetting by Georgina Hewitt
Printed and bound in the Czech Republic by Finidr

Contents

Tragic Heroines

Partners and Lovers

Mystical, Magical
and Allegorical Women

Acknowledgements

I am most grateful to my editor Alison Moss, whose vision and experience have been invaluable in the production of this book. Her patience and advice over cups of tea in the staff restaurant at the British Library kept me on track when I might have veered off course or become discouraged. In addition, huge thanks goes to Calum Cockburn and Jonathon Vines, who worked under pressure and in trying circumstances to ensure that all the many images required were available and of exceptional quality; they were helped by Virginia Mazzocato. Calum has given encouragement and expert advice throughout. Georgina Hewitt has once again done a wonderful job on the design of this book, supported by colleagues in British Library Publishing, including Sally Nicholls who arranged the sourcing of images. And a big thank you to Carolyn Jones for her expert copy editing, helpful suggestions and attention to detail. Furthermore, I am grateful to John Lee for the initial concept and for seeing this project through a somewhat challenging process. Additional thanks to Ursula Sims-Williams and Rob Williams for their helpful suggestions on the Persian and Arabic material.

I have used reasonable endeavours to verify the truthfulness of any statement made; any errors are my own.

Thank you as ever to my husband Stephen and family for your support and encouragement over the past year and more. Especial thanks go to George for helpful suggestions on a number of chapters and to Ella, whose expert opinion has been invaluable.

Au chief du mois ma maistresse
Pour qui viuoye a destresse
Conuint partir du manoir
Deuant dit et plus manoir
N y pot si sen deppuy
Sont moult fust en dur party

Introduction
Women in Medieval Legends: Challenging Attitudes

The names Guinevere, Mary Magdalene and Helen of Troy may be familiar to today's readers, while Melusine, Penthesilea and Shirin are probably less well known. They are all female characters who were popular in the Middle Ages and in this book I explore how they were portrayed in both words and images in medieval manuscripts. Manuscripts are the handwritten books that were copied and illustrated in the period between AD 800 and 1600; most of the works featured in this book are from the British Library's collection of Western European manuscripts, but there are notable examples from Eastern Europe, Asia and Africa. These are priceless objects of great beauty, as fascinating today as they were when they were first made, both for their contents and for the exquisite images that are preserved within the pages. Just as we go to see our favourite characters portrayed on screen, those who were wealthy enough to have access to books in the Middle Ages must have enjoyed looking at scenes from the stories they knew, as they were imagined by contemporary artists.

Anyone who has read or listened to stories, and there are few who have not, will know that the same themes recur in a wide variety of literary traditions across world cultures. The quest, forbidden love, the battle between right and wrong (and so on) are plots that have been reimagined many times by poets and

1 A courtly lady with her entourage, in the *Book of the Queen*, a collection of works by Christine de Pisan (Paris, *c*.1410) Harley MS 4431, f. 153r.

2a (left) Eve is tempted by a female serpent, in *Speculum humanae salvationis* ('Mirror of Human Salvation') (Germany, mid-14th century) Harley MS 4996, f. 4v.

2b (right) Virgin of the Annunciation, in the Book of Hours of Henry VII (France, *c.*1500) Add MS 35254, f. Vr.

writers. This is true of the earliest classical epics, of medieval legends and saints' lives, of the great nineteenth-century novels, and of popular TV series today. Moreover, in the retelling of old stories and in the invention of new ones, the characters and themes have been adapted to reflect the hopes, fears, prejudices and tastes of the society in which and for which they were recorded.

Throughout history men have dominated the spheres of education and power, so most storytellers were male, and men have tended to drive events both in the real and the fantasy world. Nevertheless, our legends are and always have been filled with extraordinary female characters, from Eve in the Book of Genesis to the Queen of Sheba and – at the time of writing – Barbie, on whom the 2023 film was based. These are women who have made things happen and continue to do so, despite their traditionally restricted roles and regardless of the consequences. The historian Natalie Haynes in *Pandora's Jar*, a revisional work on women in classical literature, points out that of the eight surviving plays written about the Trojan War by Euripides over two thousand years ago, only one is named after a male character, *Orestes*. The others are named for women (*Andromache, Electra* and so on).[1] In the Middle Ages, some of the most popular stories were about female saints, classical heroines and contemporary female protagonists; and each chapter of this book focuses on one of these.

3 A haughty Olympias giving instructions to her women, in *Roman d'Alexandre en Prose* ('Prose Alexander Romance') (Paris, *c.*1420) Royal MS 20 B XX, f. 7r.

The portrayal of female characters in fiction tends to conform to the prevailing views of women and their place in society at the time of writing. In the ancient and medieval world, these views differed widely from the attitudes of the twenty-first century, where women have freedoms that were previously unimaginable. During the classical era and in medieval and early modern societies, powerful and politically active women were problematic for the (mostly) male authors who recorded their stories. Stereotypes from Greek and Roman legend were adopted by medieval writers, and to these was added the Christian ideal of the pure, chaste, Madonna-like persona promoted by the all-powerful Catholic Church. In Persian literature women might represent the goal of a spiritual quest, unattainable and perfect, though still unable to challenge the rules of their religion and community. Women in the past were expected to confine themselves to the domestic world, and if they wished to influence public events they were required to do so indirectly so as not to be seen as invading male-dominated spheres. And there were double standards; male acts of violence and brutality were portrayed as great achievements if they were considered as politically necessary (even the idealised King Arthur and his knights shed the blood of countless enemies), but any violent deeds by women, no matter how insignificant, attracted moralising judgement. Literature and historical fiction are full of unlikeable male characters who are treated as complex, flawed individuals deserving respect for their achievements on the world stage, but women tend to fall into two categories: conniving seductress or sweet, selfless martyr. Eve and the Virgin Mary are the most famous examples of this dichotomy in medieval Christian literature.

Elizabeth Carney, in her study of Olympias, the mother of Alexander the Great, explores the 'unstated presumption that women should/ought to be/are nicer, kinder than men'. She concludes that when men commit atrocities (Alexander, for example, destroyed whole cities and caused many thousands of deaths) they are assumed to be doing so 'for rational reasons, out of Realpolitik', whereas the implication is that women act out of personal passion. They are 'simply vengeful'.[2] After Alexander's death, when Olympias moved to protect her grandson in the chaos of competing claims to his empire, she was portrayed as violent, manipulative and irrational for having allegedly ordered the murder of rivals. This version of events, recorded in the early histories of the Hellenistic period, has persisted to this day. Sadly, nothing that Olympias said or wrote has come down to us directly; it is filtered through the male Greek and Christian historians and chroniclers who distorted her story to serve their goals. And so she remains a controversial figure.

Cleopatra – arguably the most famous woman of the ancient world – became the subject of legend shortly after her death. She provides a potent example of the judgemental attitude towards women at the time; her life story was deliberately distorted in Roman accounts to serve the propaganda goals of the Romans in the Augustan era. Her character was reimagined by subsequent authors and historians and she has been portrayed as an exotic temptress, a woman who challenged the patriarchal order and ultimately lost catastrophically. As moves to subordinate women within the domestic sphere gained influence in the later Middle Ages and Renaissance, Cleopatra's story came to focus on her personal appearance and her relationship with Mark Antony rather than her role as ruler of the Egyptians. In illuminated manuscripts she is most often pictured beside the dying Antony, holding snakes to her bare breasts in an erotic pose (Image 4), and Shakespeare described her 'infinite variety' as making men hungry for more. Fast-forward to the films of the 1930s and 1960s, where the languid, heavily made-up character portrayed first by Claudette Colbert, then by Elizabeth Taylor, fed into the popular view, promoted by advertising companies, of women as 'dreamers and shoppers'.[3]

Heroines of medieval romance, perhaps most famously Guinevere, are no more exempt from harsh judgements than their classical predecessors. Arthur's queen, like Cleopatra, is portrayed as the beautiful temptress who

4 Cleopatra, naked to the waist, holds two asps to her bare nipples, while Mark Antony plunges a sword into his chest, in Boccaccio, *De casibus virorum illustrium* ('On the Fates of Famous Men') in French (Bruges, c.1480) Royal MS 14 E V, f. 339r.

caused the downfall of Camelot and the end of the 'perfect' society envisioned by her husband. But in much of the story she is a mere pawn with little agency: she is married off to Arthur by her father, languishes at court while Lancelot and his companions ride off on their adventures, is abducted several times and is rejected by her husband for a period in favour of the 'false Guinevere'. The powerful ego of Lancelot, Arthur's ambitions of conquest, and the evil machinations of Mordred notwithstanding, she is ultimately blamed for causing the rift between the Knights of the Round Table that leads to the final battle in which the king and his dreams perish.

5 A distressed Guinevere watches as Lancelot and knights commit violent acts, in *Lancelot du Lac* (N. France, c.1325) Royal MS 20 D IV, f. 260.

Women in Persian epic poetry of the twelfth century and beyond experience the longings of love; they are often destined to wait for their respective lovers for long periods before they can be together. While the male characters go off on quests and overcome evil, they are confined to gardens and palaces under the watchful eye of their women. Though Humayun and Shirin are less passive than some (they manage to escape and ride off in search of their lovers), their lives remain subject to the laws of religion and community imposed by male figures of authority. In *Layla and Majnun* (Image 6) Layla does not have the luxury of proclaiming her love to everyone in poetry, nor of roaming wildly in the desert like her lover Majnun (or indeed the Christian saints in Chapter 7). She must wait, pine in solitude and finally die unfulfilled. Nizami, who composed the well-known poetic legends about both Layla and Shirin, has been praised for his sympathy towards his female characters, but they do not have the same agency as their lovers, Majnun and Khusraw (Chapter 23).

It falls to Chaucer's bawdy, well-loved female character, Alison the Wife of Bath, to confront these prejudiced medieval views head on. She is the very antithesis of virtuous womanhood, and proud of it. The prologue to her tale in *The Canterbury Tales* ends with her fifth husband, Jankyn – who is determined not to be hen-pecked, as were her previous husbands – reading to her from his favourite collection of tales, the 'Book of wikked wyves'. Before long Alison has had enough of this litany of women who reputedly caused the downfall of worthy men. She describes her violent reaction in the following passage.

6 Majnun is brought to Layla's tent, in Nizami, *Layla and Majnun* (Tabriz, *c.* 1540) Or MS 2265, f. 157v.

And whan that I saugh he wolde nevere fyne	And when I saw he would never finish
To reden in thus cursed book al nyght,	With reading this accursed book all night
Al sodeynly thre leves have I plyght	Quickly I tore three pages
Out of his book, right as he radde, and eke	Out of his book, while he was reading, and also
I with my fest so took hym on the cheke	I hit him with my fist on the cheek
That in our fyr he fil bakward adoun.[4]	So that he fell backwards into our fire.

So what was in this book that so angered the Wife of Bath? It was a collection, of a kind popular in Chaucer's time, in which moralists and Church authorities brought together *exempla* from the Bible and classical sources. In this case the examples were tales of famous female characters who caused the men who loved them untold suffering; it was just one of the *exempla* collections that were widely disseminated in the Middle Ages and quoted in treatises and sermons. This practice is adopted in the love-allegory *Roman de la Rose* ('Romance of the Rose'), a famously misogynistic work that objectified women by portraying the conquest of a castle and the plucking of a rose as an obvious allegory for sexual conquest. The author of the second part, Jean de Meun, used *exempla* in his satirical overview of medieval life and thought. Favourite examples of predatory women were Eve (judged to have brought catastrophe on all humankind); Delilah, who betrayed Samson by cutting his hair to rob him of his strength (Image 7); Deianeira, who murdered Hercules with a poisoned shirt; and Xantippe, who poured a pot of urine over the head of her husband Socrates when she grew weary of his philosophising (warning to readers: do not try this at home).

Another recognised practice of medieval orators was to demonstrate their rhetorical skills by marshalling arguments against marriage. Walter Map, Archdeacon of Oxford under King Henry II, wrote the following diatribe against women and marriage in his *Dissuasio Valerii ad Rufinum philosophum ac uxorem ducat* ('Advice of Valerius to Rufinus Not to Marry') in 1180:

> *The very best woman (who is rarer than the phoenix) cannot be loved without the bitterness of fear, anxiety, and frequent misfortune. Wicked women, however – who swarm so abundantly that no place is free from their wickedness – sting sharply when they are loved; they give their time to tormenting a man until his body is divided from his soul.*[5]

7 Delilah cutting Samson's hair while he sleeps, in the *Roman de la Rose* (Bruges, *c*.1495) Harley MS 4425, f. 83v.

It is tempting to imagine that Chaucer, for one, did not agree with such sentiments. Perhaps he shared the views of the women who – just like his Wife of Bath – questioned the intelligence of those who expressed them. Yet he does not reveal whether the satire in his prologue is directed against his much-loved female character or against her husband who is unable to control her. Perhaps it is both.

The negative stereotyping of women that so incensed Chaucer's heroine was attacked in writing by a justly well-renowned author and early 'feminist'. She was Christine de Pisan, an Italian-born poet living at the French court in the early fifteenth century. She rightly remarked that although men are quick to point out the faults of the female sex, they demand higher standards of virtue from women than from men. Christine's stated objective in writing her *Livre de la Cité des Dames* ('Book of the City of Ladies') was the defence of women from unjust criticism. Although this work was composed hundreds of years ago, the indignation expressed by the author remains remarkably relevant today when female stereotypes are constantly being questioned. In the introduction she reveals opinions that are both timeless and surprisingly modern:

> *[I] wonder how it happened that so many different men – and learned men among them – have been and are so inclined to express both in speaking and in their treatises and writings so many wicked insults*

8a Christine de Pisan writing (left); 8b the narrator 'Christine' with a group of women at the gate of the City of Ladies (right), in the *Livre de la Cité des Dames*, from the *Book of the Queen*, Harley MS 4431, ff. 4r, 323r.

about women and their behaviour. Not only one or two...but, more generally, from the treatises of all philosophers and poets and from all the orators – it would take too long to mention their names – it seems that they all speak from one and the same mouth. Thinking deeply about these matters, I began to examine my character and conduct as a natural woman and, similarly, I considered other women whose company I frequently kept, princesses, great ladies, women of the middle and lower classes, who had graciously told me of their most private and intimate thoughts, hoping that I could judge impartially and in good conscience whether the testimony of so many notable men could be true. To the best of my knowledge, no matter how long I confronted or dissected the problem, I could not see or realise how their claims could be true when compared to the natural behaviour and character of women.[6]

In *Livre de la Cité des Dames* (Images 8a, 8b) Christine de Pisan includes summaries of the lives of 128 women, from characters in Greek mythology to famous women in the Bible, from saints to historical and contemporary women.

9 Queen Fredegunda as regent, showing her infant son to her Merovingian troops after the death of her husband, in *De Stede der Vrouwen*, a Flemish translation of Christine de Pisan's *Livre de la Cité des Dames* (Bruges, 1475) Add MS 20698, f. 63r.

The allegorical framework for the collection of short, moralised biographies has the narrator, 'Christine', instructed by the three female characters who represent womanhood (Reason, Rectitude and Justice). They build a fortified city where women are to be safe from misogynist attacks. A further attack on the male establishment was her *Querelle de la Rose* ('Debate of the Rose'), in which Christine denounced the immoral content and attitudes to women in the popular medieval work, the *Roman de la Rose* (see above).

It must be said that although Christine expressed some fairly radical ideas for her time, she was not a feminist revolutionary who envisaged the overthrow of her society; in fact she was conscious of women's role as wives and mothers. In her *Livre des Trois Vertus* ('Book of the Three Virtues'), a manual of education for women in all sectors of society and dedicated to a noble patron, the 'Virtues' advise women on correct behaviour. For them, a wife should 'ensure that [her husband] is well served and his peace and quiet are uninterrupted. Before he comes home for dinner everything should be ready and in good order...If [he] is bad or quarrelsome, she ought to appease him as much as she can by soothing words.'[7] This advice would have been only too familiar to our mothers and grandmothers. Based on the opinions expressed here some modern critics have seriously questioned whether the term 'feminist' should be applied to Christine. It seems anachronistic to speak of feminism in a society with rigid gender-stereotyped roles and few choices open to women, but few would dispute the fact that Christine was exceptional for her time.

The *Livre de la Cité des Dames* is the work that provided inspiration for this collection of tales of women. For the contents, Christine de Pisan borrowed extensively from Giovanni Boccaccio's *De mulieribus claris* ('On Famous Women'), a collection of biographies of famous women from history and mythology. When examining attitudes to medieval heroines I often rely on the opinions expressed by these two authors. However, it should be noted that, whereas Boccaccio focused more on the sexual relationships of his women and portrayed them as exceptional to their gender, Christine took a different stance. Boccaccio's attitude is summed up in his preface:

> I have been quite astonished that women have had so little attention from writers...[and] that they have gained no recognition in any work devoted especially to them, although it can be seen in the more voluminous histories that women have acted with as much strength as valour. If men should be praised whenever they perform great deeds (with strength which Nature has given them) how much more should women be extolled (almost all of whom are endowed with tenderness, frail bodies and sluggish minds by Nature), if they have acquired a manly spirit and if with keen intelligence and remarkable fortitude they have dared undertake and have accomplished even the most difficult deeds.[8]

This might be considered a somewhat back-handed set of compliments, though to his credit Boccaccio does show awareness of some of the issues.

This book does not aim to be comprehensive in its subject matter: my choice of heroines is confined to those whose stories are told and illustrated in medieval manuscripts in the British Library. So while Cleopatra, Guinevere and the Queen of Sheba appear here, heroines of northern legend including Brunhilde and notable medieval characters such as Eleanor of Aquitaine do not, as there are very few or no images of them in British Library manuscripts. The focus is largely on medieval European and Persian manuscripts, so it goes without saying that there are many powerful and fascinating female characters

10 Women spinning and carding wool in the lower margin of Psalm 105, Luttrell Psalter (Lincolnshire, 1325–40) Add MS 42130, f. 193r.

in other cultures (for example Hua Mulan, Nefertiti and the warrior Itzpapalotl) whose stories are not told. And then there are the generations of women throughout the Middle Ages who were not princesses, had no magical powers and whose lives were not the stuff of legend. They were midwives, nuns, mothers, spinners and weavers, running households and estates while their husbands were away and teaching their children to read. They, too, had stories to tell, but few have survived.

I set out to focus on the legends themselves, but found that as I wrote I was confronted with the issues that so incensed Christine de Pisan over 600 years ago. Though there have been countless strong, independent women throughout history – as reflected in the characters in this book – it took generations before women achieved the equality we enjoy today. The huge disruptions of the Enlightenment, the Reformation and the Suffragette movement and changes in the world economic order created an environment in which serious questioning of the roles of both fictional and real women became possible. Nevertheless, the female characters of the past – historical and fictional, ancient and medieval – remain powerful role models for us. They still fascinate and inspire readers and writers of the twenty-first century, and we continue to reimagine and retell their stories.

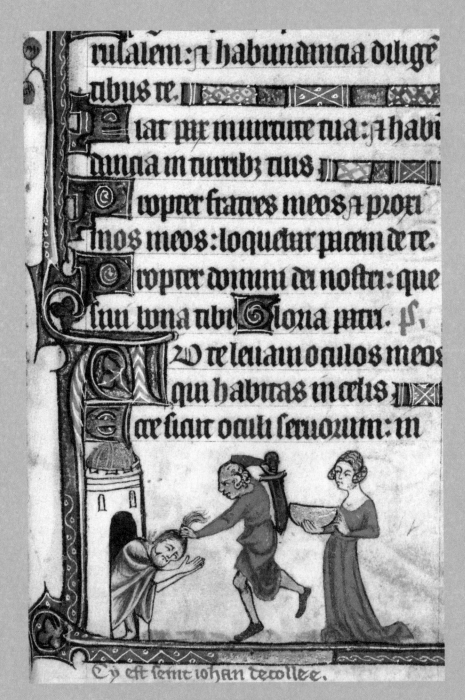

Salome holding a bowl at the execution of John the Baptist,
in the Taymouth Hours (London, mid-14th century)
Yates Thompson MS 13, f. 107r.

Warriors, Murderesses and Femmes Fatales

Part One

The Amazon Women

The mythical race of Amazons, ruthless female warriors who fiercely resisted masculine domination, were reputedly as beautiful as they were violent. In the ancient Greek sources their epithet, *antianeirai*, can mean either 'against men' or 'equivalent of men'.[1] They were described by the historian Hellanikos of Lesbos as 'golden-shielded, silver-axed, man-loving, boy-killing women',[2] and by the tragedian Aeschylus as 'virgins fearless in battle' who 'feed on flesh'.[3] Their images appear on more Greek vases than any other mythological characters apart from Hercules (Greek Herakles) and they are shown in a dynamic battle against the Greeks on a magnificent marble frieze of *c.*350 BC from Halicarnassos, now in the British Museum. A fascinatingly varied tradition of legends grew up around them; they were popular characters in the Middle Ages and remain the inspiration for female superheroes from Wonder Woman to Xena: Warrior Princess. Spanish explorers named the Amazon River after the native women of Brazil who fought alongside their men against the European invaders.

The ancient Greek historian, Diodorus Siculus (first century BC), reported that:

> *on the bounds of the inhabited world [there was once] a race which was ruled by women and followed a manner of life unlike that which*

1 Queen Penthesilea with her army of Amazons, from Christine de Pisan, *L'Épître Othéa* ('Letter of Othea') in the *Book of the Queen* (Paris, c.1410) Harley MS 4431, f. 103v.

2 The Amazon women led by their queen, in Raoul Lefèvre, *Le Recueil des histoires de Troyes* (Bruges, c.1480) Royal MS 17 E II, f. 349r.

prevails among us. For it was the custom among them that the women should practise the arts of war and be required to serve in the army for a fixed period, during which time they maintained their virginity; then, when the years of their service in the field had expired, they went in to the men for the procreation of children, but they kept in their hands the administration of the magistracies and of all the affairs of the state.[4]

Some said that after they had given birth, boys were either killed off, maimed or given back to their fathers (the sources differ on this point). They kept the

3 Hercules meeting Hippolyta, queen of the Amazons, a bas-de-page image in the *Histoire ancienne jusqu'à César* (Naples, *c*.1330) Royal MS 20 D I, f. 25v.

girls, drilling them in military arts and leading their female troops to victory over their enemies. Diodorus and others claim that the Amazons cut off or cauterised the right breasts of female offspring so that they would not be in the way when they used a bow in later life. Later writers expanded this idea, so that Strabo claimed that this amputation was to assist javelin throwing and the idea arose that the name 'Amazon' originated in a combination of the Greek prefix *a* ('without') and a variant of *mastos* ('breast'). However, alternative derivations may be from the Greek words for 'without husbands' or 'belt-wearing'. Whatever the origins of their name, it seems that the ancient Greeks – who believed that their womenfolk should be confined to the home, far from the excitement and danger of fighting – may have liked to imagine a world where heroes could dominate these mythical females with their spears.

Ancient writers located the home of the Amazons on the south-eastern coast of the Black Sea (in modern Turkey) around their city of Thermiscyra. They had lived in the distant past – in the Heroic Age of Hercules and the Trojan War. Their Queen Hippolyta had been given a girdle (or belt) by the god Ares (Roman Mars), which was the source of her power. Natalie Haynes, in her revisional study of women in Greek literature, questions the use by translators of the word 'girdle' to translate *zōstēr* in ancient Greek. *Zōstēr* is used by Homer and others to describe the war belt carried by male heroes, whereas the word 'girdle' has unfortunate connotations as the old-fashioned equivalent of Spanx 'shapewear'. And so it makes Hippolyta seem 'less alarming' and in a way 'less impressive' in the English translations than in the Greek original.[5]

The ninth Labour allotted to the demi-god Hercules in Greek mythology was to capture Hippolyta's belt, so he sailed to the land of the Amazons to find her. When he arrived at Thermiscyra, he was met by the queen and she promised to give the belt to him (Image 3). She later went to visit him at his ship, but the goddess Hera (Juno), who hated Hercules, had told some of the Amazon women that he planned to kidnap their queen. So they rode, fully armed, towards the ship and when Hercules saw them he immediately killed Hippolyta with his sword, taking her belt and axe from her body. The two sides attacked one another (Image 4) and many Amazons were slaughtered before Hercules sailed away towards Troy.

In the battle, Hercules captured Queen Melanippe as his slave. Theseus was in turn awarded her sister, Antiope; some say she fell in love with him and they married and had a son, Hippolytus. In other versions of the story she was taken to Athens as a captive, so the Amazons mounted a rescue. They invaded the city and besieged the Acropolis for three months until they were finally defeated. In the fray Antiope was accidentally shot dead by an Amazon named Molpadia, who was in turn killed by Theseus. A marker at one of the gates of Athens was said by the ancient Greeks to indicate the place where Antiope was buried, and there were other tombs in the area reputed to mark the burial places of Amazons who had died in the battle.

According to the fifth-century poet Quintus of Smyrna, a small group of Amazon warriors escaped with Queen Penthesilea and made their way to Troy to help defend the city against the Greeks. Spurred on by a dream sent to her by the deceitful goddess Athena, Penthesilea promised the king that she would personally defeat Achilles, hero of the Greeks. Some, including Boccaccio, say that she greatly loved and admired the Trojan hero, Hector, and that she wanted to avenge his death at the hands of Achilles. At first, she and her band of twelve warriors faced the Greek army, fighting like lionesses so that the soil turned red with the blood of both armies. Then at last Penthesilea came face to face with the great Achilles, who had already cut down five of her companions in rapid succession. Having first warned her that she could not win against him, he threw his spear and wounded her, then stabbed her horse. When she was down he thrust a spear into her breast and as she fell backwards, he caught a glimpse of her beautiful face and was filled with remorse. Some say he fell in love with her instantly, but it was too late – she was already dead. He carried her body carefully to the Trojans, who in gratitude gave her a burial fitting for a beloved Trojan princess.

4 Theseus and Hercules in combat with two Amazons, while an Amazon offers an olive branch to the Greeks, a bas-de-page image in the *Histoire ancienne jusqu'à César*, Royal MS 20 D I, f. 25r.

The Greek historian Plutarch, and medieval chroniclers who followed his example, placed the Amazons in the historical setting of the late fourth century BC. For them Alexander the Great met a troop of Amazon warriors led by their Queen Thalestris in the north of the Persian Empire at this time (Image 5). Accounts of the celebrated encounter diverge greatly. For some, Thalestris rode with a group of retainers to meet Alexander in the wilderness, where they hunted lions together and enjoyed thirteen nights of lovemaking (thirteen is a sacred number associated with fertility). She wished to conceive a daughter who would grow up and follow in the footsteps of Alexander to rule the world, but she did not live long after the encounter and her dream of world domination died with her. The story may have its origins in the historical accounts of a Bactrian warrior princess who was offered by her father to Alexander, and so Thalestris may have been based on a real person.

An entirely different account emerges in the medieval *Greek Alexander Romance*, where the Amazons submit to Alexander as their overlord; they offer to pay him 100 talents of gold, and to provide 500 female warriors and 100 horses to serve him for a year. Here the Amazons describe themselves as a race of 270 000 virgins, and forbid any sexual relations between their forces and the Greek soldiers.[6]

Christine de Pisan devotes four chapters to the Amazons in her work on famous women, *Livre de la Cité des Dames* ('Book of the City of Ladies') and she also references them in several other works (Images 1, 6). In her account, the ravages of war left a group of Scythian women without husbands and they courageously banded together to govern themselves without the interference of men. They then armed themselves, formed battalions and set off to take revenge for the death of their husbands. A detailed account is given of how their society is organised, followed by tales of the individual queens, including Lampedo, Marpesia and Melanippe.

Elles sassemblerent...et en conclusion delibererent que de la en avant par elles maintentroient leurs seignourries sans subgecion dommes et firent un tel edit que homme quelconques ne seroit souffert entrer en leur iuridicion. Mais pour avoir lignee elles yroient es contrees voisines a certaines saisons de lanneee et puis retourneroient en leur pays et se elles enfantoient masles les envoyeroient a leurs peres et se femelles estoient les nourriroient. Pour parfournire ceste ordenance establirent des plus nobles dames dentre elles ii que a roynes couronerent...	*They met...and decided that in future they would govern the kingdom without male supervision and so they proclaimed a law forbidding any man access to their lands. However, to assure the continuation of their race they would visit their neighbours at certain times of the year, returning afterwards to their own country; if they then gave birth to male children, they would send them back to their fathers; if they had daughters, they would bring them up themselves. To enforce these laws they chose two of the most noble among them to be crowned queens...*[7]

Much of Christine's material is based on Boccaccio's earlier work, *De mulieribus claris* ('On Famous Women'). He focuses on Marpesia and Lampedo, who he says call themselves 'daughters of Mars' (Image 7). Taking the Amazons' man-hatred a step further, he claims that after they had fought off the marauding invaders who had killed their husbands, they realised that although they were only women they could win battles, and in fact they were better off without men. Their subsequent actions are rather shocking, though Boccaccio presents the 'facts' without comment: '*[C]omuni consilio irruentes in eos,omnes interemere; inde in hostes furore converso*' ([T]hey, with common accord, murdered all those [husbands] who had not been killed by the enemy and then turned their fury on their enemies').[8]

Allegedly they then went on to conquer large swathes of Europe as well as a good portion of Asia, and were feared by all men.

Excavations in locations around the Eastern Mediterranean have uncovered more than 100 graves of women buried with weapons in burial mounds known as *kurgans*, which have been dated to the era when this region was controlled by the nomadic tribes known as Scythians. Many of the bones showed signs of

5 The queen of the Amazons ('*la royne mazomeus*') and her women meet Alexander the Great, in the *Roman d'Alexandre en prose* ('Prose Alexander Romance') in the Talbot Shrewsbury Book (Rouen, 1445) Royal MS 15 E VI, f. 15v.

arrow wounds. The high proportion of females with weapons suggests that at least a quarter of these fighters were women, so the Amazon myth may have originated with them. But they were not the only women in the ancient world with possible links to the Amazons. According to the Greek war-historian Polyaenus, Cynane, the half-sister of Alexander the Great, was a renowned warrior and reportedly killed an Illyrian queen in one-on-one combat.

For Boccaccio and the (mostly) male authors of the Middle Ages, the Amazons and other warlike females represented a threat to the natural ordering of society. So they are sometimes portrayed in both image and text as more

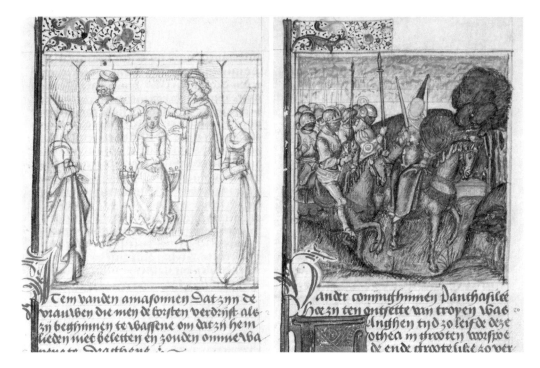

Cem vanden amafonnen Dat zijn de
vrauwen die men de borsten verdrijft als
zij beghinnen te waffene om dat zij hem
lieden met beletten en zouden ommeuba...

ander comjnuthinneu Danthafilee
hoe zij ten ontfette van tropen was
Angthen tijd zo leifde deze
othea in grooten worfpoe
de ende droote like so ver

6a (left) Coronation of an Amazon queen; **6b** (right) Penthesilea at the head of her army, in a Flemish version of Christine de Pisan's *Cité des Dames, De Stede der Vrouwen* (Bruges, 1475) Add MS 20698, ff. 43v, 51v.

male than female, conveying their renunciation of domesticity and the realms of activity suitable for women. Nevertheless, their popularity as mythological characters is attested by the many different versions of the Amazon story to survive in legends and chronicles of the period.

So were they victims of male aggression in the form of Hercules and Alexander, or did they really murder their husbands and go on to rule the world? The answer depends on the source, though all agree that they were fearsome adversaries who fought to the death. As Natalie Haynes emphasises, a common thread in their story is their solidarity and cooperation as a fighting force.[9] In contrast to the most famous male warriors in classical and medieval legend – larger than life supermen such as Achilles and Hector who fought alone for personal glory – the Amazons are most often portrayed as fighting together, cooperating for the common good. This was their strength.

7 Marpesia and Lampedo, queens of the Amazons, with women and armed female attendants, in Giovanni Boccaccio, *De Cleres et nobles femmes*, a French version of *De mulieribus claris* (France, c.1410) Royal MS 20 C V, f. 20v.

et auctorite delle est nommee
libie de son nom.

Cy sensuit listoire de marpe

Die fame van deser bruloerst van iasoun en
reusa was ter stont gheserreyt door al
tlant van thornten de coninck woude hoef hoff
houden ende sende sijn boden door al zijn lude
En int ander landen mede vergadet De heerre
zijn vrunden en maghen En steron gulden ia
krent ende zeden dit tot der bruloerst van noode
waeren Om altijt te volghen de rechte natra en
van onser matern ghecodurande al dus dese belof
te tusschen iason ende reusa medea dit mijn
up en hielt nacht noch dach va haer vrunt iason

2.

Medea

Of all the women in ancient myth, few have proved to be as fascinating as the fiery witch-princess Medea, who committed atrocious acts of betrayal and murder for love of the hero Jason. She was grand-daughter of the ancient Greek sun god Helios, so therefore part-divine, and as a character she has always raised many questions. Is she a fiercely independent woman who controls her own destiny, or a vengeful and violent priestess of Hecate who uses dark arts to achieve her goals? Or is she simply a young woman with medicinal skills who is manipulated by the gods into an obsessive relationship with the faithless Jason? The motivations for her cruel and disastrous actions have been endlessly debated from the time of the ancient Greeks through the Middle Ages and continue to be explored by feminist critics today.

The two best-known ancient Greek accounts of Medea's tale are in Euripides' tragedy *Medea* and Apollonius of Rhodes's *Argonautica*, the epic tale of Jason and the Argonauts. There were a number of other classical and contemporary sources available to medieval authors, so in the various adaptations of the story by Boccaccio, Chaucer and others, even major aspects may vary. But there is one central and inescapable action: Medea's murder of her own children (Images 1, 8). It is her motivations that vary, depending on the view of the author.

1 Medea murdering her child in front of Jason and Creusa at their wedding feast, in the *Historie van Jason* ('Story of Jason') (N. Netherlands, *c.*1480) Add MS 10290, f. 138r.

Medea's lover Jason was the son of King Aeson of Iolcos in Thessaly, on the Greek mainland. The old king entrusted his kingdom to his brother, Pelias, while his son was too young to rule. But when Jason grew up and claimed the throne, Pelias told him he must first bring back the mythical Golden Fleece of the talking ram, gift of the god Hermes (Roman Mercury). The Fleece was kept by King Aeetes of the kingdom of Colchis (on the shores of the Black Sea in what is now Georgia), but the people of Iolcos believed they were the rightful owners. It was in a sacred grove guarded by a fierce serpent with a hundred coils. So, having built his ship, the *Argo*, Jason set off for Colchis. For the Greeks in the time before the Trojan War, the lands beyond the Mediterranean were places of legend, inhabited by barbarians, monsters and dragons. Among these was Aeetes himself (said to be brother of the witch, Circe), and his daughter, the sorceress Medea. She had been taught the art of spells and potions by Hecate, the goddess of witchcraft; some said she could stop rivers from flowing and halt the stars in their course across the night sky.

After an eventful sea journey, at last the *Argo* and its crew docked at the harbour of Colchis and they made their way to Aeetes' palace. They were hidden by a thick mist that was spread by the goddess Hera (Roman Juno) to protect them; she was determined that Jason should capture the Fleece and dethrone his uncle Pelias, who had angered her in the past.

Inside the palace, Medea was wandering the corridors looking for her sister Chalciope. Hera had diverted her from her usual duties in Hecate's temple and had asked Aphrodite (the goddess of love, Roman Venus: see Chapter 12) to instruct her son Eros (Cupid) to fire an arrow into Medea's heart. Her plan was to have Medea fall for Jason and help him in his quest. The effect of the arrow was immediate, as described by Apollonius:

> speechless amazement seized her soul….and ever she kept darting bright
> glances straight up at Aeson's son [Jason], and within her breast her
> heart panted fast through anguish, all remembrance left her, and her soul
> melted with the sweet pain.[1]

From this moment the young woman was in thrall to Jason and the agent of a manipulative goddess.

The involvement of Hera and Aphrodite in Medea's story was generally omitted in medieval versions, where Medea was seen as responsible for her own actions. Boccaccio claimed that it was Jason's beauty, royal birth and reputation that attracted Medea and that she deliberately set out to captivate him with her charms and sorcery, as she felt he would be a very good match. For whatever reason, Medea was overcome with desire for Jason and became

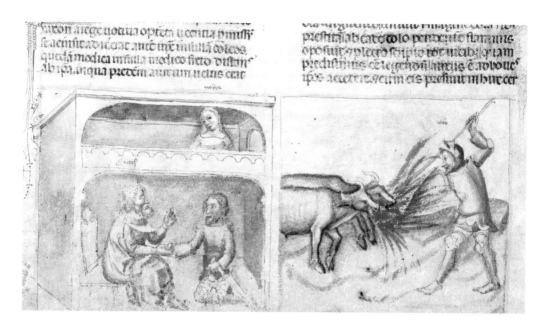

2 Jason before King Aeetes, with Medea seated on a balcony above them (left); and Jason subduing the fire-breathing bulls (right), in Guido delle Colonne, *Historia destructionis Troiae* ('History of the Destruction of Troy') (N. Italy, c.1370) Add MS 15477, f. 6v.

his willing helper and accomplice; she was prepared to use her considerable skills and to make huge sacrifices to help him achieve his aims.

A feast was provided for the newcomers, and Medea could not take her eyes off Jason while her father Aeetes proceeded to set him a series of impossible tasks in order to earn the Fleece (Image 2). He must yoke two fire-breathing bulls and plough the field of Ares (Roman Mars), then he must sow the ground with the serpent's teeth given by Athena (Roman Minerva: see Chapter 4). Aeetes knew that if Jason managed to survive an encounter with the bulls, the teeth would sprout into armed men who would kill the sower.

Using her magical powers, Medea gave Jason a flask of potion (the juice of the crocus) to cover his body and protect him from the bulls (Image 3). She told him he should throw a huge boulder into the midst of the armed men in the field so that they would fight among themselves, allowing him time to escape. In return Jason charmed her, 'soothing her with gentle converse'[2] and calming her fears; he promised to take her back with him to Iolcos where she would be honoured by all. The young and naïve Medea believed him, though she wept at the thought of leaving her home and family.

With Medea's help, Jason completed both tasks, but then King Aeetes reneged on the deal, refusing to give him the Fleece and threatening to burn

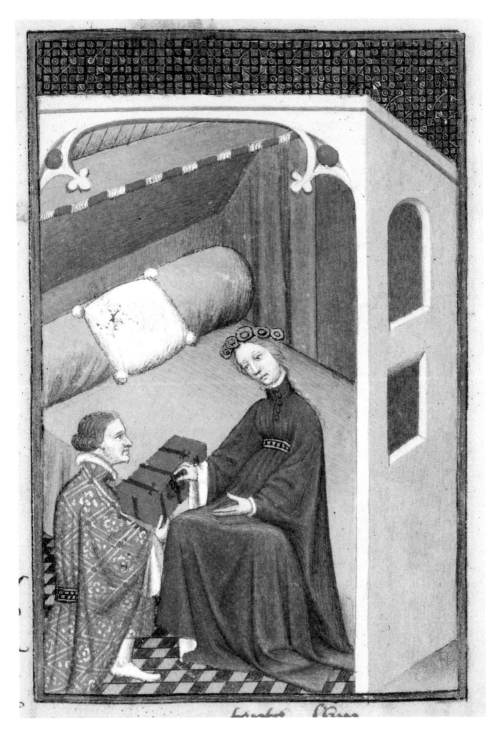

3 Medea gives Jason the potion, in *L'Épistre Othéa* ('Letter of Othea') (Paris, c.1412) Harley MS 4431, f. 122r.

4 Jason completes his tasks and carries off the Golden Fleece, while King Aeetes watches from a tower, in the *Histoire ancienne* (Paris, late 14th century) Add MS 25884, f. 108v.

the *Argo*. Once again Jason needed Medea's help, and once again he vowed by the gods of Olympus that he would make her his wife on their return to Iolcos. Medea showed him the way to the sacred grove where the Golden Fleece was hidden and used her charms and incantations to pacify the terrifying serpent that guarded it. Jason easily captured the Fleece and escaped with Medea and the Argonauts on their waiting ship (Image 4).

They were hotly pursued by the furious Aeetes, his young son Apsyrtus and the Colchans. Medea, in her unquenchable desire to please Jason, lured her brother Apsyrtus into a trap to be murdered by her lover. She then chopped the boy up and threw his body parts into the sea, thereby delaying Aeetes and his

dee qui fut tres
auel exemple en

fleet while they stopped and gathered up the pieces of the body for a proper burial. Meanwhile the Argonauts were able to escape with their prize (Image 5).

Zeus (Roman Jupiter), king of the gods, was furious at the brutal murder of Apsyrtus; he condemned the Argonauts to wander homeless on the oceans, where they faced many dangers including Sirens, wandering rocks and monsters. As they sailed past the island of Crete, they were attacked by Talos, the near-invincible bronze man, and Medea once again used her magic powers to protect them by attacking Talos in his one weak spot – his ankle. She made him graze it on a sharp rock so that his *ichor* (the substance the gods have instead of blood) flowed out of his body and he crashed to the ground.

At last the *Argo* neared the shores of Iolcos, where Medea promised to restore Jason's father Aeson to youth and take revenge on Pelias the usurper. Here, as told in Ovid's *Metamorphoses*, she donned long robes and mounted a chariot pulled by dragons, which carried her up to the magic mountain-tops where she gathered herbs and waters from the rivers. Then, calling on dark spirits of the earth, she mixed the herbs with the blood of a black ram, the slime of a water-snake and other ingredients known only to her. She then cut Aeson's throat so that his aged blood flowed out and she replenished his veins with her concoction so that he was miraculously restored to youth. Nothing more was heard about him after this.

Next Medea went to the palace of the wicked uncle, Pelias, and promised to use supernatural powers to rejuvenate the old king. She gained the confidence of his daughters by conjuring up a lamb from the body parts of an old ram that she had cut up and stewed in a cauldron. Somehow she persuaded them that if they cut Pelias into pieces and placed them in the same cauldron she would be able to use her magic potions to reassemble him as a young man. They did so and naturally that was the end of King Pelias (Image 6).

Jason, however, disapproved of Medea's barbaric methods and refused the crown of Iolcos, instead accepting the banishment imposed by the horrified citizens. Fortunately Medea inherited the throne of Corinth through her father and by some accounts they ruled there peacefully for some time. But Jason, unable to remain faithful for long, decided he should marry the princess Creusa (also called Glauce), thereby allying himself with her father, King Creon. He rejected Medea, citing her evil machinations and claiming that the Corinthians preferred him as their ruler.

5 A crowned Medea uttering a spell; Jason watches while a knight in armour cuts off the arm of her brother, Apsyrtus, in Boccaccio, *De mulieribus claris* in a French translation (Rouen, c.1440) Royal MS 16 G V, f. 20r.

6 Medea rejuvenates Aeson in a cauldron and Pelias is cut to pieces in another, in the *Historie van Jason*, Add MS 10290, f. 130v.

dont prist les pieces de ses en
fans z les ieta deuant liu. z deu.r
tous les barons qui seoiēt au
mengier auec liu. z atant sen
part z sen ala p diuisses terres
abantonnie a toute deshone
ste z ensint usa son tps. z a la fin
p vigoine de liem eismes. z p des
espration se noia en la mer. Cō
pres ne demeura pas met
grament que ca iason aso mort
vne maladie le prist si meruell

ste ne giant qu le peust icōre
uaincu. si prist a fame une ta
me mlt bele q ui out a nom de
ginura a la menoit auec liu par
tout la ou il aloit. Et cest time
amoit mlt neu itaum i qui estoit
mo itie buef z moitie homē z
nē taurus l amoit ausi. si que
il auint i iour que faules trou a
.l. fprut si gut z si miueilleus q
il mengioit .i. buef mes q sit
il cui t si le uest z vne forete

7 Medea, in a chariot pulled by fire-breathing dragons, killing her children and throwing their body parts in front of Jason, Creusa and Creon, in the *Histoire ancienne* (Naples, *c*.1330) Royal MS 20 D I, f. 37v.

This abandonment was too cruel, when Medea had given up home and family for Jason; her world fell apart. With swift and awful revenge, she sent her children to Creusa bearing a wedding gift of a golden crown and long white robe, but they burst into flames as soon as the bride put them on. She, her father and the wedding guests all died in the resulting conflagration, though Jason survived. Medea then murdered her two children in front of him and rode off in a chariot pulled by dragons (Image 7). The most famous version of this incident is in Euripides' *Medea*, and it was later described in horrific detail by Ovid in *Metamorphoses*:

> *Then savagely she drew her sword and bathed*
> *It in the blood of her own infant sons;*
> *By which atrocious act she was revenged.*[3]

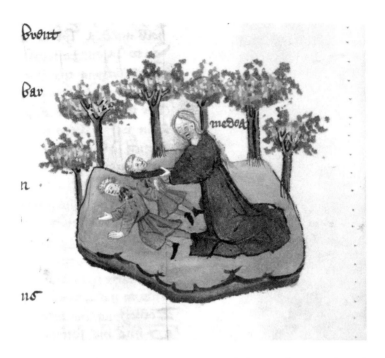

8 Medea murders her children, in John Lydgate, *The Fall of Princes* (Bury St Edmunds, c.1455) Harley MS 1766 f. 33r.

And this is the version that was retold and illustrated in chronicles and story collections in the Middle Ages, including the *Histoire ancienne* ('Ancient History'), an account of world history that included the legends of Troy and of the Argonauts.

In some versions of the tale the final outcome for the tragic couple was grimly ironic: Jason died, homeless and broken, killed by a falling beam of the *Argo*, while Medea became a female demon. However, others end on a rather more positive note. Boccaccio (in his *De mulieribus claris*, 'On Famous Women') relates that after her horrific vengeance Medea used her magical powers to escape to Athens. There she married the elderly Aegeus, king of that city, and they had a son, Medus, who founded a dynasty. After attempting to poison Theseus, she was again forced into exile but was reconciled with Jason and together they returned to Colchis. Though he allows her a satisfactory end, Boccaccio judges her with characteristic harshness as 'the most cruel example of ancient wickedness'.[4]

The English poets John Lydgate (Image 8) and Geoffrey Chaucer both retold the story of Medea based on Boccaccio's account. Whereas Lydgate describes her '*envie and venymous hatreede*' and her '*herte of malis, cruel and horrible*',[5] Chaucer places the blame firmly on Jason:

Thou rote of false lovers, duk Iasoun!	*You source of false lovers, Duke Jason!*
Thou sly devourer and confusioun	*You sly devourer and confuser*
Of gentil-wommen, tender creatures,	*Of gentlewomen, tender creatures,*
...	...
If that I live, thy name shal be shove	*If I live your name shall be made known*
In English, that thy sleighte shal be knowe!	*In English, so that your type will be recognised!*[6]

The *Roman de la Rose* ('Romance of the Rose') takes a similar view, describing Jason as '*Le faux, le traitre, le felon*' ('lying, treacherous, villainous'),[7] whereas Medea is described as having to overcome her motherly tenderness to revenge herself on her false lover. Christine de Pisan does not mention Medea's murder of her children, but rather sympathises with her plight.

Apres ce quil fu du tout advenu a son entente [Jason] la laissa pour une autre. Elle qui plus tost se laissast detruire que luy avon fait ce tour fu comme desespere ne oncques plus bien ne ioye son cuer not.	*After he had got everything he wanted from her [Jason] left her for another. She who would rather die than play this trick on him was left so desperate that never again would [she] know happiness in her heart.*[8]

Like Christine de Pisan, those who play the role of Medea, or rewrite her story for modern audiences, may not conjure up fiery chariots and would certainly be horrified by her more violent acts. But they can identify with her furious reaction as a woman scorned and abandoned by a faithless man, for whom she gave up so much. Thus her character continues to be analysed and reinterpreted in different and perhaps more sympathetic ways.

3.

Salome, Daughter of Herod

Salome's dance before King Herod and the presentation of John the Baptist's head on a platter have been the subjects of literary and artistic works since the early Middle Ages. For medieval authors and illustrators of the Christian story, Salome plays a supporting role in the life of John, cousin of Jesus, who prophesied his Lord's coming and baptised him in the River Jordan. She was blamed for John's death and was used as an example to women of how not to behave.

In Jewish history there were three women named Salome in the Herodian dynasty that ruled Judea in the period of the Christian Gospels, as well as a number of kings of Judea named Herod. This caused some confusion in the retelling of Salome's story in the Middle Ages and Renaissance. Firstly, there was Salome I, sister of Herod I (the Great). He was the infamous King Herod in the Nativity story who, when he heard from the three Magi that the 'king of the Jews' had been born in Bethlehem, ordered the massacre of all boy infants in the surrounding area to eliminate any future threat to his rule. He also had a daughter called Salome. Herod the Great died in 4 BC and his son, Herod Antipas, ruled part of the kingdom (under the Roman emperor) until AD 39. So Herod Antipas was ruler of Galilee for most of Jesus's life and ministry and was

1 Salome performing before Herod, Herodias and their guests, who are seated at the dinner table, on a scroll or *flabellum* (fan) with scenes from the life of John the Baptist (Alsace, Hohenbourg, 1175–1200) Add MS 42497, f. 1av.

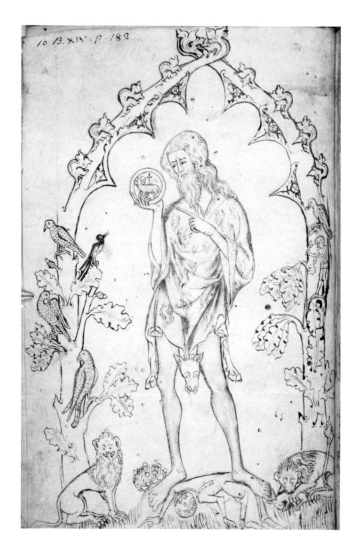

2 An unusual image of John the Baptist holding a disc with a lamb, and Salome under his feet with two lions on either side, in John Dumbleton, *Summa logicae et philosophiae naturalis* ('Handbook of Logic and Natural Philosophy') (Oxford, mid-14th century) Royal MS 10 B XIV, f. 3v.

involved in his death and that of John the Baptist. In the Gospels he was called King Herod or Herod the Tetrarch.

Herod Antipas left his first wife and married Herodias, the wife of his brother Philip (confusingly sometimes known as Herod II!), and she had a daughter, Salome. Furthermore, there was a Salome who was a follower of Jesus, who was present at the Crucifixion, and it was suggested by some that she was a sister of the Virgin Mary (see Chapter 5). Here we are concerned

3a St John the Baptist accuses Herod and Herodias; she demands that he be punished and Herod's guard beats him as he enters the prison, in the Holkham Bible Picture Book (London or S.E. England, 1327–35) Add MS 47682, f. 21r.

with Salome, daughter of Herodias and stepdaughter of Herod Antipas.

The source of Salome's legend is the Gospels of Matthew and Mark but her name is not mentioned in either. Both accounts record that Herod had John the Baptist arrested after John condemned his marriage to Herodias as illegal because she had been married to his brother. Herod did not at first want to execute John because he was a holy man and had many followers, so he imprisoned him. These and subsequent events are depicted in a series of dramatic images in a picture book of Bible stories made in London or the south-east of England. It has captions in Anglo-Norman French (the version of French spoken in England in the fourteenth century) describing the action in each picture. They follow the Gospel account quite closely, except that here it is not Herod but Herodias his wife who insists that John be imprisoned:

(Image 3a) Heroudie de ceo estoyt curuce et requyt Heroudes que yl le fesoyt mettre en prison et isi fesoyt yl

And Herodias was very angry at [John's accusation] and demanded of Herod that he put him in prison and he did this.[1]

The remainder of the story, as told in the captions, mirrors events as they are reported in the Gospels, but with details added which lay the blame squarely

3b Salome dances before Herod at his feast; Herodias advises her daughter what she should demand of Herod.

3c John the Baptist is beheaded and Salome takes his head to Herod on a platter, in the Holkham Bible Picture Book, Add MS 47682, f. 21v.

at the feet of Herodias and her daughter. Herod is shown as a man in thrall to two strong-willed, seductive women and he is unable to refuse even their outrageous demand that he murder a holy man. Again, Salome's name is not mentioned; she is *la filie Heroudie* ('the daughter of Herodias'). Nowhere in the Gospels does it mention Salome's dance, but she is shown here with her legs in the air. Such acrobatics would have been associated with medieval jugglers and tumblers, who were regarded as amoral by the Church. Her twisted, distorted movements are indications of her wickedness and depravity (see also Image 1).

(Image 3b) Comment Heroudes seet a table a une feste ouvekes tu pleyn de genz. E la filie Heroudie se meyt devaunt ly: ceo est asavoir de toumber et de autre abatement. Dount Heroudes en out graunt ioye. E disoyt: filie: demaunde ce que tu voys cuveyter deu harrayt qui la te courdie. Et ele allat a sa mere Heroudie pour la cunteher quoy ele devoyt demander. E ele la disoyt la text Seyn Jan en une esquele qui estoyt en prison. E ele allat demander la teste Seyn Jan le Baptist que estoyt en la prison. E Heroudes la ottreat.

This is how Herod was seated at the table for a feast with a crowd of people. And the daughter of Herodias came before him, performing a dance and other frolicking. And Herod was delighted at this. And he said: 'Daughter, ask for whatever you desire and Herod will grant you this'. And she went to her mother Herodias to ask her what she should request of Herod. And she [Herodias] said to her 'The head of John the Baptist, who is in prison, in a bowl'. And she [Salome] went and asked for the head of John the Baptist who was in prison. And Herod agreed to this.

(Image 3c) Comment seyn Jan le Baptist estoyt decole de un turmentour. Et la teste mise dedenz une esquelle. E la filie Heroudie la aportat devaunt Heroudes et Heroudie sa mere qui en out graunt ioye.

How St John the Baptist was beheaded by an executioner (or torturer). And his head was put in a bowl. And the daughter of Herodias carried it before Herod and Herodias her mother who was very pleased about this.[2]

The historian Flavius Josephus, who wrote his *Antiquitates Iudaicae* ('Antiquities of the Jews') in the latter part of the first century AD, was the first to mention Salome by name, and he claims she was first married to Herod's son Philip, but they had no children. After he died she married his brother Aristobulus and they had three sons. This historical account does not mention a dance performed by Salome, nor does it allude to any involvement by women

4a (left) Salome presents the head of John the Baptist to her mother; **4b** (right) they bury the head, in the Taymouth Hours (London, mid-14th century) Yates Thompson MS 13, f. 107v, 108r.

in the death of John the Baptist. Salome's portrait is found on coins of the period, where she is portrayed as a conventional wife, and certainly her legs are not in the air. Some biblical scholars have suggested that it would not have been possible for a young princess of Judea to dance in public at a banquet. Only prostitutes or courtesans would have been permitted such behaviour.

Many argue that it is more plausible that Herod gave the order to execute John for political reasons, as he feared the holy man's power to provoke civil unrest in the kingdom. Nevertheless Herod is portrayed in the Bible as an honourable man who reluctantly orders John's execution to keep his promise to Salome, and to appease Herodias. Mark's Gospel says 'And the king was exceeding sorry; yet for his oath's sake, and for their sakes which sat with him, he could not reject her'.[3] It is quite possible that the biblical account may have been embellished, but this was the image of Salome that was adopted in medieval literature and art. Her reputation as a dangerous seductress was firmly established by the Renaissance and she was considered frivolous and foolish, an attitude that led to John the Baptist's death.

In the Taymouth Hours, a private prayer book made for an English royal princess or queen, Salome's story is portrayed in the lower margins across four pages. Once again her dance is portrayed as acrobatic rather than seductive, and (even more so here) there is no doubt that she and her mother are responsible for the murder. In the two lower miniatures Salome brings the head on a platter to her mother, and then the pair bury it under a tree (Image 4). The caption states '*Cy la royne od sa file ensevelient la teste seint Johan en un erber de souz un perere*' ('Here the queen and her daughter bury St John's head in an orchard under a pear tree').[4]

In the fourth century and beyond, leaders of the early Church attacked dancing as an immoral pagan activity and Salome was used as an example of the

5 A smiling Salome with the head of St John the Baptist, in the *Histoire tripartite* ('Tripartite History') (Bruges, *c.*1475) Royal MS 18 E V, f. 371r.

consequences of such self-indulgence. Stories of her punishment proliferated in early Christian apocryphal texts, and Salome's death by drowning in a frozen river is described in legends of the Eastern Orthodox Church. After falling through a hole in the ice, she sank down up to her neck. In some accounts Herod tried to save her, but when he grasped her head it was cut off and her body was swept away. In others, her body continued to dance and wriggle under the ice so that her head was severed from her body by the sharp edges of the ice. This 'dance of death...brought to mind what she had done'.[5]

Artists of the Renaissance continued to be inspired by the contrast of Salome's seductive dance at the banquet and the gruesome severed head of John the Baptist on a platter. Scenes are found in mosaics in both St Marks, Venice and the Florence Baptistry, and in paintings and sculpture by some of the greatest artists from Donatello and Giotto to Lucas Cranach. And in the nineteenth century, with Flaubert's *Trois Contes* ('Three Tales'), Oscar Wilde's play *Salome*, introducing the famous 'Dance of the Seven Veils', and the 1905 opera by Richard Strauss, her reputation as a *femme fatale* was firmly established.

la deesse mmerue et la deesse pallas ensemble

pallas dune isle qui ot nom palle
elle fut nee et pour ce que elle tient
en toutes choses fu sage et maint
nouuellement trouua belles et
ses sappellerent deesse de sauoir
nommee mmerue a ce qui appar
a cheualerie / et pallas en toutes
qui appartiennent a sagece Et
veult dire que il soit aiouster s
a cheualerie qui moult bien y p
sant / et comme armes doient es
de la foy peut estre entendu
propos ce que dit hermes adiou
mour de la foy auec sapience

allegorie xxiiii

Et dicomme pallas qui n
doit estre aioustee auec cheualer
estre la vertu desperance adiou
bonnes vertus de lesprit cheuale
la quelle il ne pourroit y iouir
peregenes es omelies sur exode q
de ce biens auene est le solas d
qui trauaillent en ceste vie mort
si comme aux laboureurs lespe
rapimient adoulcist le labour d
besoingne et aux champions q
en bataille lesperance de couron
victoire attrempe la douleur de
playes. Et a ce propos parle sa
lapostre fortissimum solaculm
qui confugimus ad tenedã p
spem quam sicut anchoram h
amme tutam ad hebreos. b

La royne panthassellee qui a
secours de t roye

textte xiiii

Aioufte pallas la deesse
Et mes auec ta prouece
Tout bien te vient se tu sas
bien siet o mmerue pallas

Glose xiiii

Apres dit que il aioufte pallas auec
mmerue qui bien y siet et doit en sauoir
que pallas et mmerue est bne mesmes
chose mais les nomes sont pris
a ij entendemens Car sa dune qui
ot nom mmerue fu auffi surnommee

4.

The Goddess Minerva

Among all the gods and goddesses of Mount Olympus, Minerva wins the prize for multitasking; the poet Ovid called her the 'goddess of a thousand works'.[1] The Romans equated her with Athena (or Pallas Athene) and so she assumed the attributes of her Greek counterpart, who was the patron of the city of Athens and was venerated in the famous Parthenon on the Acropolis. Homer praised her in one of his hymns: 'I begin to sing of Pallas Athena, the glorious goddess, bright-eyed, inventive, unbending of heart, pure virgin, saviour of cities...'.[2]

Minerva was the daughter of Jupiter (Greek Zeus), king of the gods, and along with her father and his wife Juno (Hera) she was one of the three principal gods of ancient Rome, known as the Capitoline Triad. She was a patroness and protector of the city of Rome and of the Republic, and some sources claimed that her wooden image, the Palladium, had been brought from Troy by Aeneas, mythical founder of the city. She was the goddess of wisdom, justice and learning, of the arts of warfare and chivalry, of crafts and of chastity. The medieval author Christine de Pisan alluded to her 'marvellously subtle mind' and credited her with the invention of numbers and arithmetic, Greek shorthand, the techniques of spinning and weaving, the forging of iron

1 Minerva with a sword and Pallas Athena with a book are worshipped by young men, with the rubric 'La deesse minerve et la deesse pallas ensemble' ('The goddess Minerva and the goddess Pallas together') in L'Épistre Othéa ('Letter of Othea') (Paris, c.1412) Harley MS 4431, f. 103r.

2 Medallion of the goddess Minerva in the frame of a portrait of a patrician of Venice, part of a Doge's commission to the Zane family (Venice, c.1590) Add MS 20916, f. 33r.

harnesses and armour, the making of chariots and carts, and of flutes, fifes and trumpets.[3] An impressive list even for a goddess!

Minerva's mother was the female Titan, Metis, who tried to change shape to escape Jupiter's unwelcome attentions, and was swallowed by him. It is said that she gave birth to Minerva and then forged weapons for her while she was still in Jupiter's stomach. The constant clattering of her metalwork gave Jupiter a monstrous headache, and so the smith-god Vulcan (Greek Hephaestus) used a hammer to split his head open and Minerva emerged through the crack. As an extremely powerful goddess, she was involved in the lives of many of her fellow gods and humans, although more often than not the outcome was not positive.

One such unfortunate mortal was Medusa. A beautiful priestess serving in Minerva's temple, she was ravished by Neptune (Poseidon) in that sacred space, an act of desecration that greatly annoyed the goddess. And even though Medusa had not welcomed Neptune's attentions, Minerva blamed her and turned her into a hideous Gorgon with snakes for hair and fangs for teeth. She

3 Arachne at her loom with Minerva watching and a spider behind, in *Ovide moralisée* (Netherlands, late 15th century) Royal MS 17 E IV, f. 87v.

was so ugly that anyone who looked at her turned to stone. Minerva then helped the hero Perseus to cut off Medusa's head and he presented it to her. Some of the blood fell on the ground and engendered the horse Pegasus, which was later tamed by Bellerophon using Minerva's magic bridle. She also placed the head of the Gorgon on her aegis (a goatskin tunic fringed with serpents) and this is shown in Greek vase paintings. In medieval and Renaissance manuscript miniatures she is most often portrayed in armour with Medusa's head on her shield (Image 7).

Minerva's arms were used in the defence of virtue and the arts of peace against the destructive forces of war represented by Mars. She was, therefore, the patron of medieval knights, who were inspired by her to protect women and the Christian Church by performing chivalric deeds. In the Trojan War she had taken the side of the Greeks, while Mars had supported the Trojans. When the two met on a plain outside the city to do battle, Minerva hurled a skilfully aimed boulder that knocked the mighty god of war to the ground.

One mortal who bitterly regretted having dealings with Minerva was Arachne, a Lydian shepherd's daughter who was skilled at working with wool. According to Ovid she challenged the goddess (who had disguised herself as an old woman) to a weaving contest. When Minerva saw that the young girl's handiwork was more perfect than her own and also that she had woven subjects that were unflattering to the gods, she ripped it up and hit her over the head with a shuttle. Arachne was mortified when she realised she had angered such a powerful goddess and she hanged herself. Minerva then felt pity for the poor girl and revived her, turning her into a spider so that she could continue to spin and weave (Image 3).

A second contest involving another of Minerva's inventions again had disastrous results for the mortal competitor. Boccaccio's account of her achievements in *De mulieribus claris* ('On Famous Women') describes how she made the first flute or shepherds' pipe, either from the leg bones of a bird or from swamp reeds. Others said she used boxwood. In any case when she tried to play it the other gods made fun of her, saying she looked extremely ugly when she pursed her lips. So Minerva cursed the flute and threw it away, but it was found by a satyr named Marsyas, who played it so beautifully that Apollo was jealous and challenged him to a musical competition. As the Muses were the judges, Apollo naturally won and poor Marsyas was tied to a tree and flayed alive.

In her role as goddess of arts and crafts, Minerva (who was one of the patron goddesses of the Greek hero, Jason) instructed the giant Argus on the building of his ship, the *Argo* (see Chapter 2). Later in Jason's legend she was the source of the serpent's teeth which King Aeetes gave him to sow in the field. She also helped Prometheus steal fire from heaven and taught Daedalus his

4 Christine de Pisan in her study, writing, and, standing outside to the right, the goddess Minerva, armoured, crowned and carrying a sword and shield, in Christine de Pisan, *Le Livre des faits d'armes et de chevalerie* (London, 1434) Harley MS 4605, f. 3r.

technical skills so that he was able to make wings for himself and his son Icarus to escape from the labyrinth on Crete. Like the goddess Venus (Chapter 12) she played a part in many of the most famous episodes from classical mythology.

Minerva was an important figure in the works of Christine de Pisan, who saw the goddess as one of her predecessors and role models in wisdom and industry. At the end of her work on the art of warfare and chivalry, *Le Livre des faits d'armes et de chevalerie* ('Book of the Deeds of Arms and Chivalry'), she asks the goddess to preside over her composition as a fellow Italian. In this work she portrays Minerva as her compatriot, inspiration and ally against misogyny (Image 4). In the *Livre de la Cité des Dames* ('Book of the City of Ladies') the allegorical 'Lady' who is instructing the narrator 'Christine' on how to build the city alludes to Minerva as one of the founders of Troy and describes

5 Minerva, wearing a helmet, blows over the ocean, with a boat below; Jason ploughs a field with two oxen (his story is alluded to by Dante in *Paradiso* II); the Muses on a bank of clouds point to a star; Dante is led by Apollo, then he and Beatrice ascend towards the Heaven of the Moon, in *Paradiso* II (Tuscany, *c.*1445) Yates Thompson MS 36, f.131r.

all her inventions. Later, when the two women discuss the multiple benefits brought to humankind by intelligent women, they name three female figures who they say have been proclaimed goddesses by ignorant men because they do not believe ordinary women capable of such achievements. The three are Ceres, Queen of Sicily, who invented the techniques of agriculture; Isis, Queen of Egypt, who brought writing, and cultivation to her people; and Minerva, 'the genius…who invented so many useful skills that mankind could not live without'.[4] Minerva is also praised for her 'outstanding chastity', as she had managed to fight off the advances of the god Vulcan, and thereby 'overcame the ardour and lusts of the flesh which so strongly assail the young'.[5]

In Dante's *Paradiso*, where he compares the reader of his poetry to a sailor in a little ship (Image 5) on the 'mighty sea of being',[6] he evokes Minerva as a celestial aide who blows the ship over the waves.

L'acqua ch'io prendo già mai non si corse;	The waves I take were never sailed before;
Minerva spira, e conducemi Appollo,	Minerva breathes, Apollo pilots me,
e nove Muse mi dimostran l'Orse.	and the nine Muses show to me the Bears [constellation].[7]

Here Dante is recalling the *Odyssey*, in which, as the divine protector of Ulysses (Odysseus), Minerva caused the North Wind to blow him towards shore and guided him towards a sheltered inlet after he had been shipwrecked in a storm. As the goddess of weaving she later encouraged Ulysses' wife Penelope to delay her persistent suitors by weaving (and secretly unravelling) a funeral shroud for his father, Laertes, to buy time until her husband returned.

For poets such as Martianus Capella and Bernardus Silvestris, whose works were popular in the late Middle Ages and Renaissance, Minerva was the personification of virtue and wisdom. This wisdom could be divine or human, either seeking harmony with others and striving for the perfection of godly wisdom (equivalent to the biblical Sapientia in the Song of Solomon) or using cleverness to further one's earthly desires. Her attribute of the owl (Image 6) was adopted from Pallas Athene (in ancient Greece it is found on the reverse of coins bearing her image) and she is regularly shown holding a book; both signify wisdom. Her name, Minerva, comes from the form *Menrva* in the pre-Roman Italic or Etruscan languages, which became *mens* in Latin (meaning 'mind' or 'intelligence') and her birth from Jupiter's head is significant. In some traditions she was patroness of the arts and Ovid invokes her as his helper in composing verse.

In John Lydgate's fifteenth-century poem on chastity, *Reson and Sensuallyte* (a translation of a French allegorical work), the narrator encounters Minerva together with Juno, Venus and Mercury. He describes Minerva as *chef goddesse of sapience* ('chief goddess of wisdom')[8] because she descends from Jupiter, source of godly wisdom. In addition she can lead men away from idleness to live prudent and virtuous lives, reveal divine secrets and lead them to eternal life:

Yf she be vertu him governe,	If she guides them towards virtue,
Lyk goddys for to be eterne,	To be eternal like gods,
To lyven in that perfyt lyfe	To live that perfect life,
Wher joye ys ay withoute stryf,	Where there is always joy without strife.
The whyche shal have ende never.	Which shall never come to an end.[9]

6 An allegorical scene of the 'Triumph of an Academic', where a learned man in a chariot pulled by Minerva's owls symbolises the Renaissance ideal of Wisdom in an illustrated collection of commissions from the Doges of Venice (Italy, c.1600) Add MS 20916, f.1r.

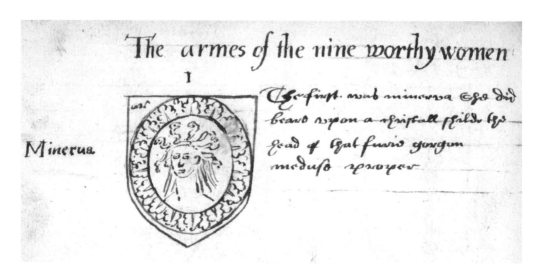

7 The arms of Minerva with a Gorgon's head, the first in a series of drawings of the arms of the 'Nine Worthy Women' (England, c.1600) Harley MS 6090, f. 3v.

Here we see the poet identifying Minerva with the Virgin Mary: both were associated with purity and wisdom; both were able to intercede with the highest authority (Jupiter/God) on behalf of humans; and both could show the path to eternal life. Lydgate provides a physical description of Minerva. Although she is old, her beauty does not fade; her eyes are like burning torches and she carries the lance of temperance and the shield of patience. Her mantle is three-coloured, symbolising the three theological virtues of faith, hope and charity, a popular concept in the fifteenth century.

Along with the biblical heroine Judith, Minerva was considered one of the 'Nine Worthy Women' in the Middle Ages. She is among the three classical women who belonged to this select group of female role models, as shown in an English collection of treatises on heraldry from around 1600 (Image 7). The arms of Minerva (a shield with the head of Medusa) are the first in the series and the other two classical heroines are legendary queens: Semiramis of Babylon and Tomyris of the Scythians. Minerva is the only goddess included, a sign of her popularity in the Middle Ages and her importance in medieval literature.

St Margaret and the dragon from a Book of Hours (Paris, c.1445)
Yates Thompson 3, f. 282v.

Holy Women

Part Two

5.

The Virgin Mary

Of all the heroines of the Middle Ages the Virgin Mary was certainly the most adored. Through religious writings, poetry, drama and images in books, as well as statues, frescoes and mosaics, she became part of the everyday lives of people, and in particular women. Magnificent cathedrals, from Notre Dame (Our Lady) in Paris, begun in 1163, to the fourteenth-century Kościół Mariacki (St Mary's Basilica) in Krakow, were built in her honour. The mosaic of Mary as mother of God enthroned in the golden apse of Hagia Sophia in Istanbul with the two great Byzantine emperors, Constantine and Justinian, beside her is one of the most powerful images in Christian art.

We learn relatively little about the life of the Virgin Mary from the Bible; surprisingly she is mentioned more times in the Quran (as Maryam, mother of the prophet Isa) than she is in the Gospels (39:14). Her first appearance in the Bible is in the Old Testament prophecy of Isaiah, though her name is not given: 'Behold, a virgin shall conceive and bear a Son, and shall call His name

1 The Annunciation: God sends his blessing down in the form of golden rays, while Mary kneels before an open book and the scroll contains the opening words of the 'Ave Maria'. Twelve scenes from the life of the Virgin surround the main image: (left from top) Joachim receives a message while tending his sheep; Joachim and Anne are expelled from the Temple; Joachim and Anne meet at the golden gates; Mary is presented at the Temple by her parents; (right from top) an angel appears to Joachim; an angel appears to Anne; the birth of Mary; Mary is given the veil to weave; (bottom row) an angel brings Mary a cushion while she is praying; an angel helps Mary with her needlework; Joseph and elders enter the Temple with rods; Mary is betrothed to Joseph. In the Bedford Hours (Paris, c.1420) Add MS 18850, f. 32r.

2 The Nativity with Mary in a bed, pointing, Joseph seated beside her, the Christ Child in the manger and the ox and ass nearby, in a Psalter (Oxford, early 13th century) Arundel 157, f. 3v.

Immanuel'.[1] Then in the New Testament at the Annunciation, the archangel Gabriel comes to her and tells her that she will give birth to the Son of God, an event related in the Gospels of Mark and Luke. Scenes of the Annunciation take pride of place in Books of Hours, the personal prayer books that were widely owned by medieval women. An example is the full-page illumination in the Bedford Hours (Image 1) where the magnificent settings and garments show the esteem in which Mary was held.

In Matthew's Gospel it is said that Joseph (Mary's betrothed) planned to divorce her quietly when he found that she had conceived a child out of wedlock, but an angel appeared to him in a dream to explain that she was a virgin and that she would give birth to the Son of God. Luke tells how Mary went to the hill country of Judea to visit her cousin Elizabeth, who was pregnant with the future John the Baptist, and they celebrated these miraculous events together. Mary's next appearance in the Bible is at the birth of Christ in Bethlehem; the

3 The Holy Family in the carpenter's shop, with Joseph working, Mary sewing and Christ playing with a spinning top, in a Book of Hours (Catalunya, 1461–1500) Add MS 18193, f. 48v.

Maidens or Monsters?

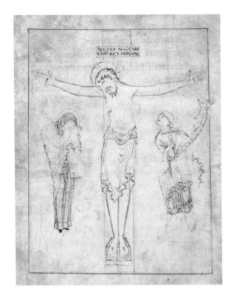

4a and 4b. Scenes of Mary sorrowing at the Crucifixion, in manuscripts of the 10th and 15th centuries:

4a. (left) With John the Evangelist in the Ramsey Psalter, a Book of Psalms (Winchester or Ramsay Abbey, 975–1000) Harley MS 2904, f. 3v.

4b. (right) With Mary Magdalene and St John in the *Bible historiale*, a book of illustrated Bible stories in French that belonged to King Edward IV (Bruges, *c*.1475) Royal MS 15 D I, f. 353r.

image of her beside the infant Christ in the stable is well known, well loved and reproduced on thousands of Christmas cards (Image 2), as is the visit of the Magi.

Little is said in the Gospels about Mary as a young mother and about Jesus's childhood, though later he is referred to as the 'carpenter's son' so medieval artists have depicted the Holy Family in the carpenter's shop (Image 3). She is present at the wedding at Cana, where she witnesses her adult son's first miracle when he turns the water into wine. At the end of Christ's life on earth she is the *Mater Dolorosa* (Sorrowing Mother) standing at the foot of the Cross, usually with St John (Image 4). The only time Jesus speaks to his mother directly in the New Testament is at his death, when he asks her to turn to John as her son in his place, and asks John to take care of her.

After the Resurrection, Mary is described in Acts as having been present with the apostles when they received the Holy Spirit at Pentecost. She then remained in the background and it is not known where she lived and died, though both Ephesus and Jerusalem have claimed to be the place of her death, which is not recorded in the Bible. Nevertheless a tradition arose about Mary's

5 The coronation of Mary as Queen of Heaven, in a Psalter produced by nuns (Germany, mid-13th century) Add MS 60629, f. 56v.

'dormition' or 'falling asleep' in the first millennium, in which she did not die but was taken up to heaven by angels and crowned by her son (Image 5). Feasts of the Assumption (from the Latin *assumptio*, meaning 'taking up') and the Coronation of the Virgin are celebrated in the Catholic and Eastern Orthodox Churches.

After Jesus's birth, the Gospels briefly relate how the Holy Family fled to Egypt to escape Herod's infanticides. From this short account there arose numerous tales about miracles performed by Mary that were popular in both eastern and western Christian traditions. The travellers were supposedly accompanied by angels and were pursued by Herod's soldiers, who were on the trail of the infant Christ. In one story, the soldiers questioned peasants working in a field about when the family had passed by. The peasants truthfully replied that it had been when they were sowing the seed; however, miraculously the corn had grown to full height in a few hours, and so the soldiers did not realise that the family had recently been there. A Syriac text describes the arrival of Mary and Joseph in an Egyptian city where people worshipped various idols. Mary entered a temple dedicated to idols and the earth shook, causing the idolatrous statues to fall and break into tiny pieces. These and other miracles associated with the Virgin Mary were a popular subject of church wall paintings and manuscript illuminations (Image 6).

With the growth of Mary's popularity in the Middle Ages, a vast repertoire of stories and legends about her was popularised. Mary's own immaculate conception and early life were described in texts known as apocrypha dating from the early Christian era, including the *Gospel of Pseudo-Matthew* (translated into Old English in the eleventh century). The events in these works were excluded from the canonical Bible as too implausible and without sufficient evidence. According to the apocrypha, Mary's birth was announced by an angel to her elderly parents, Joachim and his wife Anne (or Anna). The couple had been persecuted in their community as they had not been able to conceive a child, until Anne miraculously conceived Mary while Joachim was away tending his flocks. She was born to great rejoicing (Image 7a) and grew into an extraordinarily talented infant who could walk seven steps at only 6 months old. When she was presented at the Temple aged 3 years (Image 7b) she danced on the steps. Mary then lived among the Temple virgins and was fed by the angels. When she reached maturity, it was revealed by a miraculous sign that she should be married to Joseph, an elderly widower in her community, and he was told by an angel that she was to bear God's son.

6 The flight into Egypt, with two roundels showing the miracles of the corn and of the falling idols, in a Book of Hours (Bruges, c.1485) Add MS 17280, f. 210v.

7a The Virgin Mary at her birth. She is already wearing a crown and is held by her mother St Anne, in a Book of Hours with captions in Dutch (Utrecht or Guelders, c.1420) Add MS 50005, f. 5v.

7b Anne and Joachim giving over Mary to the service of the Temple, and the angel bringing food to Mary in the Temple, in a Book of Gospels and other works in Ge'ez (Ethiopia, 17th century) Or 481, f. 99r.

In the writings of the early Church, Mary became an example of Christian virtue, and a companion to women. Her womb was described as a hall of purity (*aula pudoris* in Latin),[2] and she was seen as the epitome of loving and consoling motherhood. Hildegard of Bingen, the twelfth-century German abbess and mystic, composed a hymn celebrating Mary's body, containing the following lines:

Ave generosa
Venter enim tuus gaudium habuit
cum omnis celestis symphonia de te
sonuit,
quia virgo Filium Dei portasti,
ubi castitas tua in Deo claruit.

Hail, noble one
Your womb rejoiced
as from you sounded forth the whole
celestial symphony.
For as a virgin you have borne the
Son of God–
in God your chastity shone bright.[3]

Representations of the Madonna and Child, in which Mary gazes adoringly at the divine child seated on her knee, were produced by some of the most famous artists of the late medieval and Renaissance periods. These

8 The Virgin Mary and Child with angels, attributed to Simon Bening, in the Prayer Book of Joanna of Ghistelles, abbess of the Benedictine Abbey of Messines in Flanders (Ghent, c.1516) Egerton MS 2125, f. 157v.

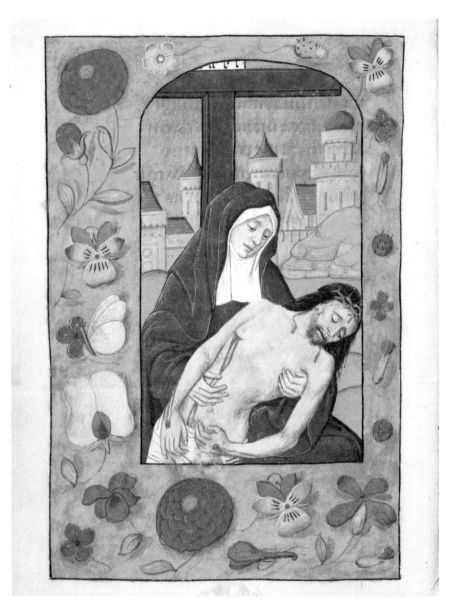

9 *Pietà*, Mary holding Christ's wounded body, in a Book of Hours (Bruges, c.1500) Kings MS 9, f. 153v.

range from manuscript illuminators such as Simon Bening (Image 8) to Duccio, Raphael and Rembrandt and many others whose images on altarpieces, paintings and statues are intimate and moving. The *Pietà*, a representation of the sorrowing Mary cradling Christ's dead body, famously depicted in marble by Michelangelo at the end of the fifteenth century, is an iconography originally

10 A full-page golden image of the 'Holy Kinship' depicts St Anne, the Virgin Mary's mother, with her three husbands in the lowest section. Above are Anne's three daughters – all named Maria – with their husbands, Joachim, Alpheus and Zebedee; in the two upper sections are Mary, Jesus and his five male cousins all with their names written underneath. In the Queen Mary Psalter (London, c.1315) Royal MS 2 B VII, f. 68r.

11. 'The Miracle of the Painter and the Devil', illustrated beneath Psalm 96, in the lower margin of the Queen Mary Psalter, Royal MS 2 B VII, f. 211r.

developed in northern and eastern European art, where the wounds of Christ are often prominently displayed (Image 9).

An extended family was attributed to the Virgin in one popular medieval work; according to Haymo of Halberstadt in his *Historiae sacrae epitome* ('Summary of Holy History'), Mary's mother Anne had two husbands in addition to Joachim and so she had two half-sisters, also called Mary. They had five sons between them who became the apostles Simon, Jude, John the Evangelist, James the Less and James the Greater (Image 10).

Devotion to Mary in the time of the crusades increased further with the popularity of a collection of stories known as the *Miracles of the Virgin*, popularised in England by the cleric and historian William of Malmesbury and others. They emphasised her intercessory power, which she used to save those who believed in her from spiritual or physical harm.

In some cases, her help was invoked in a variety of extreme and bizarre circumstances:

·   when a child was thrown by his pagan father into an oven as punishment for going to church, she rescued the child, who emerged unharmed from the oven to convert his parents;

12a A monk and a lady meet and embrace, while a neighbour and a dog watch.

12b The couple beg Mary's forgiveness for their adultery and are pardoned.

12c Mary escorts the monk back into his monastery.

12d The lady is welcomed home by her husband.

12 a–d 'The Miracle of the Monk and the Knight's Lady' pictured in the lower margins of the Smithfield Decretals (Toulouse, 1300; decorated London, c.1340) Royal MS 10 E IV, ff. 185v–191r.

- when an inexperienced young monk spilled wine on the chapel's altar linen and stained it, she made the stain disappear;
- when a son hid the best meat when his widowed mother came to dinner, though she had bequeathed him her fortune, she attached two frogs to his face;
- when a monk painting a fresco high on a church wall had his ladder broken by the Devil (who did not like the way he was being portrayed), the Virgin in the fresco came to life to rescue the painter from falling to his death (Image 11).

The *Miracles of the Virgin* survive in numerous copies, but few of the manuscripts are illustrated as they were intended for daily use, for instance as *exempla* (examples) in sermons. Nevertheless the stories are pictured in the margins of a number of luxury manuscripts, including an English royal book, the Queen Mary Psalter (Images 10, 11). Another series (Images 12a-d) is from a law book known as the Smithfield Decretals, a work of Canon law formerly owned by the priory of St Bartholomew at Smithfield in London. It was produced in southern France, but after it arrived in London a vast array of illustrations were added in the margins.

The subject matter of the *Miracles* is wide-ranging, varying from comic to serious, and from morally uplifting to violent and scandalous, but in all of them Mary is a true heroine, acting decisively against lions and devils, while treating repentant sinners with compassion. The British Library holds one illustrated manuscript in English containing five of the *Miracles of the Virgin*. In one of the stories a young man uses the dark arts to try to seduce a young woman; she prays to Mary, who appears and confiscates the book of magic spells, and the maiden's virtue is preserved (Image 13).

Out of gratitude, all those who the Virgin rescued in these stories immediately became her virtuous followers. Her miraculous deeds have been pictured and retold in popular literature and drama. Around the globe, from Walsingham to Tamil Nadu, Guadalupe, Wisconsin, Lourdes and Rwanda, wherever Mary has appeared – often to young girls from poor backgrounds – important shrines have become sites of pilgrimage for Catholics and Protestants alike. And though the official Church was dominated by men throughout the Middle Ages and beyond, she has remained a prominent symbol of the role played by women in the origins of Christianity and has long represented the female face of this religion. More recently the stereotype of the pure virgin – in contrast to the temptresses, Eve and Mary Magdalene – has been explored and questioned by some women, but for many Mary remains a powerful representation of motherhood and an intercessor with Christ.

13 The 'Miracle of Love gained by the Dark Arts' in a Carthusian miscellany (N. England, 1460–1500) Add. MS 37049, f. 95r.

6.

St Margaret of Antioch

Anyone who visits art galleries and old churches is likely to have come across an image of a saintly woman either emerging from the belly, or standing on top, of a defeated, supine dragon, often holding a cross, or plunging it down the creature's throat. This would be St Margaret who – alongside St Catherine and St Mary Magdalene – was one of the most popular female saints in the Middle Ages. She was revered across all strata of society, judging by the variety and number of surviving artefacts associated with her cult. Her easily recognisable image is found in numerous manuscripts, statues, stained-glass windows, paintings and embroidery from the eighth to the sixteenth centuries. In England alone more than 200 churches were dedicated to her during this period, including St Margaret's Westminster, the parish church of the Houses of Parliament in London. In a number of early churches her life story is depicted in series of wall paintings, and the Queen Mary Psalter, a magnificently illustrated manuscript from London or East Anglia, has an extended series of fifteen or

1a–d St Margaret and the dragon in personal prayer books from England and Europe:

1a (top left) The Alphonso Psalter (London or Westminster, c.1316) Add. MS 24686, f. 2v.

1b (top right) Book of Hours (S. Netherlands, 1425–50) Harley MS 2846, f. 48v.

1c (below left) The Hastings Hours, or London Hours of William Lord Hastings (Netherlands, c.1480) Add MS 54782, f. 62v.

1d (below right) Margaret emerging from the dragon and attacking the demon with a cat-o'-nine-tails, in the Huth Psalter (Lincoln, late 13th century) Add MS 38116, f. 13r.

2 Olibrius the Roman governor rides by and calls to Margaret, who is spinning and watching her sheep, in the Queen Mary Psalter (London, c.1315) Royal MS 2 B VII, f. 307v.

more miniatures in the lower margins illustrating all the key events of her life (see Images 2–5). It is a story that is perhaps the most fascinating of all the female saints; alongside all the standard elements, such as high birth, being pursued by a powerful figure and torture, it includes supernatural encounters with hideous creatures that have inspired artists through the ages.

Margaret lived in the early fourth century AD, a period of harsh persecution of Christians under the emperors Diocletian and Maximian, particularly in the eastern Roman empire. According to Eusebius of Caesarea (d.340), lists were made of believers and they were forced to offer sacrifices to the Roman gods outside the baths and markets. If they refused, they were sent to work in the quarries for the remainder of their (short) lives, but not before they had had an eye plucked out or a tendon in their leg severed. At this time there lived a young girl called Margaret, daughter of Theodosius, the pagan archpriest of Antioch. She was sent away into the countryside as a young girl to be fostered by a nurse, who was a Christian and secretly educated her in the Christian faith (no explanation is given as to why Margaret's parents sent her to be brought up in the country by a woman who they obviously had not vetted very closely, and they play no further part in her story). It then transpired that at the age of 15 she was guarding a flock of sheep beside the road when Olibrius, the Roman governor of the province of Syria rode by on his way to persecute the Christians of Antioch (Image 2). He was immediately overcome with desire for the beautiful shepherdess, and

3 Margaret is brought before Olibrius and berates him for his paganism, while he threatens her, in the Queen Mary Psalter, Royal MS 2 B VII, f. 308r.

sent his men to bring her to him, intending to have her for himself while she was still young.

When the soldiers tried to abduct her, she prayed to God for help and, hearing this, they returned to Olibrius to tell him that she was a Christian and so he was wasting his time on her. But he was determined to have this young maiden who was as 'lovely as a pearl'[1] (*margarita* is Latin for 'pearl') and ordered that she be brought before him (Image 3). Unafraid, she told him that she was a virgin of high birth who had given her life to Christ and would never forsake her vow, so he immediately had her thrown in prison, possibly hoping that this would endear him to her. The next day he used bribery and flattery to try to win her over, then threatened her with dire consequences if she did not succumb to his advances and worship his pagan gods. But Margaret stood firm, declaring that she was not afraid to suffer for her faith. When Olibrius admitted that he knew of Christ's Crucifixion from reading the books of Christians, she berated him for knowing these things but continuing to deny the Christian faith.

At Olibrius's command Margaret was put on the rack, beaten with rods and her flesh raked with iron combs until her bones were exposed and her blood flowed as if from a spring (Image 4). Bystanders wept and even her torturers tried to persuade her to recant and save herself from further mutilation, but she retorted, 'Be gone, evil counsellors! This torture of the flesh is the soul's salvation'. The governor returned to see what progress had been made and was so horrified at the severity of her wounds that he covered his face with his cloak.

The poor young woman was then taken down from the rack and thrown back in her cell, where she was visited by her nurse and by a holy man called

4 Margaret is tied up by the hair, whipped and lacerated, in the Queen Mary Psalter, Royal MS 2 B VII, f. 308v.

Theotimus, who fed her with bread and water through the window. As she prayed for strength to face her persecutors, her cell was filled with holy radiance, but then a monstrous dragon named Rufo appeared and leapt at her, devouring her in one gulp. She cried to God for help and the cross she was holding grew to a huge size and ripped open the dragon's stomach so that she emerged unscathed. No sooner had she done so than a black demon emerged in the corner of her cell, but she pushed him to the ground, holding him down with her foot on his neck and interrogating him (Image 1d). He admitted that he was a servant of Satan named Beelzebub who had been imprisoned by Solomon in a vessel along with his fellow demons until they were released by the armies of Nebuchadnezzar. Margaret commanded him to 'Lie still, thou fiend, under the feet of a woman'. The Devil replied, 'O blessed Margaret, I am overcome. If a young man had overcome me I had not recked, but alas! I am overcome of a tender virgin; wherefore I make the more sorrow, for thy father and mother have been my good friends'[2] (the words here are attributed to William Caxton, who printed his translation of the *Legenda aurea,* 'Golden Legend', in 1483). The fiend then admitted that the reason he tempted virtuous men and women was a malicious desire to lead them astray. Margaret dismissed him contemptuously and he vanished.

cena bona retribuas.

5 Margaret praying in a cauldron, in the Queen Mary Psalter, Royal MS 2 B VII, f. 311v.

The next day the young woman was brought before a judge and an assembled crowd, but still she refused to worship pagan gods and was further tortured. She was tied up and thrown into a cauldron (Image 5), at which point there was a sudden earthquake and a dove descended from heaven, setting a golden crown on her head.

Seeing this, 5,000 men and numerous women were converted to Christianity and were immediately beheaded by Olibrius. Fearing that more conversions might take place, he decided that Margaret should be beheaded outside the city. She requested time to pray for pardon of her persecutors, forgiveness for sinners, and special protection for women in childbirth, and a voice from heaven promised to grant all these requests. Margaret bowed her head before the soldier, Malchus, who had been chosen to execute her. He refused on account of the miracles he had seen but she persuaded him to go ahead, saying that he would be forgiven. Afraid and trembling, he chopped off her head and fell dead beside her (Image 6).

Margaret was brought a palm of victory by angels, and Theotimus, who had witnessed everything, promised to write down her story. He had a tomb built for her, where many miracles occurred (Image 7). Her relics were stolen from Antioch in 908 and taken to Italy, where some ended up in Montefalcone cathedral and others in Venice. An oval glass-fronted reliquary purporting to

6 Three angels descend to carry the decapitated St Margaret to heaven, while demons lament and Malchus lies dead beside her, in *Life and Passion of St Margaret* (N. Italy, 14th century) Egerton MS 877, f. 11r.

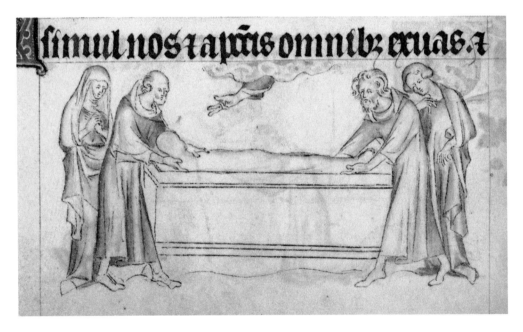

7 As Margaret is laid in her tomb by Theotimus and others, the hand of God points to her, in the Queen Mary Psalter, Royal MS 2 B VII, f. 313v.

hold 'first class *ex ossibus* (from the bone), relics of Margaret of Antioch on a red silk background' (origin: Italy) is offered online at 'The Russian Store' in Boston, USA, marked 'sold!'.

So many versions of St Margaret's life were produced throughout Europe that it would be a mammoth task to edit and collate all of them. The first known example was in Greek (where she was called 'Marina', causing confusion among later hagiographers) and then Latin. A version of her story survives in an Old English manuscript now in the British Library, Cotton Tiberius, MS A III, from c.AD 1000 (*Seinte Marherete the Meiden ant Martyr*) and hers is one of the earliest saints' lives to be written down in the French vernacular language. It is the *Vie de sainte Marguerite*, by the Norman author Wace (d. c.1180), who was born in the Channel Islands and to whom the *Roman de Brut* (an early version of the King Arthur story) is attributed.

A prose version of her story, *The Liflade ant te Passiun of Seinte Margarete*, was copied in the thirteenth century in several manuscripts (including two now in the British Library), as part of a group of texts in a West Midlands dialect of English that is known as the 'Katherine Group'. It includes lives of two other female martyrs, Saints Katherine and Juliene, and a letter on virginity, *Hali Meidhad*, as well as a guide for anchoresses, the *Ancrene Wisse*. All the texts focus on the subject of virginity and especially the idea of the virgin as the bride of Christ.

Hercneth! Alle the earen ant herunge habbeth, widewen with tha iweddede, ant te meidnes nomeliche, lusten swithe yeorliche hu ha schulen luvien the liviende Lauerd ant libben i meithhad, swa thet ha moten, thurh thet eadie meiden the we munneth todei with meithhades menske, thet seli meidnes song singen with this meiden ant with thet heovenliche hird echeliche in Heovene. This meiden thet we munieth wes Margarete ihaten.

Listen! All who have ears and hearing, widows with the wedded and the maidens especially, let them listen very eagerly to how they should love the living Lord and live in virginity, which to him is the best-loved virtue, so that they may, through that blessed maiden whom we commemorate today, with the strength of virginity, sing that holy maiden's song both with this maiden along with that heavenly host forever in heaven. This Maiden that we commemorate was called Margaret.[3]

St Margaret was one of a select group of medieval saints known as the 'Fourteen Holy Helpers' whose intercession was believed to be especially helpful

in times of trial, and she is often pictured in the company of the Virgin Mary (Image 8). Nevertheless she has long been a somewhat controversial saint; as early as the fifth century Pope Gelasius raised questions about the authenticity of her story and she does not appear among the female saints in the earliest Syrian martyrologies. Jacobus de Voragine, who included her life story in his collection of hagiographies known as the *Legenda aurea* describes parts of it as 'apocryphal and not to be taken seriously'.[4] Nevertheless she appears in Pope Gregory's martyrology of official Roman saints in the sixth century and not long afterwards in an English calendar of saints' days (seventh century).

Margaret is listed in dictionaries of saints as the patron saint of farmers, teachers, soldiers, nurses, and women in childbirth. Hers was one of the voices heard by Joan of Arc, calling her to rescue France from the English invaders. The English Sarum breviary as it is still used today has the following entry for her: 'those who invoke her on their deathbeds will enjoy divine protection and escape from the devils, that those who dedicate churches or burn lights in her honour will obtain anything useful they pray for'.[5]

St Margaret's association with childbirth, fertility and motherhood possibly stems from the prayer she offered just before she died, asking God's help for pregnant women and their babies, and because she emerged unscathed from the dragon's belly. Childbirth would have been a terrifying prospect for medieval women in a time of high mortality for both mothers and infants. The many written prayers and amulets which survive show that they relied on these to see them through the experience. Prayers to St Margaret were often included in Books of Hours, Psalters (books of psalms) and other personal devotional works owned by women, in which some images appear worn. A page from an Italian manuscript of the *Life and Passion of St Margaret* (Image 9) shows signs such as smudges and patches of colour that suggest it may have been touched or even placed on the stomachs of women in labour as a charm or talisman. Above the drawing is a prayer beginning, '*Exi infans, Christus te vocat*' ('Come forth, infant, Christ is summoning you').

The Middle English poem, John Lydgate's *The Lyfe of Seynt Margaret*, was commissioned from him by Anne Mortimer, Countess of March, in the early fifteenth century when she was a young wife, perhaps contemplating childbirth. Margaret was a popular name in the Middle Ages, at least for the royal and noble ladies whose records survive. One royal namesake became a

8 The Virgin Mary seated on a throne and holding the Christ Child, with her feet resting on a dragon and a lion; the niches around her canopy contain angels, St Katherine (bottom left) and St Margaret (bottom right), in the De Lisle Psalter (East Anglia, early 14th century) Arundel MS 83, f. 131v.

9 A woman lying in a bed screened by a curtain, with a swaddled infant held by a midwife; an illustration in a manuscript of the *Life and Passion of St Margaret*, Egerton MS 877, f. 12r.

saint herself: St Margaret of Scotland, who was born in Hungary in 1045 to Edward Aetheling, a pretender to the English throne, and married Malcolm III, King of the Scots, in *c*.1070, bearing him six sons and two daughters (Images 10a and b). A devout Christian, she still found time to rise at midnight to attend Holy Mass and feed the poor and orphans every day. She was canonised in 1250 after several miracles occurred, including the rescue of her gospel book from a stream where it was submerged but remained unharmed, and flashes of light from her tomb at Dunfermline Abbey in 1245.

Despite Margaret's popularity in the Middle Ages, in 1969 she and a number of saints of doubtful origin were removed from the official calendar of the Roman Catholic Church through an apostolic letter from Pope Paul VI. However, she continues to be venerated by the Church of England (feast day, 20 July), the Coptic and the Eastern Orthodox churches.

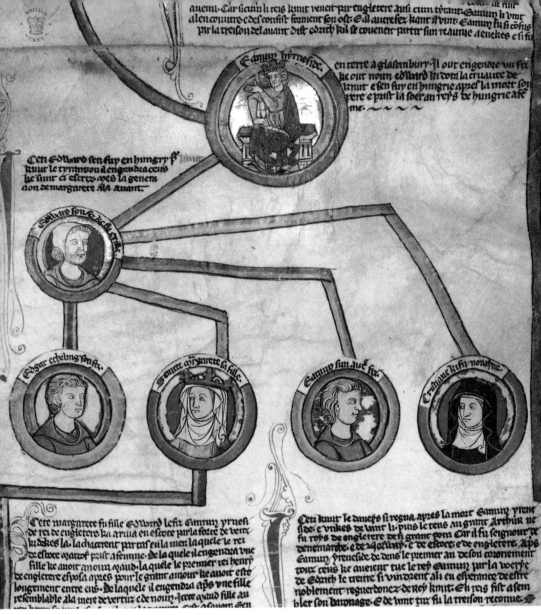

10a St Margaret of Scotland, granddaughter of Edmund Ironside, shown with her sisters, in a Royal Genealogical Roll (England, c.1300) Royal MS 14 B VI.

10b Detail of St Margaret, with a line of descent just visible beneath leading to her daughter, Margaret, who married King Henry I of England.

7.

Hairy Saints and Harlots

The deeds of three harlots-turned-holy-women are perhaps the most extreme of all the improbable saints' lives of the medieval period. Not only did they reform their lives from the depths of sin to the heights of asceticism and saintliness, but to achieve that one of them was prepared to masquerade as a man, in an unusual example of cross-dressing in medieval religious writing.

St Mary of Egypt

Perhaps the most eccentric of all three is the sixth-century St Mary of Egypt, also known as 'Hairy Mary' (hair features prominently in her story). In her early teens, Mary ran away from home to the fleshpots of Alexandria, where she enjoyed a life of debauchery, and 'never refused her body to anyone',[1] though apparently at least she did not take payment for her favours. Then when she was almost 30, her life changed completely. She joined a group of pilgrims travelling to Jerusalem for the festival of the Holy Cross, and took pleasure in seducing them on the journey – until one day she had a sudden conversion. Following some young men to the doors of the church where the Cross was kept, she found that an unknown force prevented her from entering. She forced her way inside, immediately experiencing the wonder of the holy relic,

---

1 St Zosima hands Mary his cloak, in the Dunois Hours (France, c.1445) Yates Thompson MS 3, f. 287r.

2 Mary, covered by hair, with three loaves of bread, in the Taymouth Hours (London, mid-14th century) Yates Thompson MS 13, f. 188v.

and from this moment onwards she renounced all earthly pleasures. She set off into the desert with only three loaves of bread (Image 2), miraculously walking across the River Jordan on the way. Living independently as a pious ascetic in the wilderness, she endured extreme hardship until her skin was blackened by the sun, her hair was scorched white and her breasts withered. In some accounts of her legend, she grew hair on her body to preserve her modesty (Image 3).

Much of what we know about Mary is based on the writings of Sophronius, patriarch of Jerusalem (c.AD 600). He relates how St Zosima, a priest who journeyed deep into the desert to meditate, had an extraordinary vision of a naked, emaciated woman. He pursued her along the banks of the Jordan until she turned around and terrified the poor man, calling him by his name and asking him to loan her his cloak to cover her body (Images 1, 4). Mary then told him her story, entreating him to return to his monastery, to come back in a year to give her Holy Communion, and not to tell anyone about her until after her death, and with that she vanished into the desert.

After a year, Zosima returned as he had promised, bringing her a basket of food, but she only took Communion, blessed him and ate three lentils. The following year when he returned there was no sign of Mary, so he prayed for a sign and the location of her body was revealed to him. Next to her in the sand

3 Mary of Egypt in the wilderness with monkeys, in the Smithfield Decretals (Toulouse, 1300; London, c.1340) Royal MS 10 E IV, f. 275r.

4 St Zosima, looking the other way, hands the naked and emaciated Mary a cloak, in the Theodore Psalter (Constantinople, 1066) Add MS 19352, f. 68r.

was inscribed a message asking him to bury her, so the old man made a futile attempt to dig a grave in the hard earth, using a piece of wood he had found. Looking up, he was terrified when he saw an enormous lion standing next to Mary's body, licking her feet, but the fierce beast willingly dug a grave with his claws. Zosima washed Mary's body with his tears and covered it with earth. When he returned to his monastery he told his brothers all about Mary, and they kept her memory alive, passing it on to Sophronius to record. To this day there are several churches dedicated to Mary of Egypt in Naples and Rome, and a chapel commemorating the site of her conversion in the Church of the Holy Sepulchre in Jerusalem.

St Thais of Egypt

Thais was a young Egyptian courtesan who was so beautiful that young men fought fierce duels to win her favour, leaving pools of blood on her doorstep. Many reduced themselves to poverty so that they could pay for her services and she became very wealthy. Her reputation was such that news of her reached a monk named Paphnutius, who decided to investigate. He donned everyday clothes, went to her rooms and gave her the going rate for a visit which, according to Caxton's translation of the *Golden Legend*, was 'a shilling, that is to say twelve pence, as it had been cause for sin with her'.[2] This is probably more than would have been paid to a prostitute in the fourteenth century, but for medieval Christians the reference to payment would have been a reminder of the link between greed and wantonness (Images 5a–5d).[3]

Entering her room, where her bed was draped with precious fabrics, Paphnutius berated Thais for leading so many men to wickedness. She knelt before him and wept, promising to repent and lead a chaste life in future (Image 5e). She then took all the luxuries that she had earned by her sinful deeds and burned them on a pyre in the middle of the city (Image 6). She followed Paphnutius to a convent where he closed her in a small cell and sealed the door with lead, instructing the nuns to give her a little food and water each day. He told her that she was not worthy to pray, but should stand always looking to the east and begging God for forgiveness. Her bodily excretions were to remain in the room with her as a reminder of the foulness of her sins. After three years Paphnutius returned and he learned from the vision of St Anthony, the desert father and ascetic, that God had pardoned Thais. She was released from her cell but only lived another fifteen days before dying peacefully. She became a popular saint with medieval Christians, who were touched by her story of punishment endured and the forgiveness that came too late. Numerous versions existed in Greek and Syriac and a play was written about her in Latin

5a Thais with a lover giving away his money.

5b Thais entertaining a lover.

5c Men fighting over Thais.

5d Father Paphnutius goes to visit Thais, who is arranging her hair.

5e Thais kneels before Father Paphnutius.

5a–e Images in the lower margins of in the Smithfield Decretals, Royal MS 10 E IV, ff. 178r, 179r, 179v, 180r, 182v.

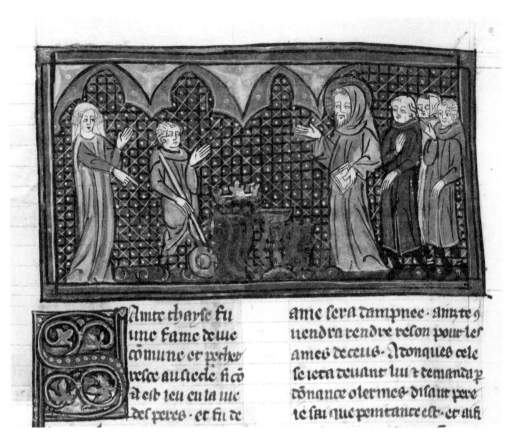

6 St Thais burns her earnings, including gold plate, in front of Abbot Paphnutius, in *La Vie des Saints* ('The Life of the Saints'), translated into French by Jean Beleth (Paris, c.1330) Add MS 17275, f. 312v.

by a nun named Hroswitha of Gandesheim in the tenth century. This was followed by English, French and Spanish versions, and the thirteenth-century *Vidin Miscellany,* a collection of religious texts for women in the Bulgarian language, contains her hagiography.

The story of Thais remained popular into the twentieth century. It was retold in a novel by Anatole France in 1890, with Paphnutius as a former libertine who declares his love for her as she is dying, claiming that faith is an illusion and that earthly love is lasting. An opera by Massenet followed shortly afterwards, and in the early 1900s an Egyptologist named Gayet claimed to have discovered Thais's mummified remains, which were placed on display in Paris. Having staged a re-creation of her burial and resurrection before a mesmerised audience, he later admitted that he had no concrete evidence for the identification.

St Pelagia

In the life of St Pelagia a dramatic story of sin and conversion in the desert is combined with the issue of transvestism, as she takes on the identity of a man in order to live the life of an ascetic. The events were recorded by an eyewitness, Jacob the Deacon, in Greek and translated into Latin by Eustochius. The beautiful actress and courtesan Margareta was seen one morning riding through the city of Antioch by a group of eminent bishops.

ecce subito transiit per nos
prima mimarum Antiochiae;
ipsaque est prima choreutriarum
pantomimarum, sedens super
asellum; et processit cum summa
phantasia, adornata ita, ut nihil
videretur super ea nisi aurum et
margaritae et lapides pretiosi;
nuditas vero pedum ejus ex auro
et margaritis erat cooperta: cum
qua maxima erat pompa puerorum
et puellarum in vestibus pretiosis
amicta, et torques aurea super
collum ejus.

lo, suddenly there came among us the chief actress of Antioch, the first in the chorus in the theatre, sitting on a donkey. She was dressed in the height of fantasy, wearing nothing but gold, pearls and precious stones, even her bare feet were covered with gold and pearls. With her went a great throng of boys and girls all dressed in cloth of gold with collars of gold on their necks.[4]

One of them, the holy Bishop Nonnus, could not stop looking at the beautiful young woman and announced to the other bishops that he was delighted by her great beauty, weeping into his open Bible at the thoughts inspired by her. He compared the long hours she spent on her appearance in order to please her lovers to the preparation Christians should make to beautify their inner selves before they met God on the Day of Judgement. The next day while Nonnus was preaching, Margareta entered the church and was 'pierced by the fear of the Lord'. She began to cry floods of tears and later wrote to him, begging for help to enter the Lord's presence. He replied, saying that she should come before him and the other bishops; he could not meet her alone as this would be too tempting for him.

Margareta came and threw herself at the bishop's feet, begging him to baptise her if she promised to turn away from her former life to become a bride of Christ. Nonnus exorcised her and baptised her Pelagia (Image 7), rejecting her former name Margareta (meaning 'pearl', and referring to her sumptuous jewellery and adornment) and appointing himself her godfather. Just then the Devil appeared and berated Pelagia for abandoning him, but she made the sign

7 The baptism of Pelagia, in Wauchier de Denain, *La Vie des Saints*, Royal MS 20 D VI, f. 221v.

of the Cross and blew him away. Two days later he came to her in the night, but again God helped her to resist him (Image 8). On the third day she called her servant and arranged to give all her precious possessions to Nonnus, who immediately distributed them to the poor widows and orphans of Antioch. On the eighth day after her baptism, when it was time to take off her white robes, she donned Nonnus's clothing and disappeared from Antioch in the middle of the night.

Years later Jacob the Deacon (narrator of the story) travelled into the desert at the request of Bishop Nonnus to visit a holy eunuch named Pelagius who had a reputation for great piety. Jacob found the saintly hermit in a small cell with one window on the Mount of Olives and was inspired by the sight of the hermit's angelic face, not realising that this was, in fact, Pelagia. He then went visiting monasteries around Jerusalem, where the fame of the monk Pelagius was widespread. But when he returned to the cell after some time there was no answer to his repeated calls and so at God's prompting he broke the window and found Pelagius's body – they had died as a result of extreme asceticism. He ran to Jerusalem to warn the other monks and they came to anoint the body in preparation for burial. Then they realised it was the body of a woman, but it

et comm ence la me de faite
pelagie · iv · xix ·
Antre pelagie fu
premierement dos
fames de la ate da
tiache · et fu plam
ne de richestes et
tres belle de cors en habit co
uonteuse namne par pensse
et en cors luxurieuse · une fois
passoit par la ate a grant or
gueil · en tele maniere que sor
lui ne ueoit on ne · or ne argent
et pierres preciouses · et prot
la quelle aloit elle resplendir
soit lair de diuerses choses sou
ef flairant · La quele simioit

dune putain deuant le regart
de ta maieste qui fer adouter cel
le pour les terriennes choses par
couueram estude ce est faire tel
te · Et ic atoi mon seigneur no
mortel ppose plaire atoi et par ma
negligence ie ne lai me fait ·
Et dist a ceus qui estoient o lui
ie uous di en uerite · elle ceste
dieux au iugement en cotre
nous amenra · Car ceste a est
painte si entontuement pre
que elle plaise a ses amis tres
et nous au celestiel espour ne
uoulons plaire · En dementres
que il disoit ces choses sembla
bles sou dampnement il condir

8 St Pelagia is visited by the Devil and a black bird while she is asleep in bed; Bishop Nonnus
blesses her, in *La Vie des Saints*, Add MS 17275, 311v.

N Antiochie bi ȝonde þe see.
A womman woned in a citee.
Dame Pelagi was heo calð
Of hir bodi was heo ful bold.
Fer womman heo was j nouȝ.
And mony a mon to synne heo þouȝ.
For commyn made heo hir bodi.
In flesch luft and lecheri.
Barouns knihtes & abbeys
Come to here from dyuse cuntes.
And riche men of vche a leode.
Come to hir for hir fer hede.
And ȝaf hir gold & riche mede.
To fulfille þe flesch luft þt dede.
Pelagi ful fere hem calð.
And good chep hire flesch heo salð
And was euer more ȝedi.
To singe þt hem in lecheri.
Of þis seruise serued Pelagi.
Til crist wold bete hire þropest.
And j wol telle on what manere.
He made hir soule hol & fere.
And made hir han repentaunce.
And for hir synne do riȝt penaunce.
þe Archebisschop of þt citee.
þere heo lived in hir jolite.
Let maken a gret sembie.
Of alle þe Bisschopes of þe cuntre
Whon alle þe Bisschop j gredercð was.
And Wasseð in þt cuttee paie.
Wfel aunt þt ȝei alle swete.
On a day in comune strete.

was so emaciated that Jacob had not recognised Pelagia. Immediately the news spread and people travelled from as far afield as Jericho and Jordan to witness the phenomenon, with nuns and monks carrying candles and lamps, singing hymns as the body was carried by the holy fathers to its final resting place. Not only had Pelagia/Pelagius rejected their sinful past but they had transcended the constraints of gender to follow their calling.

Pelagia's story survives in Middle English in a late-fourteenth-century devotional poem known as the 'Northern Homily Cycle'. It is part of a collection of religious texts copied in a northern dialect in a large book known as the Simeon manuscript, now in the British Library (Image 9). The verses on Pelagia begin with a large decorated initial 'I' as follows:

In Antiochie bizonde the see	*In Antioch beyond the sea*
A wommon woned in a Citee	*A woman lived in a city*
Dame Pelagi was heo cald	*Dame Pelagia she was called*
Of hir bodi was heo ful bold	*With her body she was very*
...	*shameless*
And riche men of uche a leode	*...*
Come to her for hir feir hede	*And rich men of every nation*
And gaf hir gold and riche mede.	*Come to her because of her fair person*
	And give her gold and rich reward.[5]

These three 'Holy Harlots', alongside the most highly revered Mary Magdalene (see Chapter 9), were extremely popular among the medieval saints, particularly with women who questioned the traditionally male-dominated, clerical ethos of the Catholic Church. From the extreme of wantonness and lechery (apparently viewed as a uniquely feminine sin) these women underwent a radical transformation to become the purest of the pure, as brides of Christ. They were models for female ascetics such as Julian of Norwich and rebel dissenters such as John Wycliffe in the later Middle Ages. However, by the sixteenth century their authenticity was being questioned by mainstream Catholics and Protestants. The mystic Elizabeth Barton, who claimed to have received a celestial letter in gold from Mary Magdalene, was condemned as a heretic under Henry VIII for her conservative views, which included strong opposition to divorce. Church authorities continued to bring women into line.

9 'Pelagia' in the Simeon manuscript (N. Worcestershire, late 14th century) Add MS 22283, f. 13r.

omne labia

mea aperies

Et os me

um anun

8.

St Helena of Constantinople

Flavia Julia Helena Augusta was mother of Constantine the Great, founder of the great eastern capital of Constantinople (now Istanbul) and the first Roman emperor to convert to Christianity. In her seventies, Helena travelled to the Holy Land and famously unearthed the wooden Cross on which Jesus was crucified, bringing it back to her son in Constantinople. Relics of the 'True Cross', as it came to be called, were distributed to churches throughout the Christian world and performed many miracles.

Helena (the name comes from the Greek word for 'torch') was born in Bithynia in the north-west of Asia Minor (now part of Turkey) in the middle of the third century AD. The Roman world was in turmoil, with emperors vying for power and assassinations having become a fairly regular occurrence. From humble beginnings, this remarkable young woman rose to a position of great power in the Roman world and was venerated as a saint after her death. According to some of the later sources, Helena started life as a lowly servant girl working in a tavern frequented by Roman soldiers stationed in an imperial outpost. She was described by Ambrose of Milan[1] as a *stabularia* ('stable woman' or 'hostess of an inn'), with the implication that she may have offered

---

1 A richly jewelled cross within a hexagonal building, surrounded by figures representing different Christian leaders; in the border, two men dig and uncover the True Cross, guided by St Helena, in the Dunois Hours (Paris, c.1445) Yates Thompson MS 3, f. 184r.

2 The emperor Constantine at the Battle of the Milvian Bridge, where the True Cross appeared to him; here it is held by one of his soldiers, in Jean Beleth, *La Vie des Saints* ('The Life of the Saints') (Paris, c.1330) Add MS 17275, f. 33r.

sexual favours to customers. As the case may be, her exceptional character and energy caught the eye of a young provincial general, Constantius Chlorus, and she became his mistress, giving birth to a son, Constantine, in around 272.

Shortly afterwards the family was torn apart by dramatic political events in the empire, when Constantius was appointed Caesar in the west and left to campaign along the Rhine frontier. Needing a higher-status wife, he married the then emperor's stepdaughter, while Helena and the teenage Constantine were sent to live in the household of one of his generals in Nicomedia. There they remained in obscurity – and Helena seemingly devoted herself to the education of her son, who soon showed great promise. When Constantius became emperor in 305, he called for Constantine to join him in Britain, where he was campaigning against the Picts. But less than a year later he died in York and his son was immediately acclaimed emperor by his troops, though he had several rivals to defeat in order to secure his position. He married the imperial princess Fausta and set off to consolidate his power in a series of battles.

de noftre pere ioseph· frel sont
ta uiolente que tu nous zem oustre
le trefor repost-et fail issir une
fumee aromatilee zesoeue ou
zeur que ie croie ou cruicefis et
quil est roy zes roys z ousiede zes
siecles amen· Ci zeuise coment

nous sauons bien que tescroit
qui sont ze ij larrons qui fu
rent cruce fie auec nre seingn
Jucrist les imst en nnla ate· et
atendi auec la gloire nostre
seingneur· Il auint azonc en
tour heure ze nonne quen por

3 The True Cross is identified to St Helena in Jerusalem, and used when a dead man is brought to life, *La Vie des Saints*, Add MS 17275, f. 34r.

The most notable of these was the Battle of the Milvian Bridge in AD 312, where Constantine and his army confronted Maxentius at the River Danube. Here he famously had a vision of a golden cross in the sky with the words 'In this sign you shall conquer' above it (Image 2). Following this miraculous victory, and perhaps on the advice of the pious Helena, Constantine issued the Edict of Milan, allowing the free practice of Christianity as a legitimate religion and outlawing the persecution of Christians in the Roman empire. Fighting under the banner of Christianity he defeated his opponents one by one, establishing himself as among the most powerful emperors of the Romans. Helena was given a prominent role as his mother and awarded the titles of *augusta* ('empress') and *noblissima femina* ('noble lady'). She was certainly a woman to be reckoned with; by some accounts it was she who advised Constantine to condemn Crispus, his eldest son, to death and to order the brutal murder of his wife, Fausta, who was scalded to death in the bath. After Fausta's death, as the most senior woman of the imperial family, Helena was given her own palace in Rome, on one of the highest points within the city walls.

During the rule of Constantine, Christianity grew into a powerful force throughout Europe and the Middle East. Helena was a key figure in establishing Jerusalem as an important site for Christians and founding key religious traditions such as pilgrimage and the veneration of relics. Eusebius of Caesarea in his fourth-century *Vita Constantini* ('Life of Constantine')[2] devotes a section to the emperor's mother, in which he portrays mother and son as Mary- and Christ-like figures. For him and later Christian hagiographers Helena became a model of obedience to the will of God, and Constantine of the pious leader and dutiful son. He was the first to visit the Holy Land, where he discovered and restored the Holy Sepulchre, Christ's tomb, and then in 326 he encouraged his mother to go on a pilgrimage to venerate the key locations of Christ's life. Constantine apparently gave her access to unlimited funds from the imperial treasury to seek out relics from the Holy Land and bring them back to Constantinople. At an advanced age but 'gifted with no common degree of wisdom',[3] Helena travelled to Jerusalem, where she visited and built churches at the sites of Jesus's tomb and the cave of the Nativity. Wearing humble clothing, she distributed alms to the poor and freed captives. Returning home aged 80, she died not long afterwards with her son at her side, leaving her considerable wealth to her son and grandsons. Having been entrusted by the emperor Constantine with important missions such as the one described above, she established a precedent for future great widows, empresses and queens. Several cities were named Helenopolis in her honour.

The legendary deed for which Helena is most famous is the discovery of the True Cross. It was Ambrose, Bishop of Milan, who first wrote a detailed account of how she was inspired by the Holy Spirit to survey the sacred hill of Golgotha where the Crucifixion took place. When she had difficulty finding the location of the Cross, she accused Satan: 'I see what you have done, Satan, to make sure that the sword which destroyed you was covered up'. She then warned him that just as Mary, mother of Christ, defeated him 'when she gave birth to the emperor' he would be 'defeated again today, when a woman uncovers your snares'.[4] Ambrose's identification of Helena with the Virgin Mary is clear; both won against Satan through the power of Christ. Having seen off the Evil One, Helena ordered the excavation of the holy ground of Golgotha and soon three crosses, nails and the inscription INRI were unearthed.

At this point accounts vary, but according to Paulinus a miraculous event revealed which of the three was the True Cross. Helena apparently ordered that each of the three crosses be placed on the body of a dead man; the first

4 St Helena with the Cross, in a Middle Dutch prayer book (S. Netherlands, 1440–1500) Harley MS 3828, f. 25v.

5 Chapel of St Helena in Jerusalem, in a German translation of Niccolò da Poggibonsi's *Libro d'Oltramare* ('Book about Overseas Lands'), an itinerary of a trip from Europe to the Holy Land and back with instructions for pilgrims to Jerusalem (Nürnberg, c.1465) Egerton MS 1900, f. 20v.

two crosses failed to revive the body, but at the touch of the third cross, the man came to life (Images 1, 3). The legend was retold by later hagiographers, who introduce a Jewish character, Judas Cyriancus, who led her to the place where the True Cross was believed to be buried. After days of searching, Helena experienced a vision of 'sweet smelling dust and a flash of lightning' which indicated the place. After the three crosses were uncovered, a leper was instructed to touch each one, and when he touched the True Cross, he was instantly healed. Helena announced, '[Mary] caused God to be seen among men. I shall give proof of his Resurrection...a remedy for sins'.[5] The Cross was then carried back to Rome where parts were housed in the Basilica of Santa Croce and fragments were distributed to many churches. The nails were given to Constantine and incorporated into his crown and horse's bridle, assuring that he would follow in Christ's footsteps as the quintessential Christian emperor and hope of salvation for his people.

Pilgrims today can visit the Armenian Chapel of St Helena in a crypt under the Church of the Holy Sepulchre in Jerusalem (Image 5); nearby is the

Franciscan Chapel of the Finding of the Cross, where, according to tradition, St Helena made her miraculous discovery. In addition, Constantine constructed a vast royal tomb for her – the Mausoleum of Helena outside Rome – and had gold coins minted with her image. Her sarcophagus is in the Vatican Museum today.

Helena, like many women of her time, had no real voice and the evidence about the historical woman is fragmentary. The events of her life were recorded mostly after her death by male chroniclers and she is best remembered for an achievement that was not hers in reality: discovering the True Cross. The sources for the historical Helena are either chronicles of imperial history (in which she plays a marginal role in Constantine's rise to power), or representations of the imperial family on coins, sculptures and other monuments, some showing changing attitudes to her role in the dynasty. But there are many gaps in the record of her deeds. Nothing is known about the period between Constantius's disappearance from her life and her reappearance in Constantine's court circles. Again, after her death nothing is written about her for some time until she reappears in hagiographies as the finder of the True Cross.

Most of what has been recorded about Helena is by Christian authors, who deal with her afterlife, her sainthood and the reception of her legend throughout the Christian world. She became an extremely important saint in the Middle Ages, seen as the new Mary who had defeated the Devil by her discovery of the True Cross. The story was depicted in historical chronicles, legendaries and Books of Hours. Her early life became the subject of various chivalric tales; in one example, as the archetypal persecuted heroine, abandoned by her husband, she reputedly kept herself and her son by doing needlework until her true identity was revealed after he came to power as the new emperor. According to Almann of Hautvillers' *Life of Saint Helena*, written on the translation of her 'relics' from Rome to his monastery in France in c.840, she was a noble lady of Trier, who lived in Germany until she moved to Rome in her old age.[6] He also described the seamless robe (said to have been worn by Jesus during or shortly before his Crucifixion) that she had discovered and brought from the Holy Land. A skull that is allegedly hers is on display in the cathedral treasury in Trier to this day and a fresco of c.310 believed to be of her survives there.

In a further addition to these remarkable stories, the English chroniclers Henry of Huntingdon and Geoffrey of Monmouth claimed that, rather than a Bithynian servant girl, Helena was the daughter of King Cole of Colchester (the 'merry old soul' of nursery rhyme fame). Wavrin's *Anciennes et nouvelles chroniques de la Grant Bretaigne* ('Old and New Chronicles of Great Britain') (see Image 6), an imaginative medieval chronicle of England from various sources, gives the following account of her early life at the English court:

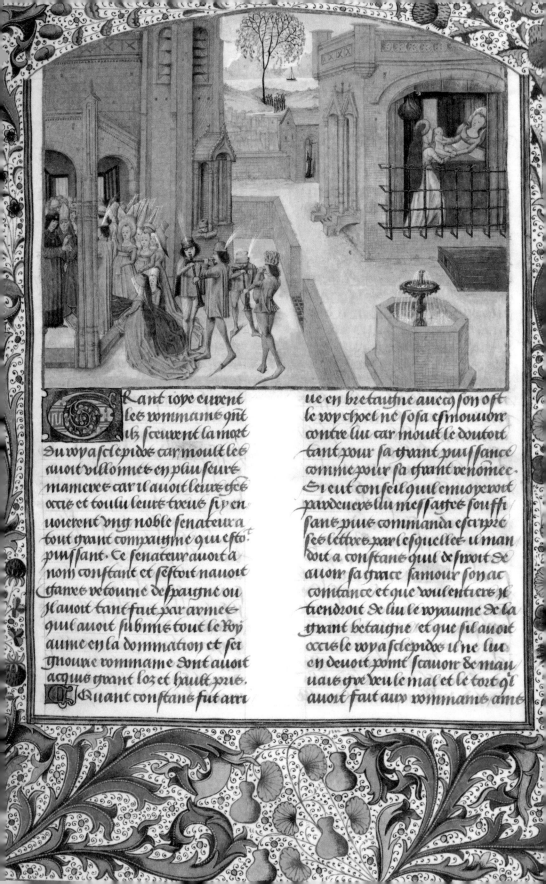

Ant roye eurent
les rommains quil
ilz sceurent la mort
du roy asclepidot car moult les
auoit villonnes en plusieurs
manieres car il auoit leurs dies
occis et toullu leurs treus si y en
uoierent ung noble senateur a
tout grant compaigne qui esto.
puissant. Ce senateur auoit a
nom constant et sestoit nauoit
gaires retourne despaigne ou
il auoit tant fait par armes
quil auoit submis tout le Roy
aume en la dommation et sei
gnourie rommaine dont auoit
acquis grant loz et hault pris.
Quant constans fut arri

ue en bretaigne aueca son ost
le roy choel ne sosa esmouuoir
contre luy car moult le doutoit
tant pour sa grant puissance
comme pour sa grant venomee.
Si eut conseil quil enuoyeroit
pardeuers luy messaiges souffi
sant puis commanda escripre
ses lettres par lesquelles il man
doit a constant quil desiroit de
auoir sa grace samour son ac
comtance et que voulentiers il
tiendroit de luy le royaume de la
grant betaigne et que sil auoit
occis le roy asclepidot il ne luy
en deuoit point scauoir de mau
uais gre veu le mal et le tort quil
auoit fait aux rommains ains

le roi coel acoucha malade et au	King Cole took to his bed and at the
bout de huit iours morut se navoit	end of eight days he died, and he

le roi coel acoucha malade et au bout de huit iours morut se navoit nulz enffans fors une toute seulle fille qui avoit a nom helaine laquel estoit moult belle courtoise sage et bien moriginee merveilleusement car son pere lavoit trop bien fait introduire en toutes sciences...afin quelle sceust bien sa terre gouveurner apres sa mort. Quant coel fut mort helaine par le conseil de ses parens print en marriage constans car il la voult avoir a femme pource que ce temps on ne scavoit pucelle ou il y eust tand te sens et bonte ed de valleur comme en elle.

King Cole took to his bed and at the end of eight days he died, and he had no children apart from an only daughter called Helena who was very beautiful, courteous, wise and marvellously well raised as her father had had her instructed in all the sciences...so that she knew well how to govern his country after his death. When Cole was dead Helena on the advice of her relatives took Constance for her husband and he wanted to have her as his wife because at this time there was no other young woman with as much sense, goodness and worth as she had.[7]

A son was born to the couple and they named him Constantine, giving thanks to God for his birth (Image 6). Constance died when his son was only 6 and so Helena governed the kingdom of Britain until her son was old enough to take over. He became an ideal chivalric ruler, raising a great army of valiant English knights to defeat the Roman emperor Maxentius who had been persecuting Christians. He deposed Maxentius and became the *seul empereur rommain* ('sole Roman emperor').

Though there is of course no historical foundation for the claim to British nationality, numerous holy wells are dedicated to St Helen in the British Isles and she is the patron saint of the towns of Abingdon and Colchester, where St Helen's Chapel is believed to have been founded by her. The Colchester coat of arms contains a cross and three crowned nails reputedly given by Helena to Constantine.

Despite her role in establishing Christianity in the Roman empire and her important position among the medieval saints, Helena is now almost forgotten in England and the Protestant world. In the Catholic and Orthodox Churches she is the patron saint of divorcées, recently converted Christians and archaeologists and her feast day is celebrated on 18 August.

6 The marriage of Constantius and Helena, and the birth of Constantine in Britain, in Jean de Wavrin, *Anciennes et nouvelles chroniques de la Grant Bretaigne* (Bruges, c.1480) Royal MS 15 E IV f. 73r.

9.

Mary Magdalene

Mary Magdalene was a hugely popular and multi-faceted saint in the Middle Ages; her portrayal in many different contexts in manuscripts and paintings reflects this quality. In collections of saints' lives or scenes from the Gospels she is variously shown washing and kissing Christ's feet (Image 4), standing beside the Cross with the Virgin Mary and others (Image 2a), or meeting the risen Christ at the entrance to his tomb (Image 3). From the thirteenth century onwards in Books of Hours and collections of prayers to popular saints, she appears as an expensively dressed and bejewelled young lady with her long, flowing locks carefully arranged, and holding a jar of ointment (Images 1, 8) or alternatively as a woman covered in hair being lifted to heaven by angels (Image 7). From a handful of appearances in the biblical narrative of Christ's life her legend grew over the centuries to encompass all these different aspects of her character.

To go back to the origins of her story in the New Testament, Mary Magdalene is first introduced among the women formerly possessed by demons who follow Christ:

> And it came to pass afterward, that he went throughout every city and village, preaching and shewing the glad tidings of the kingdom of God: and the twelve [disciples] were with him,

1 Mary Magdalene holding a jar of ointment and an open book, with a woman kneeling before her; this may be the owner of this Book of Hours from Spain (Catalunya, 1461–1500) Add MS 18193, f. 143v.

2a Mary Magdalene with the Virgin Mary and St John, looking up at Christ on the Cross, in a Book of Hours, Use of the Church of Sint Hermeskerk, Ronse (Bruges, 1465) Harley MS 1211, f. 14v.

2b An early image of Mary Magdalene and the two other women meeting the angel at the entrance to Christ's tomb, from a Book of Psalms (Canterbury, AD 1000–1050) Harley MS 603, f. 8r.

And certain women, which had been healed of evil spirits and infirmities, Mary called Magdalene, out of whom went seven devils,
And Joanna the wife of Chuza Herod's steward, and Susanna, and many others, which ministered unto him of their substance.[1]

Apart from his mother, the Virgin Mary, Mary Magdalene is portrayed in the Bible as the woman who is closest to Christ; she was present at his Crucifixion (Image 2a) and was the first person to witness his Resurrection. According to John's Gospel she went to the tomb early on Easter morning to anoint Christ's body (in Luke's Gospel she was accompanied by Joanna and Mary, mother of James, see Images 2b, 3). She found the tomb open and, having shown this to Peter, she remained in the garden alone to watch. Then she saw

3 Scenes from the Resurrection (from top left): Christ rises from the tomb; the three women including Mary Magdalene speak to an angel guarding the empty tomb; Mary Magdalene and Christ at the Resurrection (*Noli me tangere*); and Christ with two disciples at Emmaeus, in the De Lisle Psalter (East Anglia, early 14th century) Arundel MS 83, f. 133r.

two angels in the tomb where the body had been and a man walking towards her. At first she thought it was the gardener but then he said her name and she recognised him as Christ, running to him and calling out *Rabbouni* ('teacher' in Aramaic). He stopped her with the words, *Noli me tangere* ('Do not touch me', or 'Do not cling to me') (see Image 3, lower left), a scene depicted by some of the greatest medieval and Renaissance artists, including Giotto, Titian and Hans Holbein the Younger.

Biblical scholars of the early Middle Ages identified Mary Magdalene with two other female characters in the New Testament: they are Mary of Bethany, who was sister to Martha and Lazarus (the man who Christ raised from the dead), and the unnamed female sinner who washed Christ's feet with her tears of repentance in Luke's Gospel (Image 4). She kissed his feet and anointed them with precious oil while he was dining at Simon the Pharisee's house and Christ described her as most deserving of being saved, because her sins and therefore her love were the greatest. As this act of conversion and repentance was attributed to Mary Magdalene she became the symbol of the female penitent. Her conversion was a popular motif in medieval hymns and her *vita*, or 'life', became a medieval best-seller. Hers was an significant summer feast day (22 July) as recorded in the Venerable Bede's *Old English Martyrology* of c.900. Important churches and abbeys were dedicated to her and she was the first female saint to have an Oxford college named after her (Magdalen College, pronounced 'Maudlin' after the French tradition). Towns and villages, mountain ranges and even a small island near Sardinia have been given her name.

In the sixth century, Pope Gregory the Great proclaimed Mary Magdalene a harlot, describing her as 'this woman, formerly addicted to forbidden deeds, [who] had used perfume to give her flesh a pleasant odour'.[2] Mary's reputation as a female penitent and example to all sinners was firmly established. She became an example to fallen women, though nowhere in the Bible does it say that she was a prostitute. This did not stop certain male clerics, who railed against female vice in their sermons and writings, from using her as an example of female sexuality and sin who had been fortunate to be redeemed by Christ's love. In a body of verses about women that included the *Blasme des Fames* (which I loosely translate as 'Women are to Blame for Everything'),[3] women were castigated for their frivolity, light-mindedness and preoccupation with fashion, and Mary Magdalene was used as an example, implying that it

4 Mary and Martha at the raising of Lazarus, and (below) Mary Magdalene washing Christ's feet, in a Psalter (Oxford, early 13th century) Arundel MS 157, f. 8r.

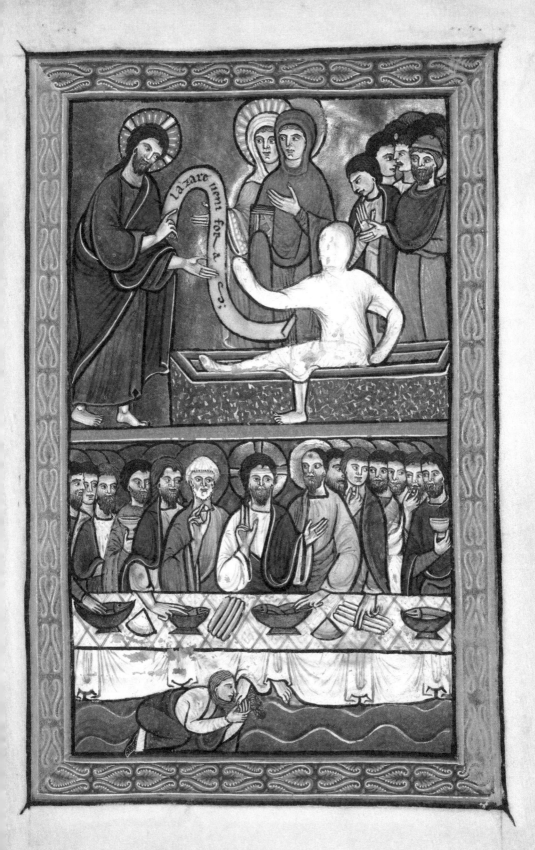

luſee le môn hére et lenr dmmna â munz a mâ n

5 Mary Magdalene (on left, wearing a head-covering) is shown as the only female among all the male apostles kneeling at the altar as Mass is said, in the Bedford Hours (Paris, c.1420) Add MS 18850, f. 98v.

was her vanity which had led to her fall into a life of ill repute. As a redeemed prostitute, she had numerous institutions for women dedicated to her, and the Order of Penitents of St Mary Magdalene spread throughout Europe, with the foundation of refuges for prostitutes, leper hospitals and hostels for pilgrims. The identification of Mary with wantonness was so pervasive that at the end of the seventeenth century repentant prostitutes became known as 'magdalens', and the notorious Magdalene Laundries for unmarried mothers operated in Ireland between the eighteenth and the twentieth centuries.

On a more positive note, Mary Magdalene was also believed to be the Mary (sister of Martha in the Gospels) who sat at Christ's feet, listening to his message while her sister busied herself with the housework. For this she was praised by Christ because she 'hath chosen that good part, which shall not be taken away from her',[4] and so she became a model for nuns and monks who had chosen cloistered lives of contemplation over worldly pursuits. But this positive quality attributed to her was used by preachers as an opportunity to

ነብ፡ተን᎘ላ፡እግዚእን፡ክርስቶስ፡ተ፟ዴዉ፡እስተርእየ፡ለማርያ፡ይ፡መግደ
ዊቅ፡ወዐዴ.ክኔል፡ዐ᎘ልአኒ።

6 Jesus appearing to Mary Magdalene, in a manuscript containing the Octateuch and Gospels in the Ge'ez language (Ethiopia, late 17th century) Or 481, f. 109r.

offer Mary Magdalene as an example to talkative women who did not sit still in church. One medieval sermon chastised them as follows: 'Some never stop moving, sometimes they stand, then they sit, or they leave and re-enter...Others while listening to the word of God show no sign of devotion. How different from Mary who also seated herself at the Lord's feet and listened to his word.'[5]

The negative attitude expressed here towards women who made their voices heard is an example of their subordinate role in medieval society. They were expected to behave demurely at all times and to rely for their opinions on the undoubtedly superior understanding of men, both at home and in church.

In some apocrypha (early Christian writings that were not included in the Bible as they were considered historically unreliable) and Egyptian Gnostic texts such as the *Gospel of Philip* and the *Gospel of Mary*, Mary Magdalene was portrayed as Christ's companion and the one among his followers whom He loved most (one even reports that the pair kissed). These texts contain a number of dialogues in which Mary poses questions to Christ, revealing a superior understanding to the other disciples and a special relationship to Him (Image 6). Because of Mary's closeness to Christ and her somewhat mysterious qualities, legends surrounding her life, death and associated miracles proliferated throughout the various Christian traditions. In the Eastern Church she was believed to have been the fiancée of the apostle John who rejected her when he was called by Christ, and this was the reason she turned to prostitution. After the Resurrection of Christ, the pair, together with the Virgin Mary, were said to have travelled to Ephesus in present-day Turkey, where they died and were buried. The English monk Willibald claimed to have seen Mary's tomb there in the eighth century.

In France a legend arose that Mary Magdalene, together with the Virgin Mary, two other women called Mary, Martha, Lazarus and other saints (depending on the version of the legend) were put to sea in a rudderless boat by persecutors of Christians. After drifting for some time, they came ashore in Provence, landing near Marseilles, some say in the town known as Les Saintes Maries de la Mer ('the Saint Marys of the Sea') in the Camargue. There they found the local people were worshipping pagan gods. Mary went straight to the Temple and began to preach the Christian faith. The people were so inspired by her beauty and the fair speech issuing from the mouth that had kissed Christ's feet that many converted.

At this time in Marseilles there lived a prince and his wife who greatly desired a child and so they made sacrifices to the idols. They were known to Mary, who appeared to the wife in a vision, telling her to give up her life of luxury and open her house to the poor and needy. The couple obeyed Mary's instructions and they conceived a son, but when Mary strongly suggested the husband go on pilgrimage to thank St Peter for the miracle, his wife insisted on accompanying him. On the voyage, the wife died while giving birth to a son during a fierce storm, leaving her baby crying out in hunger. The father was forced to leave his wife's body with his son at her breast on a rocky outcrop in the middle of the sea; he covered them with a mantle and called out to Mary Magdalene for help before continuing his voyage. After spending two years visiting the holy sites in Jerusalem with St Peter, the prince boarded a ship for Marseilles. As they sailed past the rock where he had left his wife and son he saw a small child playing on the shore, and he found his wife's body lying where he had left it (Image 7). He prayed again to Mary, who had nurtured the child in his absence and who now brought his wife back to life. The family joyfully sailed on to Marseilles, where they found Mary Magdalene still preaching and converting the people. The prince and his wife were baptised and destroyed all the pagan temples in the city.

7 A kneeling hermit (on the right) sees a vision of Mary Magdalene, covered in hair, being carried to heaven by angels; on the left the prince on his ship spies his son beside his dead mother on a rock, in a miniature by Giovanni Pietro Birago accompanying prayers to Mary Magdalene, in the Sforza Hours (Milan and Ghent/Brussels, *c.*1500) Add MS 34294, f. 211v.

After many years preaching and performing miracles, Mary Magdalene went to live in a grotto high up in the *massif* of Sainte Baume, where she passed thirty years in fasting and penance and her hair grew long to cover her body (here her legend bears remarkable similarities to St Mary of Egypt, see Chapter 7). By some accounts she was lifted to heaven seven times a day by angels who fed her. This was witnessed by another hermit, who went to Marseilles to report what he had seen. When she died she was buried at the church of St Maximin in Aix-en-Provence, which is still a site of pilgrimage.

However, in the thirteenth century, Mary Magdalene's most important shrine became the abbey of Vézelay in Burgundy, on the pilgrim route from Germany to Santiago in Spain, where her relics were kept. According to the popular book of saints' lives known as the *Golden Legend*, a monk was sent from the abbey to Aix in 771 by one Gerard, Duke of Burgundy, who was childless, to find and bring back the relics of Mary Magdalene. When the monk arrived in Aix he found that the city had been destroyed by pagans, but luckily he happened upon a tomb with an inscription saying that it contained the remains of the saint. He opened it secretly in the night and took the bones to his lodgings, where Mary Magdalene appeared to him and told him to complete his task forthwith. So he set off towards Vézelay, but when he was half a mile away he was unable to carry the relics any further until the monks came with a suitable procession to receive them. Soon afterwards the duke and his wife had a child.

Mary Magdalene remained an extremely popular saint in France. Her tomb at Vézelay became the departure point for the second crusade and in 1254 the saintly King Louis himself visited the grotto at Sainte Baume where Mary had lived as a hermit. He called her:

la sainte femme: ne l'a-t-elle pas ardemment aimé? n'a-t-elle pas mérité de lui un pardon abondant de ses péchés; ne lui a-t-il pas permis enfin des contacts familiers.

this most holy woman: did she not love Christ passionately? Did she merit in exchange the abundant pardon for her sins which she received from him; did he finally not allow her to be close to him.[6]

Medieval writers focused on the closeness of the relationship between Christ and Mary Magdalene after she was converted. St Anselm, Archbishop of Canterbury, wrote a prayer to her in 1081 dedicated to Adelaide, daughter of William the Conqueror. In a series of striking images Mary Magdalene was compared to the Bride seeking the Bridegroom in the Song of Songs of the Old Testament.[7] Foundations in her name spread across the Holy Roman

8 Mary Magdalene, in the Breviary of Queen Isabella of Castille (Bruges, *c*.1490) Add MS 18851, f. 408r.

empire and Italy, decorated with paintings or sculptures of her by well-known artists of the Renaissance. In the nineteenth century the large new church of La Madeleine in central Paris was dedicated to her and the madeleines (little cakes made famous by Proust in his *À la recherche du temps perdu*) are named after her (or her namesake). Her former reputation as a woman of ill repute has now been rejected by the Catholic Church. In 2016, in recognition of her presence and role at the Resurrection, a decree was issued in which she was to be designated *de apostolorum apostola* ('apostle to the apostles') in the Mass celebrated on her official feast day in July.[8]

Solomon receives the Queen of Sheba, in the *Bible historiale*
('History Bible') (Paris, early 15th century) Royal MS 15 D III, f. 285r.

Powerful
Women

Part Three

pu faire herodes se par prieres
fery tout lui eust pardonne.

Cy ensieut listoire de cleopa
tre royne des egipciens

Cleopatre féme
egipacenne fu
renommee par
tout le monde

10.

Cleopatra, Queen of Egypt

The last Ptolemaic queen of Egypt, lover of two Roman emperors, has been portrayed in historical writing, art, literature and theatre as intelligent, seductive, devious, tragic, mysterious and ruthless. From the earliest Roman propaganda through Chaucer's *Legend of Good Women* to Elizabeth Taylor's 1963 screen portrayal, her 'infinite variety' (Shakespeare)[1] has excited both admiration and censure. Plutarch, who wrote the first and most detailed early description of her in his *Life of Antony*, claims that:

> her beauty, as we are told, was in itself not altogether incomparable, nor such as to strike those who saw her; but converse with her had an irresistible charm, and her presence, combined with the persuasiveness of her discourse and the character which was somehow diffused about her behaviour towards others, had something stimulating about it.[2]

Cleopatra's lifetime, from 70 BC to 30 BC, coincided with civil wars between four of the greatest of all the Roman generals: Pompey (who she helped with supplies), Julius Caesar and Mark Antony (both of whom were her lovers) and Octavian (later Augustus Caesar, the first Roman emperor) who defeated and captured her.

---

1 The death of Cleopatra, with dragons not snakes, in Giovanni Boccaccio, *Des Cleres et nobles femmes* (*De mulieribus claris* in French translation) (Paris, 1400–25) Royal MS 20 C V, f. 131v.

Cleopatra VII (there were many other queens named Cleopatra – it means 'glory of her father') was a descendant of the Greek Ptolemy I Soter, Alexander's general, and was given the epithets Thea Philopater ('father-loving goddess'). An independent and adventurous woman, she rode, hunted and led her troops into battle. She may have been the first in her line to speak Egyptian, though her first language was Greek and she is believed to have been proficient in five or six other languages. She was the daughter of Ptolemy VII Auletes, who had almost lost the throne through the machinations of his stepmother, Cleopatra Selene, and had been exiled in Rome for some time, probably accompanied by his daughter. In the end he retained power with the help of the Romans, who were the new power in the Mediterranean.

Ptolemy VII died in 51 BC and our Cleopatra inherited the throne of Egypt aged 17, together with her brother, Ptolemy XIII Philopater, who was just 10 years old. The young boy-king's eunuchs advised him that he would be better off ruling alone, and that he should depose his intelligent and dynamic sister who was outsmarting them at every turn. Hearing this, Cleopatra travelled to the eastern border of Egypt to raise an army against her brother's faction. There she met Julius Caesar and the meeting between the Egyptian Queen and the most famous of all the Roman generals has been portrayed many times. In Plutarch's version Cleopatra is delivered by her servant wrapped in a carpet, which is unfurled to present her at the feet of Julius Caesar. In Plutarch's words:

> So Cleopatra, taking only Apollodorus the Sicilian from among her friends, embarked in a little skiff and landed at the palace when it was already getting dark; and as it was impossible to escape notice otherwise, she stretched herself at full length inside a bedsack, while Apollodorus tied the bedsack up with a cord and carried it indoors to Caesar.

> It was by this device of Cleopatra's, it is said, that Caesar was first captivated, for she showed herself to be a bold coquette, and succumbing to the charm of further intercourse with her, he reconciled her to her brother on the basis of a joint share with him in the royal power.[3]

A scene from a fifteenth-century French history of Julius Caesar, *La Grande histoire César*, portrays something of Cleopatra's bewitching quality, as she and her brother Ptolemy play host to Caesar at an elaborate banquet in Alexandria (Image 2). The setting and costumes imagined by the artist are entirely medieval and the accompanying text gives a detailed description of Cleopatra's elaborate costume, jewels and physical appearance, comprising an inventory of the features considered most attractive in a medieval woman.

2 Julius Caesar, Ptolemy and Cleopatra at a rich banquet in Alexandria, in *La Grande histoire César* or *Les faits des Romains* (Bruges, 1479) Royal MS 17 F II, f. 299r.

For example, her figure is moderately curvaceous: '*plus grossette ung pou par entour les hanches que par le pis*' ('a little wider in the hips than in the ankles'). She has '*la bouche bien faite et le menton la couleur fresce et vermeille et le fardement que elle y ot is enluminoit tout son affaire*' ('a well-shaped mouth, a chin that was fresh and pink; and the make-up that she used made everything sparkle'). The luxurious feast is then laid out before the reader, from the crystal water decanters to the bowls made of precious stones and gems. The wines and sumptuous meat and fish dishes are flavoured with cardamon and other spices, and everything is of the highest quality. Caesar is suitably impressed by what he sees, and he dreams of conquering Egypt, the richest land by far of any he has seen. Meanwhile the author of this history comments that Ptolemy and Cleopatra were unwise to display their riches to a potential enemy, making Egypt ripe for conquest.

According to the historical sources, Caesar tried to mediate between Cleopatra and her brother Ptolemy XIII in their struggle to control Egypt, finally taking Cleopatra's side. With his help, Ptolemy was defeated and he and his advisers killed. Cleopatra was restored to the throne with her younger brother Ptolemy XIV as consort, and effectively ruled Egypt from this time, underpinned by Roman power. Caesar, then in his fifties, fell in love with the young queen and he took her to Rome, where he had a golden statue of her made for the temple of Venus. Cleopatra bore him a son, Caesarion, and they stayed together in his villa outside the city for two years. He may have planned to marry her and create a new dynasty to rule Egypt, though the Romans were horrified at this idea of their ruler marrying a foreign woman and acquiring dynastic power. In any case, Caesar's murder in 44 BC cut the relationship short, leaving Cleopatra in a perilous position. As a Hellenistic queen, her objective was to ensure that her son succeeded to the throne, so she quickly returned to Egypt to consolidate her position. Her brother was poisoned at around this time, clearing the way for her son, though there is no conclusive proof that she was involved.

Only three years later Cleopatra found another powerful champion; Mark Antony, member of the triumvirate (the coalition of three men who ruled Rome for ten years from 43 BC). The pair met when he visited Egypt while campaigning in the eastern Roman empire. According to Roman historians, Antony, like Caesar before him, fell completely under her spell and they soon became lovers. The most famous description of their meeting is in Shakespeare's *Antony and Cleopatra*, where she is described as a seductive siren sailing on a golden barge down the Nile:

...For her own person
It beggar'd all description: she did lie
In her pavilion, cloth of gold of tissue,
O'erpicturing the Venus where we see
The fancy outwork nature[4]

Antony left his Roman wife Fulvia for her and they had three children: twins named Cleopatra and Alexander, and a son named Ptolemy. In 40 BC Antony was forced to return to Rome, and when his first wife died, he married Octavia, half-sister of his fellow triumvir, Octavian (Augustus Caesar). He then returned to Egypt and he and Cleopatra held a great celebration, announcing that they were emperor and empress of the east. Cleopatra sat on a golden throne and Antony proclaimed her queen of Egypt, with Caesarion, her son by Julius Caesar, as her co-regent. Other provinces were given to their three children, with the implication that they were founding a new Egyptian dynasty. Over the next few years they led a life of excess and debauchery at the Egyptian court, as described by the medieval author Boccaccio.

> As the insatiable woman's craving for kingdoms grew day by day…she asked Antony for the Roman empire. Perhaps drunk or rising from such a noble supper, Antony, who was not in full possession of his mental faculties… promised to give it to her, as if it were his to give…Good Lord, how great was the audacity of the woman who requested this! And the man who promised it was no less! How generous was this man…[5]

Boccaccio bases this description on Roman sources, which blame Cleopatra, claiming that Antony had fallen completely under the spell of her charms and great wealth. When he divorced his wife, Octavia, this was the final straw for her brother, Octavian. He defeated the combined forces of Antony and Cleopatra at the battle of Actium, and the pair were captured by his troops in Alexandria. Both committed suicide in 30 BC. Their hopes of founding a new Egyptian dynasty were over and Egypt became a province of Rome.

Cleopatra's magnetic personality and the dramatic events surrounding her life and death have led to a multitude of interpretations over the last 2,000 years. The earliest portrayals in surviving portrait heads of ancient origin and on coinage were no doubt carefully curated; masculine facial features and royal iconography were apparently designed to establish her legitimacy as ruler of Egypt. In reliefs, she sometimes wears a headdress associated with divinity and sometimes even the apparel of a (traditionally male) Egyptian pharaoh, such as a man's kilt and royal beard; her right to rule is emphasised rather than her femininity. The perception of her as a *femme fatale* begins with the Roman writers; she was subjected to a deliberate propaganda campaign by Augustus, so that poets of the period including Horace and Virgil portray her as exotic, even barbaric, and blame her non-Roman wantonness for Mark Antony's defeat and death. Following the classical sources to which they had access, medieval writers focused on Cleopatra's seductive qualities and on the circumstances surrounding the double suicide. Boccaccio dismisses Cleopatra as '*totius orbus fabula*' ('the object of gossip for the whole world')[6] and focuses on how she seduced and led Antony astray: 'She gained glory for almost nothing else than her beauty, while on the other hand she became known throughout the world for her greed, cruelty and lustfulness'.[7]

Geoffrey Chaucer, in his *Legend of Good Women,* devotes a chapter to Cleopatra among the women who were 'trewe in lovinge al hir lyves'. In this work he is at pains to portray women in a positive light in line with courtly values, though he ascribes Mark Antony's all-consuming love for Cleopatra as leading to the tragic outcome, and therefore in a sense he is blaming her, just as Boccaccio does:

> *Al for the love of Cleopataras,*
> *That al the world he sette at no value.*[8]

Chaucer describes the disastrous battle of Actium in detail and focuses on the laments of the two lovers as they take their own lives. Cleopatra dies as a tragic heroine, proclaiming her faithful love to the last:

> *The same wolde I felen, lyf or deeth.*
> *And thilke covenant, whyl me lasteth breeth,*
> *I wol fulfille, and that shal wel be sene;*
> *Was never unto hir love a trewer quene.*[9]

There are various myths surrounding Cleopatra's death, the most famous being the one dramatised by Shakespeare in *Antony and Cleopatra.* Here, after the defeat at Actium, Cleopatra hides in her tomb at Alexandria. Antony, believing she is dead, stabs himself. Barely alive, he is brought to her hiding place and dies in her arms, prompting her famous line 'The crown o' the earth doth melt – My lord!'[10]

When Cleopatra discovers that Octavian plans to parade her through the streets of Rome as a captive, she arranges for asps (poisonous snakes) (Image 4) to be brought to her in a basket of figs, and she dies from their bites. This is the scene most often chosen by illuminators of historical manuscripts, where two snakes usually are shown, one applied to each of her breasts (Image 3). In some cases the snakes resemble dragons, as in medieval French the word *serpent* could be applied to either a snake or a dragon (Image 1).

Though she is probably best known for her dramatic suicide by snakes, extravagant stories have circulated about Cleopatra from Roman times. Pliny the Elder told in his *Natural History*[11] how she owned the two largest pearls of all time, and she dissolved one of these (worth close to half a million dollars today) in a dish of vinegar and swallowed it. This was to win a bet against Antony that she could provide the most expensive dinner they had ever eaten (no mean feat in the context of their conspicuous consumption). The plausibility of this tale has been tested by scientists who discovered that it is not possible to dissolve even a small pearl in vinegar. Nevertheless the incident has inspired

3 The death of Antony and Cleopatra in *Histoire tripartite or Chronique de Baudouin d'Avennes* (Bruges, c.1475) Royal MS 18 E V, f. 363v.

artists from the Italian Tiepolo to the Dutch Golden Age artist, Jordaens, who portrayed Cleopatra as an oriental seductress. From the time of the Greeks and Romans 'the East' was seen by Europeans as an exotic, debauched place, where women were sensual and wealth was a corrupting force. The image of Cleopatra as a sensual, mysterious *femme fatale* fits perfectly with these long-held misconceptions. It was rejected by the Egyptian author Ahmed Shawqi in his 1927 play, *Death of Cleopatra*, as imperialist propaganda.

One of the key questions about Cleopatra as a cultural icon who has been reimagined by succeeding generations has always been – was she Greek or Egyptian (North African) in appearance? A historical scroll from southern

separaf corpuf. qd unū diuidif spmē. Nat̄e adūlt̄iū
ē. Sz hoc docet murene & uipe n̄ uire geniſ. Sz ardore
libidinis expetituf amplecit. Discite ō uiri quia alie
nā pmollire queretr uxorem. Qui serpentis sibi asciscere
cupiat contubernium. Qui etiam cōpanduf ipe serpenti
sit. Festinat ad uipā que se in gremiū ū non directo
amore uirtatiſ sz lubrico deuii amoris infundit. Festinat
ad eā q̄ uenenū suū resumit ut uipa. Que ferr pacto
coniunctioniſ munie. uenenū q̄d euomuerat rursus
haurire.   Aspis.

spiſ uocata q̄d morsu uenena imittit & spar
git. Ioſ em̄ grei uenenū dicutr. & inde aspiſ
q̄ morsu uenenato imittit. Ctutr q̄dm sep pa

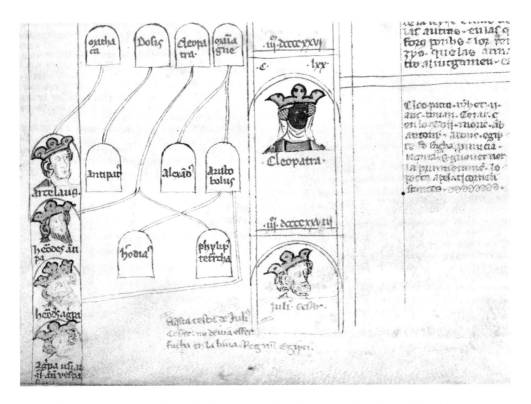

- ontha ca
- Dolis
- Cleopa tra·
- oxta gne
- ·iij· dccccxvj
- ·c· ·lxx·
- · Cleopatra ·
- Cleopatra·rober·ij· aug·tuun·Cesar·e en lo·xxvij·monk·ab antonij· atauc·egip re·&·fugla·puu·ca· Kouisl·G·gouuer·uer la pumdemine·lo pum apdaij comeli femae·
- antipat
- Alexão
- Azulo bolus
- arcelaus·
- hedes ān pa
- hodia⸗
- phylup tetrcha
- hedz agru
- ·iij· dccccxxvij·
- aqua usij as al au vefui
- Julj· Cesar·
- Agfta cesbe de Julj Cefret no dena effet fachu en la hira·Regni Egypi·

5 Cleopatra and Julius Caesar depicted among the rulers of Egypt in a chronological table of kings and emperors of the world, in Paolino Veneto's *Abbreviamen de las Estorias* in the Occitan language (Avignon, 1323–50) Egerton MS 1500, f. 15v.

France depicts her as dark-skinned (Image 5). And a painting by the artist Gérôme, *Cléopâtre apportée à César dans un tapis* ('Cleopatra brought to Caesar in a Carpet'), which was displayed at the Royal Academy in London in 1871, was criticised for impropriety, for 'obtaining more notice from gentlemen than ladies' and for flesh tones that were 'black and opaque'.[12] The debate over her ethnicity has resurfaced recently owing to the controversial choice of an Israeli actress, Gal Gadot, to play her in a planned Hollywood biopic and the casting of the mixed-race actress, Adele James, in the Netflix drama, *Queen Cleopatra*. An actress of Arabic or African ancestry has been proposed as more appropriate, though there is no conclusive evidence as to the real Cleopatra's exact ancestry. The most likely answer is that she was of mixed Greek and Egyptian descent.

4 A man with an asp ('Aspis') in a Bestiary (Salisbury, England, 1225–50) Harley MS 4751, f. 61r.

Esgardant les
disgraces et infe=
licitez des sei=
gneuries et roy=
aulmes et deul=
lant moustrer que en leurs
maleuretez avort sexcusent
les roys sur faulte de bon peu
ple le peuple sur faulte de

bons roys Et tous deux sur
la voulente de dieu ou de for=
tune Je treuve que la divine
providence pourroit touhãs
et assortist tels roys de tels
peuples tels peuples de tels
roys et que fortune ny fait
riens Car en regardant les
crvissances et les chentes des

11.

Olympias, Empress of Macedon

Daughter of the king of Molossia, wife of Philip of Macedon and mother of Alexander the Great, Olympias lived an extraordinary life in the fourth century BC. Although she is a historical figure, surviving accounts of her life and deeds are so astonishing that it is difficult to distinguish the real character from the fictional. Even her name is disputed; she bore no less than four during her life. Originally called Polyxena, she was also known as Myrtale, Olympias and/or Stratonice (meaning 'victor in war'). Her husband Philip apparently named her Olympias when on the same day he received three important pieces of news: a great victory had been won by the Macedonian army at Olympia; his horse had won its race at the Olympic Games; and his wife had given birth to a son (the future Alexander the Great, see Image 1). She has gained a reputation as the first woman to play a major role in Greek politics; while her son was away conquering distant lands, she wielded a good deal of power as his mother, then after his death she acted as regent for her grandson. At almost 60 years old she won the support of the army and fought off rival contenders to the throne

1 Queen Olympias attended by her ladies at the birth of Alexander; the eagles on the roof announce his future greatness, in Vasco da Lucena, *Les Fais d'Alexandre le grant* ('The Deeds of Alexander the Great'), a French version of the *Historia Alexandri Magni* by Curtius (Bruges, c.1490) Royal MS 20 C III, f. 15r.

2 Nectanebo disguised as a serpent seducing Olympias, in the *Roman d'Alexandre en prose*, in the Talbot Shrewsbury Book (Rouen, c.1445) Royal MS 15 E VI, f. 6r.

for several years until she was forced to surrender – when her enemies allied against her in favour of a male leader.

The ancient sources paint a picture of a determined and vengeful woman, manipulative and ruthless in her devotion to the success of her son and her dynasty. From a later perspective, she is an example of how impossible it was for even a strong and aggressive woman to retain real power in the Greek world. As daughter of the king of Molossia, her marriage to the older Philip II of Macedon (who already had at least one wife) was a dynastic one. It had been arranged by Olympias's uncle to unite the two kingdoms of Molossia and Macedon. Some say, though, that they met on the sacred island of Samothrace during their initiation into the orgiastic cult of the Kabeiroi and Philip was captivated by her beauty. They had two children, Alexander and Cleopatra, in the early years of their union but their violent natures led to stormy disagreements. Olympias particularly detested the other women and children in Philip's life; according to Plutarch she may even have poisoned one of Philip's sons by another woman. He adds that she introduced wild Dionysian rituals involving snakes into the palace milieu. She is even accused of sleeping with her pet snakes, a symbol of heightened sexuality and a habit that did not endear her to Philip. According to the Latin historian, Justin, he finally divorced her 'on suspicion of adultery'.[1]

Historical accounts of Olympias's marriage and the conception of Alexander were fictionalised in the *Roman d'Alexandre en prose* ('Prose Alexander Romance'), a collection of popular medieval legends about the life of Alexander the Great in French verse or prose, based on an earlier Greek original. Manuscript copies of this work show Olympias being seduced by a dragon-like creature (Image 2), illustrating the story that she had slept with a serpent (snakes and dragons are often conflated in medieval miniatures as the French word *serpent* could refer to either). Apparently Olympias was worried that Philip was about to divorce her because she had not yet given him a child. She consulted the Egyptian pharaoh-magician Nectanebo, who was exiled at her court, and he instructed her to have intercourse with a god to produce a son who would avenge her for Philip's neglect and cruelty. His advice to her was:

> You must know…that the following sign will be given before the god enters your room. If, as you rest at evening in your chamber, you see a serpent creeping towards you, order everyone to go outside. But do not put out the lamps, which I have prepared to give proper honour to the god, and which I will light and give you; no, go to your bed and make yourself ready, cover your face and do not look directly at the god whom you saw come to you in your dream.[2]

With his plan now in place, Nectanebo disguised himself as the Egyptian god Ammon in the form of a serpent and slept with the queen. She conceived a son who was, of course, Alexander. In Plutarch's *Life of Alexander*, Philip saw them sleeping together and as a result lost the eye with which he saw the god. This story of Alexander's conception was widely represented in the literature and art of the Roman empire and the medieval period. Olympias and the snake are often depicted in bed together (Image 2), or, in a scene from the *Roman d'Alexandre*, Nectanebo as a snake kisses Olympias while she is seated beside Philip at a banquet (Image 3).

A Roman copper medallion of c.AD 400 in the British Museum shows Olympias reclining as a serpent rests its head on her hand; on the other side is a profile of Alexander the Great. A 2017 Indian television series called *Porus* (about the great Indian ruler who was defeated by Alexander) contains a scene in which Olympias is played by the actress Sameksha Singh. Taking refuge from her violent husband in the temple of Zeus, she asks the god to give her a son who will restore her pride and conquer the world. In response, Zeus sends her thousands of black snakes who, in a horrifying scene, crawl all over her body as a representation of Alexander's divine conception.[3]

When he was old enough. Alexander murdered Nectanebo for deceiving

3 Olympias is kissed by a dragon-like serpent as Philip shows his disapproval, in the *Roman d'Alexandre en prose* (N. France or S. Netherlands, early 14th century) Royal MS 20 A V, f. 7r.

his mother. Nevertheless he himself spread the story that the god Zeus Ammon, not Philip, was his father and that he was therefore divine. When he visited the shrine of Siwah in the Egyptian desert, he claimed that he had a vision confirming that Ammon was his father. In the 2004 Oliver Stone film *Alexander*, where Olympias is played by Angelina Jolie, she states that it was Zeus who came to her and gave her a son.

The affair with Nectanebo was used in some versions of Alexander's story, including the Middle English *Kyng Alisaunder*, to portray Olympias as an exhibitionist seductress, and to pass judgements on her and on women in general that can only be described as misogynist.

For men seith by north and south	*For men say, by north and south*
Wymmen beeth evere selcouth	*That women always succumb to odd whims.*
Mychel she desireth to shewe hire body	*She greatly wished to show her body,*
Her faire hair, her face rody	*Her fair hair and rosy complexion,*
To have loos and ek praisying	*So as to be famous and admired.*
And al is folye by heven-king.	*All this is folly, by the King of heaven.*[4]

Comment li rois alixandre crownie la mere la royne olimpias garie de la grant maladie.

Quant li message s'en furent partis alixandre ordena en son lieu pour

4 Olympias and Alexander talk, in the *Roman d'Alexandre en prose* (Paris, *c*.1340) Royal MS 19 D I, f. 14r.

Later in the poem we are told that Olympias longed for her lover Nectanebo to return to her bed; she showed no shame or remorse, and the narrator comments, 'So dooth womman after mysdoying' ('A woman acts in this way after doing wrong'). The fact that her husband is already intent on leaving her for another woman is not mentioned.

In spite of her marital difficulties, Olympias took great care over the education of her children, ensuring that both her daughter Cleopatra and her son were well prepared for public life. The account of Alexander's youth in the

Roman d'Alexandre relates how he took his mother's side in the strife between his parents, telling Philip that Olympias had given him no cause for complaint. He arranged a reconciliation between the pair and later protected his mother from Philip's guard Pausanius, who tried to abduct her. When Philip rejected Olympias and took a new wife – a Macedonian woman also called Cleopatra – her son took her to shelter in her brother's court in Molossia. Her life changed dramatically when Philip was murdered at the wedding feast of his daughter, Cleopatra, at his palace in Agai in 336 BC. Many believed that from her exile Olympias had conspired with Alexander to have Philip killed, though other accounts blame Pausanius (who still lusted after the queen) for the murder. Shortly afterwards, Philip's new wife and young infant were also murdered, probably at the instigation of Olympias.

During Alexander's subsequent reign (336–323 BC) Olympias, as mother of the king, became a significant political figure, carving out a more powerful role for herself during the long period he was away conquering the world. However, women had little independent status in her world and so any power she had was dependent on her son. And mother and son had a close bond, as demonstrated in a scene from the *Roman d'Alexandre* (Image 4); just before Alexander left on his campaign against the Persians, hearing she had been ill, he went to visit her and was overjoyed to find her fully recovered. As he travelled further from home on his long journey of conquest, mother and son wrote to one another across the vast distances and it seems that she retained some influence over him in this way. One of these exchanges (preserved in a much later 'transcript' in the *Noctes Atticae* of the second century AD) shows how Olympias tried to temper her son's hubris. Alexander wrote to his mother:

Rex Alexander Iovis Hammonis filius Olympiadi matri salutem dicit

King Alexander, the son of Zeus Ammon, sends his greetings to his mother Olympias.

She replied:

Amabo...mi fili, quiescas neque deferas me neque criminere adversum Iunonem; malum mihi prorsum illa magnum dabit, cum tu me litteris tuis paelicem esse illi confiteris.

My son... hush! Lest you defame me or incriminate me before Juno! [the Greek goddess Hera, Zeus's jealous wife]. She will certainly cause me some great harm once you have confessed in your letters that I am her husband's adulteress.[5]

5a Iskandar (Alexander) writes to his mother to warn her of his impending death (left); 5b Olympias receives the letter from a messenger (right), in Firdawsi, *Shahnamah* ('The Book of Kings') (?Bukhara, *c.*1600) Or 14403, f. 332r-v.

The letters show a touching concern between them; Alexander addresses her as 'sweet mother' and in one instance he asks her to send Persian robes and regalia for his bride Roxana. He admits to missing his mother during the years he is away and instructs Roxana to treat her mother-in-law with respect.

The *Roman d'Alexandre* contains copies of letters Alexander supposedly wrote to Olympias and to his teacher Aristotle about his adventures in faraway lands, where he describes all manner of strange beasts and peoples that he encountered. But back at the court in Macedonia, Olympias was involved in political intrigue, waging war against various powerful figures through letters to her son, and conducting a protracted feud against Antipater (the regent he had appointed), who became her bitter enemy. In fact she made so many enemies in Macedonia that she went to live with her daughter in Molossia. Meanwhile Alexander, travelling ever further eastwards, continued to keep an eye on his mother, sending her gifts from the lands he had captured. When the oracle predicted his imminent death he asked if it would be possible to embrace her one more time before he died, and even sent her advice on how best to accept his death (Images 5a, 5b).

But from the moment her powerful son died, Olympias was left unprotected against the many enemies she had made, and she took part in a ruthless struggle to retain the throne for her grandson (son of Alexander the Great and Roxana). With the support of the Macedonian army, she defeated her

6 The capture of Pydnia and Olympias's murder, in the *Roman d'Alexandre en prose* (Paris, c.1420) Royal MS 20 B XX, f. 97r.

female rival Eurydice (granddaughter of Philip II by another wife), imprisoning her so that she took her own life and having her husband put to death. However, reports of her cruel treatment of her rivals turned her supporters against her and, following a siege at Pydnia, during which she apparently ate both elephants and the corpses of her maids, she was captured and imprisoned by the forces of Cassander (Image 6). She died bravely and with composure but Cassander refused to bury her and cast her body out to be devoured by wild animals (if we are to believe the *Roman d'Alexandre*) (Image 7). Her daughter Cleopatra was also murdered and Alexander's great empire was divided among his generals.

No confirmed images of Olympias survive from the Hellenistic period, though in later periods her image in surviving literature and art is more frequently found than that of her husband Philip. Greek historians who first wrote about Olympias are largely critical of her as a woman who tried to influence events in a world where respectable women were confined to the domestic sphere and restricted to the roles of wife and mother. Her relationship to her son is often the subject of jokes and remarks about the negative qualities of women. Even Alexander, while he allowed his mother a certain amount of power in his absence, reminded her early on that wives should obey their

7 Olympias's head and body are thrown to wild beasts outside the city, in the *Roman d'Alexandre en prose*, in the Talbot Shrewsbury Book (Rouen, *c*.1445) Royal MS 15 E VI, f. 24v.

husbands, and declared that the Macedonians would never submit to being ruled by a woman.[6]

Nevertheless, Olympias managed to exert some direct influence in a highly patriarchal culture; she had to be strong and think for herself in order to survive and protect her descendants and so naturally she made enemies. Ultimately all of Alexander's female relatives were murdered by the men who seized power after his death and any surviving historical evidence about his mother is fragmentary and contradictory; nothing that she wrote or said can be conclusively verified. The *Roman d'Alexandre* is only very loosely based on the real events of Alexander's life, and so her reputation is gleaned largely from the legends therein and from the descriptions of male historians who lived centuries after she died. They judged her as ruthless and held her responsible for her involvement in murders of a handful of enemies at court, whereas her son Alexander has been largely admired for his remarkable conquests, though he caused the death of thousands and the destruction of entire civilisations. It is only recently that historians have questioned this view of her and tried to uncover the real Olympias – a woman who managed to wield influence in a world dominated by larger-than-life men.

amoureux et pour ce sont cy figurez
amans qui lui presentet leurs cueurs.

texte. 6
De venus ne fais ta deesse
ne ne chulte de la maistresse

12.

Venus, Goddess of Love

In Christine de Pisan's didactic work, *L'Épistre Othéa* (Image 1), Othea, the goddess of prudence and wisdom, advises her pupil, a young knight, to beware of Venus. Her opinion of the goddess is clearly summarised in a translation made by an English knight named Stephen Scrope in *The Boke of Knyghthode*:

Off Venus in no wyse make thi godesse,
And for no thynge sette store by here promysse.
To folowe here it is rauenous,
Both vnworchippefull and peryllous.[1]

Nevertheless, the smiling medieval courtiers in this image are all eagerly offering the enthroned goddess their hearts.

Venus has been described as 'the most original creation of the Roman pantheon'[2] and she was certainly the most desirable of all the goddesses. Hers was the beauty of love, but also of temptation and sexual desire; with her exquisite looks and grace, she was famous for her romantic adventures and affairs with both gods and mortals. Those who were under her protection were safe from harm but she was proud and haughty and could be a ruthless adversary, especially to women who might threaten her self-proclaimed status as beauty queen of Olympus. She delighted in interfering in the love-lives of

1 Othea shows Hector courtiers giving their hearts to Venus, in Christine de Pisan, *L'Épistre Othéa* ('Letter of Othea') (Paris, c.1412) Harley MS 4431, f. 100r.

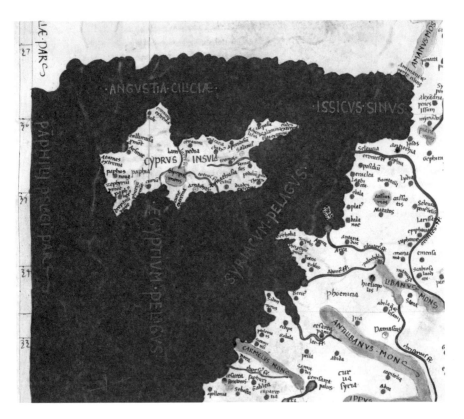

2 A medieval map of Cyprus, in Ptolemy, *Geography* (Florence, *c.*1470) Harley MS 7182, f. 92v.

her fellow gods and of those on earth, and so she plays a role in a wide variety of legends from the *Aeneid* to the earliest surviving version of the Sleeping Beauty story in the medieval legend of *Perceforest,* where she helps the hero Troylus to wake the sleeping princess Zellandine.

Originally an Italian goddess of fertility, fruit and flowers, Venus had temples dedicated to her at least as far back as the third century BC. She was later identified with Aphrodite, the Greek goddess of love, so in books on mythology the two are commonly treated as two manifestations of the same goddess. In medieval legends, which are almost exclusively descended from the Roman literary tradition, she was known as Venus. In the Greek tale of Aphrodite's origins (adopted by the Romans for Venus) she was born from the seafoam (*aphros* in Greek) that gathered around the genitals of Caelus (Uranus) after they had been cut off and tossed away by his son Saturn (Cronos). She came ashore on the island of Cyprus and it is said that wherever she stepped grass grew under her feet. Surprisingly, there are also mentions of a bearded male Venus, described by Macrobius in his *Saturnalia* of the fifth century:

3 Vulcan, Venus and Mars, in Jean de Meun, *Roman de la Rose* (Bruges, c.1500) Harley MS 4425, f. 122v.

There's also a statue of Venus on Cyprus, that's bearded, shaped and dressed like a woman, with sceptre and male genitals, and they conceive her as both male and female. ...In his Atthis *Philochorus, too, states that she is the Moon and that men sacrifice to her in women's dress, women in men's, because she is held to be both male and female.*[3]

Venus was married to the blacksmith god, Vulcan (Haephestus), who was clumsy, hairy and sooty, and who forged iron thunderbolts for Jupiter (Zeus), king of the gods. Unsurprisingly, she was never faithful to him; her true love was Mars (Ares), the god of war. One day the sun god Sol (Helios) came to Vulcan and told him he had seen Venus lying with Mars, in his (Vulcan's) own palace. The blacksmith was enraged and went to his workshop where he made a net of metal so fine and light that it was almost invisible, but so strong that it was impossible to break. He installed it in Venus's bedroom and the next time she was with her lover the net was released and bound the pair so tightly together that they could not escape. Vulcan invited all the gods to come

Cy commence le liure intitule ouide methamorphose. qui contient
en somme quinze liures · et commence le prologue dudit liure ·

Outes escri-
ptures soiēt
bonnes ou
mauuaises
sont pour
nostre prouffit et docterme
faictes. les bonnes affin
de y prendre exemple de bien
faire et les mauuaises
affin que on se garde et

abstiengne de mal faire ·
On dist communement et
il est vray que sens respons
ou mussié est perdu sy est
chose moult a despriser · et
pour ce ne le doit on celer-
ains publier et monstrer
a ceulx qui ne le scevent -
Pour laquelle cause
le veul traicter selonc mon

MVSEVM
BRITAN
NICVM

and witness the trapped lovers, causing much hilarity among them. Scenes of Venus and Mars in art of the Roman period tend to ignore their adultery, portraying them as a good-looking couple attended by their son Cupid (Eros) or a group of cherubs, and husbands and wives were regularly portrayed as the divine couple, presumably at their own request.

The adultery scene is illustrated in a manuscript of the medieval love-allegory, the *Roman de la Rose* ('Romance of the Rose') (Image 3), in which the second part is a satirical commentary on medieval society. Here the tale of Venus and Mars is retold by the Old Woman, an allegorical character who has an extremely cynical view of contemporary sexual morality. She first gives advice to young women to be just as promiscuous as men, using potions or any means at their disposal to make themselves attractive, and keeping 'Venus's chamber' neat. Referring to the Mars-Venus story, she comments on Venus's shame at being seen by all the gods in a compromising position, but adds that they were amazed and delighted at her beauty. She also justifies Venus's action by saying that Vulcan was so ugly it was not surprising that such an attractive woman would not be satisfied with him as a husband.

In addition to Mars, Venus was said to have a penchant for several other gods including Mercury (Hermes) and Bacchus (Dionysus), and also various mortals. She bore many children, and there are diverse traditions relating to these among the medieval mythographers who retold and commented on the classical material. Most agree that Cupid was her son by Mars. However, the philosopher Bernardus Silvestris described Venus as having two children (Jolcus and Cupid) by Vulcan; the French theologian Alan of Lille claimed that Jolcus, the child of darkness, was born of her adulterous union with Antigamus; Alberic of London said she had a son named Hymenaeus with Bacchus. According to Boccaccio, Venus conceived two children without fathers, called Amor and Cupid, and Mercury gave her a child named Hermaphroditus. Apparently at the time of his birth neither masculine nor feminine planets had superior influence, so he shared the attributes and desires of both. In addition, Aeneas was believed to be her son by the Trojan prince Anchises (more on this Trojan connection later).

Among Venus's mortal lovers Adonis is perhaps the most well known; the Roman poet Ovid tells their story in his *Metamorphoses*, one of the most important sources of classical mythology in the Middle Ages. Here he describes how Venus became besotted with Adonis:

4 Opening page of the *Ovide moralisée* showing the birth of the children of Saturn, the future gods of Olympus (Netherlands, late 15th century) Royal MS 17 E IV, f. 13r.

A most beautiful child, then a boy, now a man, now more beautiful than he was before, now interests Venus herself, and avenges his mother's desire. For while the boy, Cupid, with quiver on shoulder, was kissing his mother, he innocently scratched her breast with a loose arrow. The injured goddess pushed her son away: but the wound he had given was deeper than it seemed, and deceived her at first. Now captured by mortal beauty, she cares no more for Cythera's shores, nor revisits Paphos... she even forgoes the heavens: preferring Adonis to heaven.[4]

Adonis had been born of an incestuous union arranged by Venus herself between King Cinras of Cyprus and his daughter Myrrha. She turned the latter into a myrrh tree and then gave the baby Adonis to Proserpine, daughter of Jupiter and Ceres, to care for until he was older. In some versions of the legend, Proserpine (who had been carried off to the Underworld by Pluto) also fell in love with the beautiful young man. She arranged for him to be killed by Mars, Venus's lover, so he could join her in Hades. As Venus ran to help the dying Adonis she trod on a thorn and her blood fell on the petals of a white rose, staining them red. For this reason roses are Venus's flower, though Boccaccio claimed it was because of their pleasing odour, which stimulated desire. The tussle over Adonis caused great strife between the two goddesses until the situation was resolved when he was allowed to spend a third of his time with Venus in the upper world, a third in the Underworld with Proserpine and a third wherever he pleased.

A version of the *Metamorphoses* was produced in the Middle Ages – known as the *Ovide moralisée* – in which Christian morality was applied to Ovid's tales (Image 4). The anonymous author described how Venus gave Adonis myrrh to drink and warned him not to go hunting but he disobeyed and so he was transformed into an oak tree.

In the late medieval and Renaissance periods love was seen in both a positive and negative light; it could be an ennobling force, a spiritual union that brought out the best in people and gave them an inner light. But many saw it as a kind of madness, and in courtly literature such as the *Roman de la Rose* and the *Tristan and Isolde* legend the pains of love were emphasised. One of the most tragic myths involving Venus, and one in which she does not emerge in a positive light, is the story of Venus and Psyche, which is sometimes considered to be more a fairy tale in the early tradition of *Beauty and the Beast* than a classical legend.

Psyche was a mortal, the youngest and most beautiful daughter of an unnamed king and queen; she was so beautiful that there were no words to describe her perfection. She was fresh and innocent and was seen by many as

Venus in human form so that people travelled from afar to admire her. Venus became mad with jealousy and she instructed her son Cupid to use one of his arrows to make Psyche fall in love with an ugly man. However, she was so beautiful that Cupid fell in love with her himself. They married and he built her a palace with jewelled floors and golden walls. But Cupid knew that as a mortal she must never look on his face, otherwise their unborn child would not be immortal, so he only visited under cover of darkness.

For a while they enjoyed a blissful union, but Psyche became lonely and invited her two sisters to stay. They were jealous of her beautiful home and persuaded her that she should find out who or what her husband was – perhaps he was a hideous monster or a horrible snake. So one night Psyche took a lamp and shone it on Cupid's face while he slept. She was amazed to see that it was sweet and lovable, but unfortunately she allowed some wax to drip on his face and he awoke and flew away in a fury. Psyche clung to him in panic, lost her hold and fell to the earth in despair. She searched everywhere for him, tormented by Venus who was enraged when her son told her about his marriage. Venus gave her a series of impossible tasks to complete, one of which was to fetch for her a box containing a beauty treatment from the Underworld. But Psyche, having managed to bring back the box (with the help of a speaking tower) once again fell prey to curiosity and opened it, falling into a deathly sleep. Cupid prayed to Jupiter who revived her, pronounced the pair officially married, and appeased Venus. He gave ambrosia to Psyche who became a goddess and gave birth to a daughter named Voluptas ('pleasure'), so Venus was now a grandmother.

For the Romans, Venus was the divine mother of Virgil's hero Aeneas, who fled from the sack of Troy to found the city of Rome. Julius Caesar gave her the epithet *Venus Genetrix* and claimed to be descended from Aeneas through his son Ascanius. Successive Roman emperors believed that their connection to Venus promised them divine blessings on all their enterprises, provided that they continued to celebrate her and offer her gifts. A temple to Mars in the Circus Flaminus in Rome was built in around 133 BC, with a colossal statue of Mars and a nude Venus inside. The emperor Augustus used the story of the Venus–Mars relationship to link *Aeneadum Genetrix*, 'the mother of the descendants of Aeneas' with the 'father of the founder of the nation' in a dynastic mission (Mars had reputedly fathered the other legendary founders of Rome, Romulus and Remus, through his rape of Rhea Silvia, their mother).

In the *Aeneid* Venus intervenes when Aeneas and his fleet are blown off course by a storm and shipwrecked on the shore near Carthage by Juno (queen of the gods and patroness of Carthage), who does not want him to succeed in his mission of founding Rome. Venus appears, disguised as a huntress,

5 Paris awards the apple to Venus, in Convenevole da Prato, the *Regia Carmina* (Tuscany, c.1340) Royal MS 6 E IX, f. 22r.

and shows him twelve swans flying overhead – they have escaped from being attacked by an eagle and she tells him that this is an omen that he will prosper. She advises him to go into the city of Carthage to meet the founder, Queen Dido, and covers him in a cloud to prevent him being seen by Juno. Then she summons Cupid to use his powers to make Dido fall passionately in love with Aeneas so that she will forget her allegiance to Juno. When Aeneas in turn falls for Dido's charms, Venus agrees to help Juno arrange a union between the pair, knowing that in fact Jupiter (king of the gods) will not allow it. The outcome is Dido's suicide when Aeneas abandons her after Jupiter orders him to leave Carthage and continue his journey to found Rome. He stops to dedicate a temple to Venus at Eryx and, though he faces further trials sent to him by Juno, Venus persuades Neptune (god of the sea) to make sure he reaches the shores of Italy safely. When he arrives Venus asks her husband Vulcan to make him new armour and later heals him from a wound he receives in a battle against his enemy Turnus, who he ultimately defeats with her help and that of Jupiter. So Venus triumphs over the wishes of Juno with the help of her husband.

Venus and Juno (queen of the gods) had a long-standing rivalry following the famous incident known as the Judgement of Paris (Image 5). One day Paris, son of King Priam of Troy, was visited by Mercury and three goddesses, Minerva (goddess of wisdom and war), Juno and Venus. Mercury asked him to decide which goddess was the most beautiful and to award her the golden apple. It was an impossible choice. Juno offered to make him king of Europe and Asia, Minerva offered him wisdom, but the clever Venus swayed him by promising to give him Helen, the most beautiful woman in the world. And so Paris chose Venus, and his decision set in motion the events that led to the Trojan War (see Chapter 20, Helen of Troy). Of course Juno was furious at this decision and she and Venus became sworn enemies.

In the *Roman de la Rose* Venus appears several times to help the lover, protagonist of the dream vision, who is intent on plucking the Rose (i.e. winning the lady). In the first part by Guillaume de Lorris (approximately 4,000 lines), she is initially portrayed as the mortal enemy of Chastity, whom she attacks mercilessly by stealing rosebuds from her at every opportunity. The Lover describes her attributes, methods and stylish air:

Mes Vénus qui tous dis guerroie
Chastée, me vint au secors
Ce est la mere au diex d'Amors
Qui a secoru main amant Ele tint un brandon flamant
En sa main destere dont la flame
A eschauffée mainte dame.
El fu si cointe et si tifée,
Et resembloit déesse ou fée
Du grant ator que ele avoit
Bien puet cognoistre qui la voit,
Qu'el n'ert pas de religion;

But Venus, who wages war
On Chastity, came to my aid.
The mother of the God of Love,
She has helped many a lover;
She held a blazing torch
In her right hand, that has
Warmed many a lady, with its flame.
She was so elegant, and adorned
And resembled a goddess, or a fairy.
From her fancy attire,
It was easy to tell
She was not a nun;[5]

6 Venus in her chariot attacking the castle and threatening the guards, in the *Roman de la Rose* (Paris, 15th century) Egerton MS 1069, f. 140r.

She then tries to persuade *Bel Accueil* (Fair Welcome), the friend of *L'amant* (the Lover), to help him seize the day and capture the Rose.

Bien est, ce m'est avis, droiture	*It is right, in my opinion*
Que uns baisers li soit gréés,	*To grant him a kiss;*
Donnes-li, se vous m'en créés;	*Allow it; for, believe me in this,*
Car tant cum vous plus atendrés,	*The longer you choose to delay,*
Tant plus sachies, de tens perdrés.	*The faster time slips away.*[6]

In the second part of the *Roman de la Rose* when Cupid/the God of Love and his army are attacking the castle of Jealousy where the Rose is imprisoned, he sends messengers to his mother on Mount Cythera to ask for her help. Venus at that time is busy hunting with and making love to Adonis, and so the story of his death is summarised here, and the author, Jean de Meun, advises young men to listen to their mistresses if they want to avoid disaster. Following this sad tale, the action returns to Venus, who immediately flies to the aid of her son Cupid in her chariot of pearls and gold, drawn by a team of turtle doves (Image 6). She vows to seize the guards, burn the defences and win the key to the tower where the Rose is held. The pair attack the castle but the defenders put

7 Venus swimming in the sea; holding her planet in the sky, in Matfre Ermengaud, *Breviari d'amor* (Toulouse, early 14th century) Royal MS 19 C I, f. 41v.

up a strong fight; Nature sends her priest Genius to their aid and he spurs them on, advocating compassion and kindness rather than chaste denial of pleasure.

Venus re-launches the assault, preparing to fire a burning arrow at the tower that is guarded by a gold statue. Venus fires the arrow and captures the castle. The lover now is able to '*pregne, debaille et colle / Rosiers et rose, flors et foille*' ('to take, reveal, and pluck / Bush and Rose, leaf and flower').[7]

From the middle of the twelfth century onwards, and particularly in the fourteenth century when large luxury manuscripts were being produced for the entertainment of wealthy patrons, classical myths were a popular subject. With the emphasis on courtly love and morality during this period, Venus played an important part in many of these works, retaining the rich and elusive qualities from her classical origins. Her association with the planet Venus is explored by a number of authors. Boccaccio, Giraldi and others expanded on Plato's idea that there were two Venuses, the heavenly and the terrestrial. As the former she was associated with the morning and evening star, one of the brightest and most beautiful objects in the night sky (Image 7). As the latter she was the first of the prostitutes on Cyprus and venereal disease (named after her) was the result. Both aspects of her reputation as a beautiful woman – the object of worship and desire, and the wanton corrupter of men – were debated and illustrated in books on the subjects of love, astrology and classical mythology.

13.

The Queen of Sheba

Born on the fifth day of January in the tenth century BC and known in Western culture as the Queen of Sheba, this powerful and mysterious woman is the only female character from the Old Testament to feature in the sacred texts of Judaism, Christianity (both the Old and New Testaments) and Islam. In the European imagination, she came to represent the supposed luxury and sensuousness of the Orient. Different cultures gave her many names. In the New Testament Jesus refers to her as the 'Queen of the South';[1] in Jewish folklore her name is Malkath and in Arabic it is Bilqis or Belqis. To the Ethiopians she is either Eteye Azreb, which means 'Queen of the South' in the Ge'ez language, or Makeda, another name for 'queen'; East Africans call her Habashia and in West Africa there is a folk figure named Bilqisi Sungbo who has also been identified with her. According to the Roman-Jewish historian Josephus, she was Nikaulis, 'the woman who ruled Egypt and Ethiopia'.[2] Josephus's historical works were key sources in the Middle Ages, and he called the capital of Ethiopia 'Saba', so she is known as the *Reine de Saba* in medieval French texts. In the nineteenth century the poet Gérard de Nerval, who wrote the libretto for an opera about her, referred to her as *Reine du Matin* ('Queen of the Morning').[3]

The Queen of Sheba reigned over a hugely wealthy kingdom whose location has been a subject of debate. There are several references to a land of Sheba and its peoples in the Bible. Genesis 10:7 lists Seba and Sheba among

---

1 The Queen of Sheba in Firdawsi's *Shahnamah* ('The Book of Kings') (Shiraz, 16th century) IO Islamic 3540, f. 2r.

2 Arabia and Ethiopia are marked on this 16th-century map by a Portuguese cartographer in the Queen Mary Atlas (?England, 1558) Add MS 5415A, f. 16r.

the sons of Cush, Psalm 72 says that the kings of Sheba and Seba shall offer gifts to Solomon, Jeremiah 6:20 mentions incense (or frankincense) from Sheba, and Joel 3.8 prophesied to the Jews that they would be sold as slaves to the men of Sheba, 'a people far off'. Ancient Assyrian texts and inscriptions refer to (male) sovereigns of 'Saba' and Arab legends evoke a powerful tribe in ancient Yemen, with a dynasty that ruled for many years. Coins with images of kings of Saba survive and there is archaeological evidence of trade in spices, perfumes and gold from southern Arabia, supplying the markets of the eastern Mediterranean. Jewellery, incense burners and household objects have been found – some dating from as early as the eighth century BC – as well as alabaster and bronze statues of female figures, though none are conclusively identified with the Queen. However, King Solomon's reign is traditionally dated to the tenth century BC by biblical scholars, and most written evidence dates from the sixth century onwards, so it is difficult to establish a chronology and firm historical or archaeological evidence for her existence.

In the Bible, the Queen of Sheba first appears in a well-known episode in the Old Testament Book of Kings, with an almost identical version in the Book of Chronicles.[4] Scholars generally agree that these accounts (dating from the

3 The Queen of Sheba presents gifts to King Solomon, while her attendants unpack gifts they have unloaded from camels, in a *Bible historiale* (Paris, c.1415) Add MS 18856, f. 157r.

fourth to the sixth centuries BC) are based on much older texts, possibly court records recording contemporary events. The Queen is introduced in terms of her relationship to Solomon:

> *And when the Queen of Sheba heard of the fame of Solomon...she came to prove him with hard questions. And she came to Jerusalem with a very great train with camels that bore spices and very much gold and precious stones, and when she was come to Solomon she communed with him of all that was in her heart.*
>
> ...
>
> *And she gave the King an hundred and twenty talents of gold and of spices very great store, and precious stones; there came no more such abundance of spices as these which the Queen of Sheba gave to Solomon*
>
> ...
>
> *And King Solomon gave unto the Queen of Sheba all her desire, whatsoever she asked, beside that which Solomon gave her of his royal bounty. So she turned and went to her own country, she and her servants.*[5]

From this short description, vague allusions to a powerful queen in other traditions, and the sparse physical evidence, a whole raft of legends and fables developed around the Queen of Sheba in medieval Europe and the Middle East. The Quran, which was completed in the seventh century AD, and therefore many centuries later than the Hebrew Book of Kings, contains two passages in which the story of Bilqis (the Queen of Sheba) is told. They are the Surat al-Naml ('The Ant')[6] and the Surat Saba ('Sheba')[7]. Both here and in the Old Testament, the Queen's name is not given, and neither is the location of her kingdom. The story of the meeting between the two great rulers was popular in Persian and Arabic literature; it was embellished by Quranic commentators and subsequent storytellers, who called the Queen Bilqis. In deluxe manuscripts from Iran – particularly those produced in Shiraz in the sixteenth century – images of Solomon and Sheba in a magnificent setting often formed the frontispiece (Image 4). The many different threads of the story in the Eastern traditions may be summarised as follows.

Solomon, who greatly enjoyed feasting, one day held a great banquet for all the kings of the East that was accompanied by an extravagant spectacle including a parade of devils, spirits and all the animals of heaven and earth. Solomon had the gift of speaking to the birds, and when he gathered them all together he found that the hoopoe was not among them. As the bird had not answered the summons, he threatened it with severe punishment for its disobedience. But the hoopoe was merely late for the gathering, and when he arrived he had an excellent excuse. Appearing before Solomon, he announced that he had just arrived from Saba, a land at the end of the earth, where he had seen something unknown even to his master. It was a country of great riches ruled over by a woman on a magnificent throne, where the people worshipped the sun rather than the true God, as directed by the devil himself. Solomon was not sure whether to believe this tall tale, so the hoopoe promised to bring the Queen to him in chains so he could see her for himself. Solomon was delighted and had a letter prepared for the hoopoe to deliver to the Queen, ordering her to come and pay him homage, or her kingdom would be conquered by the birds, spirits and demons at his command.

When Bilqis received Solomon's letter, knowing his noble reputation, she first asked the advice of her people, then decided to send a return letter and offer him many precious gifts and treasures from her kingdom. Solomon, who was not interested in material wealth, refused the gift and – in a strange gesture – had her throne stolen and brought back to him so that he could alter it and test her ability to recognise it as a sign of her intelligence. After a journey of seven years the Queen reached Solomon's court in Jerusalem with an entourage of sixty elephants, camels, Ethiopian attendants and caravans

4 A double-page miniature within an illuminated border of the Queen of Sheba at the court of King Solomon, in Firdawsi, *Shahnamah*, IO Islamic 3540, ff. 1v–2r.

filled with gold and precious stones, incense, perfumes, ebony and ivory and sumptuous fabrics. She passed the throne test and was welcomed by the king in a lavishly decorated pavilion where he sat on a magnificent throne surrounded by his attendants.

Solomon had arranged for the pavilion to have a glass floor and this unnerved the Queen, who had never seen anything of the kind. She mistook the glass beneath her feet for water, raising the hem of her robe so that it would not get wet, and this allowed Solomon to admire her legs (Image 5). He soon realised that they were rather hairy; this was acceptable for a man but extremely unattractive in a woman and he turned away in disgust (in some versions she also had hooves like a donkey). Solomon ordered a *jinn* ('genie')

5 Solomon watches the Queen of Sheba raising her skirts as she approaches his throne, in *Speculum humanae salvationis* ('Mirror of Human Salvation') (London, *c.*1500) Harley MS 2838, f. 44v.

to create a depilatory for the Queen to rid her of the unsightly hair, as he had realised she was otherwise extremely attractive and intelligent. Her pride was wounded and she in turn decided to put Solomon in his place by setting him a long series of riddles. However, as Solomon was so wise and clever he was able to solve them all easily. Bilqis was convinced by this performance that she should worship Allah, the true God.

The 'trick' that Solomon apparently played on the Queen to allow him to admire her legs has fascinated researchers, who have come up with various explanations. In ancient Greek legend there is a female demon with the legs of a donkey, who goes by the name of Empusa or Onoskelis and who appears in Aristophanes' comedy, *The Frogs*. A Judeo-Christian text of the third century or earlier tells us that some of the demons under Solomon's power believed that the beautiful queen who entered Solomon's court with her impressive train was not a human but a rival female devil. Fearing that the king might fall victim to her charms and give her power over them, they convinced him that under her robes she was hiding the hooves of a donkey like Onoskelis, and so that is why the king tricked her into believing she had to wade through an expanse of water to reach his throne. In some versions Solomon saw she was not a donkey-devil but a beautiful woman with shapely legs, though a rumour spread that she was excessively hairy and so she was given the name Bilqis (derived from Onoskelis).

The *Qisas al-anbia* ('Tales of the Prophets') claims that Solomon married Bilqis and that she bore him four children, three daughters and one son,[8] but other authors state that Solomon gave her in marriage to the king of the Hamdan tribe. Later it was said that her grave was discovered by a group of Himyarites (peoples of the present-day Yemen) digging in a royal cemetery; they found a woman's corpse wrapped in golden robes buried under a marble slab, on which verses showing it to be Bilqis's tomb were inscribed.[9]

Another Eastern legend tells of a royal alchemist at the court of Saba who made a small rug that could hover above the ground. The Queen was delighted with this invention and had a large version made of beautiful green silk embroidered with gold and silver and studded with precious stones. She sent it to King Solomon as a token of her love but when it arrived he was busy supervising the building of the Temple. Preoccupied with his task, he gave it to one of his courtiers instead. The Queen was heartbroken when she heard her gift had not been well received and resolved to have no more to do with magic carpets. It is said that nobody else could afford to buy these magnificent objects, so the alchemist and his workmen stopped making them and the knowledge was lost forever.

An Ethiopian monk named Yetshak, who in 1320 wrote down a compendium of stories called *Kebra Negast* or 'Glory of the Kings', said that when the Makeda (the Queen of Sheba) visited Solomon, she was seduced by him. The king had warned her that while she was welcome to his hospitality, she must not take anything without asking. During the night, Makeda suffered from thirst caused by a spicy meal she had been offered by Solomon and she drank the water beside her bed. As she had broken the taboo, Solomon decreed that she must offer him her body in repayment and nine months later she gave birth to a boy called Menelik. When he was old enough, Menelik wanted to know his father and so he travelled to Jerusalem where he met King Solomon. Returning home, he brought with him the Ark of the Covenant, the sacred container of the Ten Commandments. In Ethiopian legend, the Ark has remained in Ethiopia ever since and Ethiopians see Menelik as the first in an unbroken line of Ethiopian kings that ruled until Haile Selassie I was deposed in 1974.

The name Bilqis appears in genealogies of the Sabean monarchs and she is associated in legend with other female rulers of the East, such as Zenobia. These women are said to have possessed great beauty, a love of riches, and attributes that are normally the preserve of kings. Stories about them contained similar themes; they were apparently manipulated by cunning enemies who posed as friends or suitors and as a result they lost their crowns.

Among the medieval European versions of Sheba's story, Boccaccio, in his *De mulieribus claris* ('On Famous Women') (Image 6) gives Nicaula (his

6 Nicaula, Queen of Sheba, presents gifts to King Solomon. Behind her are the 'barbarous' peoples of Ethiopia that Boccaccio alludes to in his *De mulieribus claris,* here in a French translation, *Des Cleres et nobles femmes* (Rouen, *c.*1440) Royal MS 16 G V, f. 53v.

name for the Queen) credit for 'good conduct' despite her being the product of the 'extreme barbarousness of Ethiopia'. He also tells that 'She gave Solomon magnificent presents among which it is believed were those small trees from which balsam comes, which Solomon later had planted and cultivated not far from Lake Asaltis [i.e. the Dead Sea]'.[10]

Christine de Pisan closely follows Boccaccio's narrative in the *Livre de la Cité des Dames* ('Book of the City of Ladies'), where she includes the Queen in her section on prophetesses, listing the lands she travelled through on her way to Jerusalem:

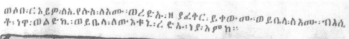

7 Christ on the Cross in an Ethiopian Bible (17th century), written in Ge'ez, Or 481, f. 105v.

[Elle] laissa son pays et chevaucha par la terre d'Ethiope et d'Egipte par les rivages de la Rouge Mer et par les grans desers d'Arabé et a tout moult noble compaignie de princes, de seigneurs, de chevaliers et de nobles dames a moult grant estat et tresor de plusieurs choses precieuses vint et arriva en la cité de Jherusalem...

[She] travelled from the regions of the Orient, from the farthest corner of the world, leaving her country and riding through the lands of Ethiopia and Egypt, accompanied by a distinguished entourage of princes, lords, knights, and noble ladies of high estate and carrying many precious treasures, she arrived in the city of Jerusalem...

Christine then includes a legend of Coptic origin whereby the Queen prophesies the Crucifixion of Christ (here, characteristically the Jews are portrayed in an unflattering light). She visits Solomon's temple and sees a huge

8 Solomon receiving the Queen of Sheba and her entourage, in a *Bible historiale* (Paris, early 15th century) Royal MS 15 D III, f. 285r.

tree trunk lying in the mud apparently originating from a tree that grew in the Garden of Eden. She stops to pay homage, proclaiming:

'Ceste planche qui ores est tenue en grant vilté et mise soubz les piez sera, tel temps vendra, honoree sur tous les fusts du monde et aournee de pierres precieuses es tresors des princes. Et dessus le fust de cette planche mourra cellui par qui sera anientie la loy des Juifs'. Ceste parole ne tindrent mie a truffe. Les Juifs ains l'osterent de la et l'enterrerent en lieu ou ilz cuiderent que jamais ne fust trouvee, mais ce que Dieux veult garder est bien gardez, car si bien ne la sorent Juifs mucier qu'elle ne fust trouvee ou temps de la passion de Nostre Seigneur Jhesu Crist. Et de celle planche veult on dire que fu faite la croix sur laquelle Nostre Sauveur souffri mort et passion. Si fu lors avoirié la prophecie d'icelle dame.

'This plank, now held in such great contempt and placed under foot, will, when the time comes, be honoured above all other pieces of wood and decorated with precious gems from the treasuries of princes. And on this plank will die the one who will annihilate the law of the Jews'. ...So the Jews removed the plank and buried it in a place where they believed it would never be found. But what God wishes to save is well protected, for the Jews did not manage to hide it well and so it was rediscovered at the time of our Saviour Jesus Christ's passion. And it is said that from this plank was made the Cross on which our Saviour suffered death and passion. So this lady's prophecy was then fulfilled.[11]

lqntin ÷ libro by x
aplo Cv rqina fa
ba audia fama
falomonis vaitm
ihilm ai magnis
mintabs aii hono
rando q quitirqina
grnalis aat Ouch
nc fiqu fical̄t gae
q onni di longtiq
ai munibs uaiic
banc adoiaie.

9 The Queen of Sheba presenting gifts to Solomon, in a *Biblia pauperum* (Netherlands, c.1400) Kings MS 5, f. 3r.

Because of this legend, the Queen of Sheba was sometimes associated with the Sibyl who foretold the coming of Christ (see Chapter 27).

The Queen of Sheba became an important symbol for medieval alchemists; in a treatise completed in the fifteenth century known as the *Aurora consurgens* she was associated with wisdom, the moon and the south wind.[12] The Book of Wisdom in the Bible is quoted extensively in this work, referring to King Solomon and his bride, the 'Wisdom of the South', as is the quotation from Jesus in the New Testament, 'the Queen of the South shall rise up in Judgement'.[13] The story of the Queen's visit to Solomon is invoked in the first line of the *Aurora,* in which she represents divine feminine wisdom who brings the wisdom of God to man.

Whether she is viewed as a beautiful but demonic partner, the essence of knowledge or a noble ancestress, the Queen of Sheba was certainly an independent woman ruling a fabulously wealthy kingdom. The historical record and subsequent legends contain the memory of a woman who held a high-ranking position in a world dominated by men, suggesting that she was a capable ruler who was able to hold her own.

14.

Candace of Ethiopia

An early description of Queen Candace is of 'a very beautiful woman, who was middle-aged, a widow, mother of three sons'.[1] In medieval literature she features in a key episode from the large body of popular legends about Alexander the Great's fictional exploits in the East. Many of these originate from a Greek text dated to the third century AD and usually called the *Greek Alexander Romance* or the *Pseudo-Callisthenes*. There are believed to have been other early versions of the stories in Pahlavi (Middle Persian) and Arabic but few traces remain, though later sources in Armenian, Syriac and Arabic survive, mostly descended in some way from the Greek romance. Alexander's meeting with Queen Candace is described in historical and poetical works from Ethiopia and Persia, Armenia and Azerbaijan, and preserved in a wide variety of languages. In the West, it features in medieval Alexander romances in Old French (Image 2), Middle High German, Slavonic, Middle English and other European vernaculars, based on the Greek text or a Latin translation made by Valerius in the fourth century.

The most magnificent surviving illuminations of the Alexander legends are found in manuscripts of two great works of Persian narrative literature of the eleventh and twelfth centuries, the *Shahnamah* ('The Book of Kings') of Firdawsi (Images 4, 5), and the *Khamsah* ('Five Poems') of Nizami (Images 1, 6,

1 Iskandar (Alexander) is shown his portrait by Nushabah (Candace), in Nizami, *Khamsah* (Tabriz, Iran, *c.*1540) Or 2265, f. 48v.

2 Alexander with Queen Candace and her two sons, in the *Roman d'Alexandre en prose* in the Talbot Shrewsbury Book (Rouen, *c*.1445) Royal MS 15 E VI, f. 19v.

7), and in copies of the French *Roman d'Alexandre en prose* ('Prose Alexander Romance') (Images 2, 8) of which a number of verse and prose versions were composed from the twelfth century onwards. The illuminated copies from both Asia and Europe mostly date from the fourteenth to the sixteenth centuries, and the British Library holds some of the most famous examples, from which the images in this chapter are taken.

In the original *Greek Alexander Romance* Candace of Meroe was a powerful queen who presided over a magnificent court and whose fame had spread far and wide. She was reputedly descended from Queen Semiramis and ruled Egypt with the god Ammon as her adviser. This fictional Candace is based on a real dynasty of queens who ruled the fabulously wealthy Kingdom of Kush (in modern-day Sudan) and were known by the title of *Kandake /Kentake* (meaning 'queen regent' or 'royal woman'). This royal matrilineal title, romanised as 'Candace', was treated incorrectly as a personal name in classical sources; the early Greek

3 Philip and Queen Candace's eunuch ride in his chariot; the eunuch hands a book of scriptures to the apostle and the river behind him is the water in which he was baptised. The rays of light streaming down show the spirit of God descending on them, in the Bedford Hours (Paris, c.1420) Add MS 18850, f. 108r.

geographer Strabo mentions a Candace of the Ethiopians, a masculine woman, who had lost an eye in battle. In the New Testament of the Christian Bible, a 'Kandake, queen of the Ethiopians' is briefly mentioned when the apostle Philip meets 'a eunuch of great authority' from her court and converts him to Christianity.[2] The episode is illustrated in the Bedford Hours as part of an extensive cycle of illustrations of the biblical Acts of the Apostles (Image 3).

In the Ethiopian legend of Alexander, known as *Zena Eskender*, Queen Candace is called 'Qendaqa, queen of Samer', and is described thus: 'And their queen was more beautiful in appearance, and had more understanding, than all the other women in the world'.[3] Having heard of her great riches, Alexander wrote to Qendaqa demanding that she turn over to him all the treasures she had captured when she conquered Egypt, otherwise he would attack her kingdom. She replied that she was not afraid of him as she had 800,000 horsemen at the ready. In the meantime she sent him gifts of 100 gold bars, 500 Ethiopians, 200 parrots, 200 sphinxes, a crown with pearls and emeralds, 80 ivory boxes, 308 elephants, 300 leopards, 13 rhinoceroses, 4 panthers, 300 man-eating dogs, 6 ivory tusks, 300 leopard skins and 1,500 logs of ebony. She also sent a painter in disguise to Alexander's camp to paint a detailed likeness of him, which she later hid in her chamber.

As both sides were preparing for battle, Kandaros (or Candaules), Qendaqa's son, was brought before Alexander by one of his generals, Ptolemy Soter. Kandaros had been attacked by bandits in the mountains while he was travelling with his family and household to celebrate a festival with the Amazons. His wife and the remainder of the party had been abducted by the bandits, so Alexander agreed to help him, planning to use this opportunity to visit Candace's court incognito. He swapped places with Ptolemy, placing him on the throne, and had Kandaros brought before him. The two arranged that Alexander, disguised as one of the Greek generals, Antigonus, would take an army of horsemen to rescue the captives. Alexander and his troops set off and before long, thanks to his skilled tactics, the prisoners were brought back unharmed to Kandaros, who was overjoyed to see his wife safe and sound. Out of gratitude for the brave rescue, he invited Antigonus/Alexander to ride back with him to visit his mother and receive royal gifts.

The legend describes how, when Alexander entered Qendaqa's chamber of red gold, ornamented with precious stones and crystal pillars, he 'wept with a great weeping'. When she reassured him that he had no need to fear, he replied, 'I weep because of joy, and because of what I see of thee and thy beauty',[4] and he compared her noble stature and royal bearing to that of his mother, Olympias (see Chapter 11). They made love for a day and a night and when he left she gave him the cloak decorated with the sun and moon on which they had lain together.[5]

The visit of Alexander to Candace is one of the most frequently illustrated episodes in the *Shahnamah* of Firdawsi, composed in c.AD 1000, and the earliest of the Persian texts that tell the story of Candace in some detail (Image 4). Here Alexander is known as Iskandar and the queen as Qaydafah, and her kingdom is located in Andalos (?Andalucia). In this version, while Alexander is in Egypt, he learns of the powerful queen and decides to visit her kingdom. Having rescued Qaydafah's son, Iskandar (in disguise) is received by the grateful queen and all three enjoy an elaborate feast together. Then the next morning Qaydafah holds an audience in her splendid marble chamber, where she immediately recognises her guest as Iskandar himself from her secret portrait of him (Image 5). Qaydafah shows him the portrait and, when he is in suicidal despair at having been outwitted by a woman, she uses the opportunity to give him a lesson in humility: even such a great conqueror can be captured by a queen who is cleverer and wiser than he is.

Nevertheless Qaydafah recognises Iskandar's valour and promises to keep his identity secret so that he can escape from her country unharmed, avoiding

4 Iskandar seated before Qaydafah in her palace, in Firdawsi, *Shahnamah* (Qazvin, Iran, c.1585) Add MS 27302, f. 414r.

the vengeance of those who would murder him while he is unprotected. In return he promises he will not send his army to invade her kingdom.

The meeting between the two great rulers is also featured in the Persian poet Nizami's *Sharafnamah* ('Book of Honour') from his twelfth-century

Khamsah (Images 1, 6, 7). Here Candace is called Nushabah (roughly translated as 'the Water of Life') and her kingdom is in the locality of Barda (in present-day Azerbaijan, and formerly known as Harum). This is where Nizami himself lived, and Nushabah features in a variety of popular legends in the area. In the *Khamsah* she is abducted by the Rus (Russians) and rescued by Iskandar, who arranges her marriage to the king of Abkhaz, a kingdom on the Black Sea.

Nushabah is described as a pure and God-loving queen who avoids men and presides over a magnificent court at Harum (Image 6):

A thousand virgin girls were at her service and, besides damsels skilful in riding, thirty thousand swordsmen in her army. However, no men had access to her court, except those who were close to her. Her counsellors were all women who had no husband... Her throne was made of crystal [bulur] embedded with so many precious stones that they shone at night like the moon.[6]

The feast Nushabah provides for Iskandar takes on greater significance as it is an opportunity for her to demonstrate her superior wisdom to the young man who is intent on world domination. Two thrones are placed side by side and cloths are laid out, one for the queen and her maidens, the other for Iskandar. And whereas the former is laden with dishes of food 'beyond limit' (lamb, ox, birds stuffed with almonds, and fragrant wine), Iskandar's feast is a tray bearing four cups of pure crystal, 'One full of gold, and the other of ruby; the third full of cornelian, and the fourth of pearl',[7] laid out on a cloth of gold. Nushabah invites Iskandar to eat, and he asks, 'How should I eat stone?' Hearing this, Nushabah laughs in his face, explaining the lesson he should learn from her actions. 'Why stretch out our hands so basely to obtain these mean stones? Why heap jewel upon jewel on this path of life that ends with the stone (i.e. grave)?' Iskandar is chastened and acquiesces, saying 'A thousand praises on this woman with a sound judgement, who guides us towards uprightness'.[8]

In the French romances, Alexander learns the same lesson from Aristotle when he is given a golden apple at the gates of paradise: worldly goods and power are ephemeral, whereas a reputation for good deeds and honour will endure. A different slant on this episode is found in a mystical medieval commentary on the Quran by Maybudi called 'The Unveiling of Secrets and Instruction of the Pious' in which Dhu'l-Qarnayn (the 'two-horned one', as Alexander is called in the Quran, probably because of his association with

5 Iskandar, in disguise, is shown his portrait by Queen Qaydafah, in Firdawsi, *Shahnamah* (Shiraz, Iran, c.1560) IO Islamic 133, f. 349v.

the Egyptian god Ammon who is often shown as a ram) is invited to a feast of pearls and gemstones by an unnamed queen of a 'country in the West'. She admonishes him for his greed and ambition, saying, 'what are you intending to do with your rule over the Universe? Your share in this world is two loaves of bread; all the rest is futile and vain'.[9]

In both the *Shahnamah* and the *Khamsah*, the wise and devout Candace imparts her queenly wisdom to Alexander, teaching him a lesson of what it is to be an ideal ruler. Success is not attained by personal prowess, but is subject to destiny and the guidance of God. However, in a later Persian romance, the anonymous *Eskandar-nama*, the meeting between the two becomes a tale of seduction, with Candace (here named Qaydafah) offering herself to Alexander. She agrees to his demands to supply his army and she comes alone to his room at night, dressed as a concubine. She says to him:

> *Draw me not from love to battle with thee; express not reproach to thy own captive*
> *Plant not the thorn in thy path of love that thou mayst not fall upon the thorn (of sadness)*
> *Be the liberator of me from straightness of heart that thou mayst be safe from captivity of heart.*

> *When from her own throne [Nushabah]; descended and performed service*
> *She sat bride-like on a chair of gold; became servant of the monarch [Sikandar].*[10]

She then extracts a promise from Alexander that he will send for her to come and live with him in Rum (i.e. Greece) when he returns home.

In the French *Roman d'Alexandre* and many of the European vernacular legends, Candace gradually mutates from the stately and powerful ruler of the early Greek and Roman accounts to a mere female love-interest. The emphasis on the relationship between the pair becomes the focus of the Candace episode and she becomes a generic heroine of medieval romance, attractive and suffering the painful symptoms of love. The original Latin text contains little description of her physical traits, rather emphasising her wisdom and foresight. By the twelfth century, in the Anglo-Norman French *Roman de toute*

6 Iskandar is entertained in the magnificent court of Nushabah (called Bhureh in this manuscript, commissioned by the Mughal emperor Akhbar), in Nizami, *Khamsah* (Lahore, c.1594) Or 12208, f. 244v.

chevalerie ('Romance about all of Chivalry') she is being described as '*bele e blanche*' ('beautiful and fair-skinned')[11] and her rich garments are similar to the long robes and headdresses of such characters as Elvide and Guinevere (see Chapters 15, 19), reflecting French court dress of the period (as portrayed in Images 2 and 8).

In the anonymous *Venjance Alixandre* ('Vengeance of Alexander') composed in Venice in the twelfth century, Candace has all the attributes of a medieval heroine, rather than a woman of North Africa or even Andalucia: long blonde hair, sparkling eyes and a complexion like a rosebud. A Middle English version of the Alexander romance, *Kyng Alisaunder*, focuses on her wealth and beauty ('Of al the werelde she was richest, / Of alle wymmen she was fairest') and on her desire for Alexander. The following lines are from a letter she writes to him:

Oo Alisaunder, thou riche kyng
Bee my lorde and my derlying.[12]

When Alexander arrives at Candace's court, he finds her walking in the garden singing a *lay* (a short French love-song) about Dido, the lovesick heroine of the French *Roman d'Eneas* ('Romance of Aeneas'). Rather than a wise and revered figure, Candace has become a frivolous charmer whose aim is to ensnare Alexander and his great wealth. In *Kyng Alisaunder*, her kingdom is named Saba, so her character has been conflated with the Queen of Sheba, (see Chapter 13). Boccaccio, in his *De mulieribus claris* ('On Famous Women') notes in his chapter on Nicaula, Queen of Ethiopia, that there is confusion in some sources with 'Candace queen of Meroe, after whom the kings of Egypt were later called Candaces for a long time, as before they had been called Pharaohs'.[13] So confusion about Candace's identity and the location of her kingdom persisted in the varied medieval versions of her story. Was she from Albania, southern Spain, the Caucasus, Ethiopia, Nubia or even India? And though she was portrayed as a strong and powerful woman by some authors, she did not merit a story of her own; hers was a supporting role as one of the many women in the legend of Alexander the Great.

7 Iskandar seated beside Nushabah on a golden throne, in the earliest illustrated copy of Nizami's work, *Sharafnamah*, from his *Khamsah* (S. Iran, *c*.1200) Or 13529, f. 48r.

8 Candace takes Alexander into her chamber and gives him a crown, in the *Roman d'Alexandre en prose* (Paris, *c*.1420) Royal MS 20 B. XX, f. 71v.

Khusaw and Shirin in a garden being entertained by her maidens; an inscription over the throne states, 'The pupil of my eye is thy dwelling, show kindness and come down, for the house is thy house', in Nizami, *Khamsah* (artist: Mirzah Ali) (Tabriz, c.1540) Or MS 2265, f. 66v.

Tragic Heroines

Part Four

Cy commence la tresppiteuse hystoire de messire Floridan jadis chlr
Et de la tresbonne et vertueuse damoiselle Elvide et leurs piteuses fins

aulx et cou-
rigeur faiz des
nobles et vertu-
euses personnes
sont dignes de
estre recompte-
et escriptz tant afin de leur baul-
lier et acquistre nom immortel
par renommee et souveraine
louenge Comme aussi pour esmouuoir et enflamber les cuers
des lisans et escoutans a ensuiuir
et faire œuures vicieuses desho-
nnestes et vituperables et entie

prendre et acomplir choses hon-
nestes vertueuses et meritoires
pour viure en gloire perdurab-
le. Et pour ce que tout
noble homme et bien renomme
Anthoine de la salle esauer
auez tousiours prins plaisir
et des le temps de vostre ieune
ieunesse vous estes delicte a
lire aussi rescripre hystoires
honnourables Ouquel exera
et continuant tout perseue
de iour en iour sans inter-
ruption Je Rasse de bruhamel

15.

Elvide

In the late medieval romance *Floridan et Elvide*, the heroine, Elvide, is renowned for her beauty and purity and she sacrifices her life for the latter in the tragic denouement. She falls in love with Floridan, a young knight from Sicily, who is described as '*beau de figure, preux, hardy et vaillant*'[1] (in other words he has all the chivalric virtues: good looks, courtesy, daring and valour). Both young lovers are of good family: Elvide, described as a lovely young woman of around 16 or 17 years, is the daughter of a rich and powerful knight. But her parents decree that she should marry a wealthy landowner who lives nearby but who is *assez ancien* ('rather old').

The young lovers meet in secret, exchanging promises and discussing plans for the future. They have only one wish – to marry and be together forever. Meanwhile Elvide's father is determined she should accept his choice of husband and sets a date for the wedding. So the young lovers have no choice but to elope. Floridan fetches Elvide in secret from her home early one morning and they flee into the woods where his servants are waiting with his horse. He leaps into the saddle, lifts her up behind him and they gallop away. Once they are out of sight, Floridan slows his horse and they choose quiet paths through the countryside to avoid being seen. Fearing that her father will have sent his men after them, Floridan orders his servants to follow him

---

1 Elvide watches the murder of Floridan, in *Floridan et Elvide* (Paris, late 15th century) Cotton MS Nero D IX, f. 109r.

on different routes, keeping watch for any pursuers. But in so doing he leaves himself and his future bride exposed to the dangers of travelling alone.

Towards evening the young couple arrive at a village where a fair is taking place. Elvide is tired and they decide to stop at a local inn to rest and await the arrival of Floridan's men. Four drunken louts from the fair see the young couple entering the inn alone and assume that Elvide is a woman of easy virtue as she has no servant with her. They decide to try their luck. The innkeeper warns them off his premises, protesting that Floridan is a high-born knight and Elvide a noblewoman. But the four troublemakers, fired up with lust and drink, force their way in and bang on the door of the room where Elvide is resting. When Floridan answers politely, they demand a turn with his wench. Floridan explains his situation, assuring them that Elvide is a virtuous lady and his future wife. They do not believe him and threaten to force their way in. Floridan has no alternative but to defend the door of Elvide's room, which he does courageously. Using his considerable fighting skill, he overcomes all four assailants and they turn to retreat down the stairs, nursing their wounds. But seeing Floridan is off his guard, one of them throws a spear, piercing him through the heart. His strength and life force ebb and he falls to the floor, dead. The young paragon of knightly virtue has been conquered by the treachery of his thuggish adversaries.

Celebrating their victory, the four revellers force their way into Elvide's chamber and when the distraught young woman pleads with them, they laugh and taunt her. She makes a desperate plan, requesting that the four men visit her one at a time to preserve her dignity. Once she is alone with the oldest of the four, she begs him to spare her and help her escape; if he does, he will be rewarded by God and by her family for his good deed. Unfortunately he is the most immoral of all and ignores her pleas:

Et, a ces motz, l'un d'eulx s'avance, qui la prent le plus rudement du monde, disant qu'il aura sa compaignie avant qu'elle luy eschappe, veille ne daigne.	And with these words one of them advances towards her, grabbing her most roughly, saying that he will take advantage of her before she escapes him, whether she consents or not.[2]

Realising all is lost, she asks him to close the window and as soon as he turns his back, she clutches the little knife she carries with her to cut meat. Plunging it into her chest, she utters a pitiful cry, and falls to the floor, bleeding. As she breathes her last the innkeeper and others arrive on the scene.

The moment of Floridan's death is depicted in a full-page illumination in a late fifteenth-century manuscript of chivalric romances (Image 1). For

2 A young couple united in marriage, in the Smithfield Decretals (England, early 14th century) Royal MS 10 E IX, f. 195r.

dramatic effect, Elvide is shown watching the struggle between Floridan and his four attackers, whereas in the story the fight takes place outside her door and she does not witness his death. Three of the evil group are escaping through a doorway, with their weapons lying broken on the floor. But one of them has his right hand raised, having just thrown the spear that has lodged in Floridan's heart. The elegant young lovers contrast with the rather unkempt appearance of the revellers. Details such as the black cushion on the bench and the blood on the carpet add realism to the shocking events unfolding in the room, and the windows in the background anticipate the tragic events to follow.

One version of the French romance *Floridan et Elvide* was translated by the French courtier Rasse de Brunhamel from a fifteenth-century moral tale in Latin by Nicolas de Clamanges, a humanist scholar and secretary at the papal court in Avignon. Surviving in only four manuscript copies, it was printed in several sixteenth-century editions. A slightly different French text was part of the *Cent nouvelles Nouvelles* ('One Hundred New Novellas'), a collection of stories associated with the court of Philip the Good of Burgundy in the fifteenth century, and versions of the tale exist in Italian, one of which is given a historical

3 The child bride Isabella of France is given by her father Charles VI to Richard II of England in Jean Froissart, *Chroniques* (Bruges, c.1490) Royal MS 14 D VI, f. 268v.

setting: the town of Nancy in the time of Joan of Arc. Though Boccaccio did not include the story in his collections of tales, Brunhamel suggests that had he known of it he would have done so.

The story of young lovers fleeing to avoid the censure of their parents has long been popular, and in the Middle Ages there were two better-known works that explored this theme: *Pyramus and Thisbe* and *Floire et Blanchefleur*. In these stories, as in our tale, young love is at first portrayed as a beautiful and lasting ideal:

Floridan et la pucelle ne estoient que ung [une] cœur, une amour et une voullenté.	Floridan and the maiden were nothing if not one heart, one love and one desire.[3]

However, ultimately the consequences of youthful rebellion are shown to be disastrous and each couple comes to a tragic end. This is unsurprising as the young couple's defiance of parental authority set a dangerous precedent and the consequences posed a threat to social order in the Middle Ages. Clandestine marriages were outlawed and only the Church could sanction the union of a man and woman (Image 2). Young ladies of good family were treated as merchandise in the marriage market, used as pawns to cement alliances and consolidate property holdings. They most often had no choice in who they married, and royal princesses especially were often betrothed at a very young age. An example was Isabella, daughter of King Charles VI of France, who became the second wife of Richard II of England in 1396, aged only 7 (Image 3). She had to leave her family and travel to England with a much older man she had never met before. The marriage remained unconsummated when Richard died in 1400, and Isabella later married Charles of Orleans. She died in childbirth at the age of 19.

Elvide's courageous sacrifice in *Floridan et Elvide* is compared by Clamanges and his translator to the suicide of the older Roman heroine, Lucretia, a beautiful and virtuous wife who was raped by her husband's cousin, Sextus Tarquinius (see Chapter 16). Lucretia's '*ardant desir de [l]a pureté*'[4] ('ardent desire for purity') is praised by the author even though she was unable to avoid Sextus's attack, and took her life afterwards to avoid the shame of having lost her virtue. In contrast, Elvide outwitted four armed men using courage and quick thinking and so she was able to preserve her purity until death, remaining an unconquered heroine.

tres estrange de toute suspecçon de non licite consentement, voult par anticipacion pourveoir qu'elle ne fust soillie par vil et deshonneste actouchement et ama mieulz la mort que d'encheoir en ce pechié.	avoiding all suspicion of unlawful consent, she managed by forethought to avoid being defiled by a vile and dishonest sexual act and she preferred death to falling into this sinfulness.[5]

So although both women take their own lives, Elvide chooses the ultimate sacrifice on the altar of purity, whereas Lucretia, a married woman, is a victim whose male relatives later take revenge for her death. Revenge is not mentioned in *Floridan et Elvide*, just the tragedy of young lives lost. And the moral for female readers of this tale is doubtless that there is no sacrifice too great for a young woman to make when her chastity is under threat. De Brunhamel describes Elvide in heroic terms worthy of a medieval knight:

Ne par manasses ne par espoentemens quelxconques ne poeut oncques estre surmontee.... Ellvide bateilla tres fermement a l'encontre de quatre grans et inhumains chartons lesquelx victorieusement elle surmonta.... Ellvide en son blanc pucellaige voult corageusement morir pour garder de rompture son noble et precieux seau virginel.

Neither by threats nor fear could she be overcome.... Elvide fought very steadfastly against four large and cruel waggoners whom she victoriously overcame.... Elvide in her pure maidenhood would rather die courageously to preserve her noble and precious hymen from rupture.[6]

In contrast to the pure and dignified Elvide, the men who attack her are portrayed as aggressive drunken louts who lack manners and are overcome by '*furieux desir, crueuse voullenté*'[7] ('angry desire and crude impulse').

Clamanges uses this tale as an example to women of Elvide's (some would say excessive) dedication to her chastity. The three virtues most admired in medieval women were chastity, obedience and humility, as inspired by the teachings of the Church, in which the ideal of femininity was based on sacrifice and self-effacement. In this respect Elvide was the perfect role model for young women; she remained passive and dignified in extreme circumstances and the only aggression she used was against herself. Although suicide was considered sinful, in her situation it was seen as justified as there was no alternative available. She was considered a true heroine for her time and a courageous female martyr.

4 Woodcut print of Floridan and Elvide (Ellinde) riding through the forest, in *L'hystoyre et plaisante cronique du petit Jehan de Saintré de la jeune dame des belles cousines sans autre nom nommer, auecques deux autres petites hystoires de messire Floridan et la belle Ellinde*, Michel le Noir (Paris, 1517) Bibliotheque nationale de France.

Du petit saintre.

Icy finist la tresplaisante hy stoire et cronicque de messire ie han de saintre/et de la ieune da me des belles cousines sans au tre nom nommer.

De messire floridan/et de la belle Ellinde.

Icy commence la trespiteu se hystoire de messire floridan iadis cheualier ⁊ de la tresbon ne ⁊ vertueuse damoyselle ellin de ⁊ de leurs trespiteuses fins.

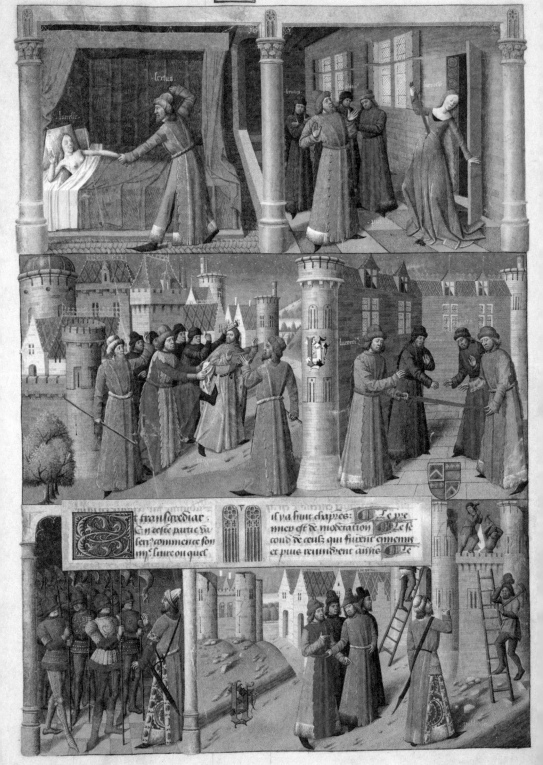

Lucresse   sextus

brutus   Lucresse

Lucresse

t transgrediar:
En este partie su
lenz comment son
me: sture on quel

il y a huit chapies: Le pre
mier est de moderation
cond de ceulz qui fuyent enemis
et puis reuiennent ainsi

16.

Lucretia

The tragic suicide of the Roman wife Lucretia was compared to the courageous act of self-sacrifice by the medieval heroine Elvide in Chapter 15. Lucretia was familiar to medieval audiences from the works of Roman historians including Titus Livius (Livy). He was the first to record a shocking event that took place in the late sixth century BC when Rome was still ruled by kings. Lucretia, a virtuous wife and the daughter of the eminent magistrate Lucretius, was raped by Sextus Tarquinius, the son of the tyrannical king Tarquinius Superbus ('Tarquin the Proud'), who had seized power by violence and ruled by fear.

It seems that Lucretia's husband, Collatinus (a relative of the ruling Tarquins), may not have been a worthy husband for such a paragon. With an irresponsible act he set in motion the series of events leading to her death. One evening during a drinking bout with his fellow soldiers including his cousin Sextus, he took part in a competition as to whose wife was the best. Determined to win, he suggested that they all ride to his house in Collatia late at night in order to surprise his wife and see how she occupied herself in his absence. In contrast to the other wives, who were out enjoying themselves, they

1 The story of Lucretia (from top left): Sextus threatens Lucretia with death; Lucretia commits suicide; Tarquinius Superbus is expelled from Rome; Lucretia's male relatives swear revenge; the new consul orders his troops to remove the symbols of Tarquinius' authority; his palace-fortress is demolished, in *Les Fais et les dis des Romains*, a French translation of Valerius, *Facta et dicta memorabilia*, (Paris, c.1475) Harley MS 4374/3, f. 211r.

found Lucretia at home, busy at her needlework. So Collatinus was awarded the prize, but he came to regret his actions. The boyish contest went horribly wrong when his wife's superior beauty and virtue were noticed by his evil and lascivious cousin.

A few days later, Sextus returned while Collatinus was away and was welcomed to the house as a guest. During the night, he entered Lucretia's room with a drawn sword, intending to rape her (Image 1, top left). When she resisted even under threat of death, he warned her that unless she gave in to him he would murder both her and his slave and leave their bodies naked together, spreading the lie that he had killed them both as a punishment for adultery (Image 2).

The next morning Lucretia sent for her husband and father, asking them each to bring along a trusted witness, and told them what had happened, demanding that they avenge her honour. Then she plunged a dagger into her chest, dying in front of them (Images 3, 4). Collatinus's relative, Junius Brutus, drew out the knife and uttered these words:

> By this blood, most chaste until a prince wronged it, I swear, and I take you, gods, to witness, that I will pursue Lucius Tarquinius Superbus and his wicked wife and all his children, with sword, with fire, aye with whatsoever violence I may; and that I will suffer neither them nor any other to be king in Rome![1]

Lucretia's story featured as an example of female chastity in a popular moralistic work, *Facta et dicta memorabilia* ('Memorable Deeds and Sayings') written by Valerius Maximus in c.AD 31 and translated into French in the fourteenth century (Image 1). For Valerius, Lucretia not only exemplified chastity, but also by her actions she liberated the Roman people from tyranny. According to Livy, Junius Brutus, true to his word, displayed her body in the public square in Collatia and, vowing to avenge her death, he led an armed mob to Rome. Tarquin the Proud was deposed and his family, including his lascivious son, was exiled. Junius Brutus and Collatinus were appointed the consuls of newly republican Rome (Image 1). As a result, Lucretia became a symbol of freedom from tyranny in Renaissance Italy, and her suicide the subject of paintings by masters from Raphael to Artemisia Gentileschi, and from Rembrandt to Albrecht Dürer.

Through collections by such writers as Valerius and Boccaccio, Lucretia's story was well known in the Middle Ages. In her *Livre de la Cité des Dames* ('Book of the City of Ladies'), Christine de Pisan criticises the attitude among some men that women invite violent attacks, and that they secretly enjoy them.

2 Lucretia's rape, in Livy, *Ab urbe condita* ('From the Founding of the City') (Padua, c.1400) Burney MS 198, f. 4r.

3 Lucretia's suicide, in Livy, *Ab urbe condita*, Burney MS 198, f. 4r.

Her character, Lady Justice, uses Lucretia as an example of a woman who was desired for her goodness and purity rather than for her beauty and who found the shame of violation too much to bear.

In the popular allegory, the *Roman de la Rose* ('Romance of the Rose'), a work noted for its misogynistic tone, Lucretia's story is alluded to by the allegorical character Jealousy as a warning to men who force themselves on married women (Image 4). He appears sympathetic to Lucretia, but ends with the comment that women as virtuous as her no longer exist, in his experience:

Si n'est il plus nulle Lucrèce,	*Alas there is no longer a Lucretia*
Ne nulle Pénélope en Grèce	*Nor a Penelope in Greece*
Ne nulle preude femme en terre	*Nor any honest woman here on earth*[2]

Shakespeare's early poem, *The Rape of Lucrece*, published in 1594, focuses on the very human feelings of the characters, here called Tarquin and Lucrece: firstly on the powerful desire that consumes him, and then on the unbearable shame felt by her. With his characteristic powerful imagery, Shakespeare brings to life the two characters in the scene immediately following the rape. His sympathy for the victim is clear:

> *He like a thievish dog creeps sadly thence, She like a wearied lamb lies panting there.*[3]

Writers from classical times to the modern day have asked themselves why a pure and innocent woman such as Lucretia should die, and their answers reflect changing contemporary attitudes. The story has been reinterpreted many times, allowing writers to explore the moral implications of both rape and suicide. For the ancient Romans the death of such a virtuous woman was a sign of a corrupt society that needed to be reformed. In medieval versions, the villainy of Sextus and the virtue of Lucretia are contrasted, so that she is presented as a model of female purity and exemplary courage. No matter how her story has been presented, she remains a character to be admired. Her distress and revulsion towards her attacker are clear and she proclaims her innocence by a final and effective act of resistance.

4 Lucretia committing suicide before her husband and father, in the *Roman de la Rose* (Bruges, *c*.1500) Harley MS 4425, f. 79r.

Cy commence le premier livre
de la bible moralisee trans-
latee de latin en francois.
In principio cre-
auit deus celu
et terram. dixit
quap deus fiat
lup et facta est
lup. Cy apres.
Au commencement dieu
cria le ciel et la terre. Se dieu
dist lumiere soit faicte et lu

miere fu faicte. La cre-
acion de lumiere emporte la
creacion des angelz. car ilz
ont lumiere denter dement.
Et dieu regarda que lu
miere estoit bonne. et la de-
uisa des tenebres et appella
la lumiere iour et les tenebres nuit. et fu celle vespe-
ree et la matinee ensieuant
compte pour le premier
iour car a midi auoit este

17.

Eve, the First Woman

Adam and Eve's Fall from grace and expulsion from the Garden of Eden is one of the most well-known stories in the Judeo-Christian world. According to the Book of Genesis in the Bible, God created Adam and all the animals of the Earth. Seeing that Adam was the only creature without a partner, and that it was not good for him to be alone, God decided to make him a helpmate in his own image. This passage from the Vulgate, Jerome's fourth-century Latin translation of the Bible, tells us how it was done:

Inmisit ergo Dominus Deus soporem in Adam cumque obdormisset tulit unam de costis eius et replevit carnem pro ea;

And the Lord God caused a deep sleep to fall upon Adam, and he slept: and he took one of his ribs, and closed up the flesh instead thereof;

Et aedificavit Dominus Deus costam quam tulerat de Adam in mulierem et adduxit eam ad Adam;

And the rib, which the Lord God had taken from man, made he a woman, and brought her unto the man.

Dixitque Adam hoc nunc os ex ossibus meis et caro de carne mea haec vocabitur virago quoniam de viro sumpta est.[1]

And Adam said, This is now bone of my bones, and flesh of my flesh: she shall be called Woman, because she was taken out of Man.

[1] The Creation, Temptation and Fall of Adam and Eve, at the opening of the first chapter of a *Bible moralisée* ('Moralised Bible') (Bruges, 1455) Add MS 15248, f. 17r.

2 The creation of Eve from Adam's rib, in the Book of Hours of René of Anjou (Paris, c.1410) Egerton MS 1070, f. 140.

And so by the end of Genesis, chapter 2, the couple are living together 'as one flesh', in harmony with their environment and without any cares in the 'paradise of pleasure'² that God has created for them. Around them the four streams of Paradise flow and there are precious stones in abundance (Image 6).

The Bible does not say how long this state of bliss continues, but in Genesis chapter 3 things begin to go horribly wrong. The 'subtil' serpent is introduced in the opening verse, and he persuades Eve that God has not been honest with them; apparently if they eat the fruit of the one tree that God has forbidden to them, the two humans will become godlike themselves, gaining knowledge of good and evil. Eve is persuaded and she picks the fruit, takes a delicious bite and offers it to Adam, who follows suit (Image 1, centre). Immediately they are aware of their own nakedness and hide themselves guiltily. God appears and sees what has happened. First Adam, then God put the blame squarely on Eve; God says to her, 'What is this that thou hast done', and to Adam, 'Because thou hast hearkened unto the voice of thy wife, and hast eaten of the tree, of which I commanded thee, saying, Thou shalt not eat of it: cursed is the ground for thy sake; in sorrow shalt thou eat of it all the days of thy life'.³

3 The Expulsion from the Garden of Eden, in the Holkham Bible Picture Book (London or S.E. England, c.1327–35) Add MS 47682, f. 4r.

The punishment is swift and brutal; an angel with a fiery sword drives Adam and Eve out of the Garden of Eden forever to begin a mortal life of sorrow on Earth (Image 3).

In the *Midrash* (a body of Talmudic commentaries on Jewish scripture) the details of Adam and Eve's story are similar in many ways to those in the Christian Old Testament, but the action takes place over twelve days. The first seven days are taken up with the Creation, then on the eighth Adam and Eve conceive their sons, Cain and Abel. On the ninth day God's commandment not to eat the forbidden fruit is given to the pair. The Temptation and Fall happen on the next (tenth) day. (Here one could make a wry observation that the first humans ignore God's command the very day after it has been issued – an early example of how humankind invariably responds to a prohibition issued from above.) The judgement and expulsion from Paradise follow immediately on the eleventh and twelfth days and humanity's fate is sealed.

Another key Jewish text, the *Haggadah* (meaning 'narration' or 'telling', and read at the feast of Passover), contains the story of the Jews from the Creation up to their Exodus from Egypt. One of the most lavishly illuminated

4 Adam naming the animals (right); the Creation of Eve and the Temptation (left), in the Golden Haggadah (Barcelona, c.1325) Add MS 27210, f. 2v.

copies to survive from medieval Spain is now in the British Library and is known as the Golden Haggadah. It has fifty-six miniatures in colour on a solid gold background illustrating the story of Genesis; they include the Creation and the Temptation of Eve (Image 4).

Just as the medieval Jews dwelt on the origin of humanity and what it meant, so too did their Muslim and Christian counterparts. In Islam, Adam is regarded as the first human being, as well as the first prophet. He was created from a handful of dust. Eve is referred to in the Quran as Adam's spouse, created from him, though her name Eve (Hawa) appears only in other Islamic texts. Notably, in the Islamic tradition, it is Satan who takes the blame for deceiving the pair into eating the forbidden fruit; the Quran says that both tasted of the tree and there is no mention of Eve being the more guilty party.

In the Christian context, scenes of Adam, Eve, the serpent and the tree of knowledge of good and evil were widely reproduced in the Middle Ages, representing humankind's origin story and a reminder of original sin. They are to be found at the beginning of illustrated liturgical books of all kinds (Images 1–3), as well as chronicles (Image 5), encyclopaedias and all manner of religious art. Eve is generally shown conversing with the serpent, picking the fruit, or giving it to Adam, so there is no doubt as to who is held responsible for this act that was so devastating for the whole of humanity.

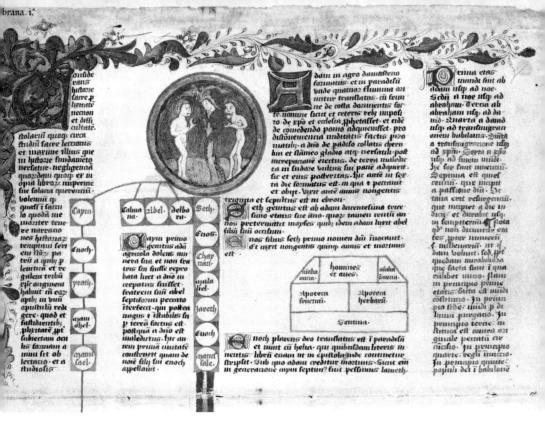

5 Peter of Poitiers, *Chronicle of World History*, showing the Fall of Man, and the descent from Adam and Eve to Noah and his descendants, with a diagram of the Ark (England, 15th century) Harley Roll C 9, Membrane 1.

Writers of medieval apocryphal texts and legends added further details that were not included in the Bible about the main characters and their actions after the Fall. In these, Eve's character and motivations are explored: was she merely a weak woman or did she face the consequences of her actions? And how did Adam treat her after their fall from grace? The Latin *Vitae Adae et Evae* ('Life of Adam and Eve') tells how Eve coped with the trials of existence, including the sorrows of childbirth and motherhood, her further temptations and her attempt to return to Paradise by doing penance while immersed in a river.

A number of religious dramas in French and English survive from the twelfth century onwards, in which the character of Eve is largely a sympathetic one. In *Le Mistère du Viel Testament* (a mystery play about the Old Testament in French), she is portrayed as a fallible human, succumbing to the Devil's flattery and to the desire to taste the appetising fruit. In *Le Mystère d'Adam* ('Adam's Mystery Play'), a drama in Anglo-Norman French, she comes across

Coment nir seig[neu]r ara adam et porta en p[ar]adie t[er]rest[re] et fait eue de son conste et leur deffent le fruit

as the nobler of the two characters. When Adam blames her in abusive terms, '*Femme desvée! / Mal fus tu unques de mei née!*'[4] ('Cursed woman! / It is bad luck that you were ever born of me') she calmly admits her fault, and her main concern is for the future of their offspring. A York mystery play from the mid-1400s presents Eve as a quasi-comic character, the target of Adam's misogynistic jibes; but also as a woman who takes responsibility for her mistakes and makes the best of a difficult situation.

The image of Adam digging and Eve spinning was used to represent their life of hard work and suffering on Earth (Image 6, bottom right). In a later image from a biblical typology, they are the only humans in an inhospitable landscape. The children are left to fend for themselves, emphasising the bleakness of their situation (Image 7). According to the Bible, the pair had three sons, Cain, Abel and Seth, the first of whom murdered his brother, becoming one of the arch-villains of the Old Testament. No daughters are mentioned in the Bible, but the *Vitae Adae et Evae*[5] states that the couple had thirty sons and thirty daughters.

The Syriac *Cave of Treasures* and medieval Irish apocryphal writings, including the *Sex aetates mundi* ('Six Stages of the World') and the *Banshenchas* ('Tales of Women'), provide further information about the children of Adam and Eve, including numbers and names. In the Syriac text, Cain and Abel both have twin sisters named Lebouda and Kelimath respectively, and Adam decides that they should each marry the other's twin. But because Lebouda is more beautiful, Cain desires her and his jealousy causes him to slay Abel. So once again it is a woman at the root of a disastrous action by a man. The Irish texts seem to have been invented by scribes who used the biblical descriptions of Noah's children for some of the details. In one version, Adam and Eve had fifty-two sons and seventy-two daughters and the *Sex aetates mundi* gives a list of the names of all the sons, including some exotic inventions from Gismus to Sile. There is no corresponding list of daughters but three are named in some of the texts: Pibb, Olla and Pithibb, and these three become the mothers of all the humans on Earth. In the *Cethror coic* poem, another daughter, Sechna, appears, and in the *Banshenchas*, Cain's daughter Ambia is the ancestor of the 'monsters of long ago'.[6]

In certain biblical legends, the story ended well for Adam and Eve: they

---

6 The whole story, as told in the Bible, is summed up in a full-page image in this magnificent prayer book made in Paris for a member of the French royal family in the early 15th century. The Creation and the Temptation of Adam and Eve are shown on the left, and on the right the consequences of their act: they are expelled through the magnificent gates of Paradise to a barren Earth where they toil in peasants' clothing; above right, their sons make offerings and then Cain murders his brother, Abel, in the Bedford Hours (Paris, c.1420) Add MS 18850, f. 14r.

7 Adam digging and Eve spinning, with their children in the background, in *Speculum humanae salvationis* ('Mirror of Human Salvation') (London, c.1500) Harley MS 2838, f. 5r.

were included among those rescued by Christ when He descended into Hell for three days after His Crucifixion, bringing salvation to the souls that had been held captive there since the beginning of the world. This episode was known as the Harrowing of Hell and is based on apocryphal texts (Image 8).

Within medieval Christian doctrine, Eve's sad tale began with her creation. In the Book of Genesis, Adam was made in the image of God and given dominion over the beasts, birds and fishes. He was given the power to name them, a sign of his superiority of understanding or reason, and was also given an immortal soul. He was created first, directly by God, and brought to life by divine breath, but Eve came later, out of his body. In other words, Adam was seen as a creature of reason and the spirit, while Eve was a creature of the flesh and was subject to him. This attitude within the teachings of the Church is widely attributed to St Augustine, the influential early Christian theologian. He taught that the possession of reason elevated Adam (and men in general) above the animals, who had limited understanding, and also above women, who were similarly ruled by the senses.

In the Middle Ages, Eve came to be seen as the archetypal female temptress whose sensuality overcame reason, and as such she was the antithesis of Mary, pure and saintly mother of Christ. Though the Bible states that she picked the fruit because it looked good to eat and the serpent told her it would not harm her, medieval authors took a more misogynistic view of her motivations. Male authors such as John Lydgate, in his *Examples against Women* written in the

8 Adam and Eve rescued from Hell by Christ, in Jean Beleth, *La Vie des Saints* ('Life of the Saints') (Paris, *c.*1330) Add MS 17275, f. 19r.

fourteenth century, cites Eve as one in a long list of women whose deliberate misdeeds have brought disaster for their menfolk (including the biblical figures Adam, Samson and Solomon). Boccaccio claimed that it was her characteristic female fickleness and a desire for power that prompted Eve's action. This theme, introduced in his first story, is developed in many of the lives in his collection of tales of famous women, demonstrating how women who aspire to glory ultimately bring disaster on both themselves and the men around them. His attitude is reflected in manuscript illustrations of his work (Image 9), where Eve is shown as a fashionable princess with a rather frivolous demeanour being charmed by a seemingly cute dragon-like serpent. Above them an angel holds his sword aloft, in the knowledge that she will succumb to temptation.

And so Eve, the first woman, was seen as the cause of humanity's downfall. It was generally agreed that her female sensuality overcame Adam's male reason. The author of an anonymous diatribe called *Le Blasme des Fames* ('Women are to Blame') written in around 1400 in Anglo-Norman French, in which women are blamed for starting wars, burning castles and generally creating chaos, claims that:

Pur ceo qe femme out fieble sens   *Because woman has weak intellect*
L'enginnat primes li serpens   *The serpent tricked her first.*[7]

In images of the Temptation scene even the serpent is regularly presented as female (Images 5, 10).

9 Eve's Temptation in Boccaccio, *Des cleres et nobles femmes* ('On Famous Women') (Paris, early 15th century) Royal MS 20 C V, f. 7r.

It was left to the female author, Christine de Pisan, writing in the fifteenth century, to finally challenge these misogynist views of Eve. In her *Épistre au dieu d'amours* ('Letter to the God of Love') she writes in the voice of Cupid (who in reality expresses her own views), attacking the churchmen and other

10 The tree of knowledge of good and evil (left) and the Temptation (right), in a *Bible historiale* (Paris, *c.* 1330) Yates Thompson MS 20, f. 1r.

polemicists who blame women for all the evil in the world. She defends Eve, saying that she did not intend to deceive her husband, but was merely taken in by the serpent.

The last word in this debate should perhaps be given to Christine in another of her works. The narrator of the *Livre de la Cité des Dames*, who is being tutored by Lady Reason, raises the subject of Eve. She quotes Cato, the Roman orator, who claimed that if the world had been created without woman, mankind would still live in the company of the gods. Lady Reason, who represents the author's own viewpoint, argues that in fact it is through a woman, the Virgin Mary, that humankind has access to the kingdom of God (see Chapter 5):

Et se aucun me dit que il en fu bani par femme pour cause de dame Eve, ie dy que trop plus hault degre a acquis par marie que il ne perdi par Eve.

And if anyone says to me that it is because of a woman, the lady Eve, that [man] was expelled from [paradise], I would say to them that [man] has gained far more through Mary than he ever lost through Eve.[8]

عحلاق بالصلوة عبد الحق وعحاو بالبر والبل والوب

المومن المسجد حالسمالا

دا دش سپہر دانش آموز

جم آن از سر شکوبسی

کہ کودکی را زامبد او زہم

با او بلافت کروستی

مشغول من ہرکہ تعلیم

با آن پسر خمد ہمور

ہم لوح شیشہ دخرتاخد

تاریخ برد و شب ادوز

18.

Nizami's Layla and Shirin

The tragic tales of Layla and Majnun and of Shirin and Khusraw have their origins in princely deeds, both historical and mythical. Originating in Arabic legends and recorded history, they were among the most important works of Persian literature as part of the *Khamsah* ('Five Tales') of Nizami Ganjavi, the influential Muslim poet of the twelfth century. His respect for and understanding of women and his tolerance of other faiths mean that his heroines, particularly Shirin, are not mere objects of male desire, but strong and rounded characters.

Layla

The story of Layla and Majnun originated in tales first recorded on the Arabian peninsula in the seventh century AD of a poet who used the pseudonym Majnun and who expressed his unrequited love for his cousin in songs about separation and longing. In the 1180s the Persian poet Nizami collected these stories into a romance in the *Udri* genre, which explores the theme of unfulfilled love among characters who are semi-historical and in many cases interchangeable. To satisfy his patron, Akhistan, the ruler of Shirvan (in present-day Azerbaijan), he included such Persian elements as the cultured court milieu, moonlight garden settings, the asceticism of the male protagonist and his companionship

1 Layla and Majnun at school, in Nizami, *Khamsah* (Herat, c.1493) Add MS 25900, f. 110v.

with animals in the wilderness. The result was one of the most imitated works in Persian and across the whole sphere of Persian cultural influence, in Pashto, Urdu, Kurdish and the Turkic languages.

Layla is described as precociously intelligent, modest and uncommonly beautiful; in sum, she is 'a heart's delight':

> Bright as the morn, her cypress shape, and eyes
> Dark as the stag's....
> And when her cheek this Arab moon reveal'd
> A thousand hearts were won; no pride, no shield
> Could check her beauty's power, resistless grown.[1]

Her young schoolmate, Qays is captivated by her beauty from the first moment and before long the pair are inseparable, passing the hours in 'soft converse' and exchanging looks of love. Qays begins to spend all his time writing beautiful love poems to Layla, who pines for him in secret; both are oblivious to the wagging tongues of friends and family. The young lover, 'maddened with excessive grief',[2] takes to wandering, scantily clad, in the desert and haunting the doorway of Layla's home at night until people begin to call him 'Majnun' ('madman'). Layla is more circumspect, keeping her feelings to herself, though all the while longing for Majnun. When her family moves to the Najd mountains Majnun follows, urgently calling her name so that it echoes through the woods and valleys. His father counsels moderation and patience, but at last in desperation he goes to meet with Layla's father and ask for her hand in marriage, although he considers her family inferior. He is humiliated and his offer rejected; Layla's family refuse to face the shame of marrying her to a youth who behaves so recklessly and is believed by everyone to be crazy.

Majnun, overcome with grief, abandons his home and family. He disappears into the wilderness, living in solitude among the wild animals and refusing to return to his mother and father. They leave food for him at the bottom of the garden, hoping that one day he will come back, but he grows ever more emaciated and isolated, spending his days composing extravagant love poems and verses in various poetic genres. He lives in a cave and travellers sometimes come across him reciting his poetry to himself, writing in the sand with a stick. When at last his parents die, he feels great sorrow and remorse at having abandoned them and is comforted by a fawn who becomes his companion in the wilderness.

2 Majnun in the wilderness surrounded by animals, in Nizami, *Khamsah* (India, 1557–8) IO Islamic 384, f. 42r.

چون خبر که حلقه

براس آن و دیار خسته

کرده آن و دان خنریز

آمده آن و دان که درکار

شخص و سر رازهم

زنا که دران مبان و ید

نظاره نیافت دربیان آه

انوه و دان بر ان که درگاه

Layla meanwhile is promised by her family to a young man named Ibn Salam who has fallen in love with her; they marry and although she is a faithful and dutiful wife she keeps herself pure for Majnun, refusing her husband's advances. She is able to arrange secret meetings with Majnun from time to time, but these are always without physical contact; they spend the time reciting poetry to each other while keeping their distance. This only increases their longing for one another. Majnun's behaviour becomes ever more erratic; he befriends gazelles in the desert, giving away his few possessions to save their lives from hunters, and then allows a beggar woman to lead him around in chains, dancing and proclaiming his poetry like a creature possessed by demons. By chance they come across Layla's family encampment and he sinks down in the dust outside her tent, pounding his head on the ground and begging her to put an end to his suffering (Image 3).

After some years Ibn Salam dies and at last Layla is free. Believing that happiness is within her grasp, she prepares for her wedding to the man she has loved for so long, but the obstacles remain insurmountable. In one version of the tale, Majnun is so focused on the ideal picture of Layla (compare Shah Ji in Chapter 23) that he runs away to the desert again. Layla dies of grief and is buried in her bridal dress. In another version she is told that she must spend two years in mourning before she can marry. This is too much for her to bear after so many years of waiting and longing; she dies of a broken heart without seeing Majnun again. Whatever the circumstances, the final outcome is the same – we are left with the image of Majnun lying prostrate on Layla's grave (Image 4). Like Romeo and Juliet – and star-crossed lovers throughout world literature – both die of longing and are buried side by side; the hope is that their souls will be reunited in the hereafter.

Along with many of the popular medieval tales in this collection, Nizami's portrayal of Layla's character raises questions about the role of women in a patriarchal society. His heroine, though unwavering in her commitment to Majnun, has no choice but to remain obedient to her father and faithful to the husband he has chosen for her. Even when the lovers meet secretly she keeps Majnun at arm's length, reminding him that she is a married woman and must obey the laws of chastity. Her loyalty to her family and society override any personal feelings or choice. Despite these questions, the poem has a strong moral message, in that sublime spiritual love is portrayed as superior to earthly physical relationships. Majnun experiences all the deprivations of a spiritual

3 Majnun is brought to Layla's tent in chains by an old woman, in Nizami, *Layla and Majnun* (Tabriz, c.1540) Or 2265, f. 157v.

4 The death of Majnun on Layla's grave, in Nizami, *Khamsah* (India, 1595) Or 12208, f.165v.

ascetic, and Nizami uses the story to comment on the themes of sacrifice, humility and death.

In Arabic *layla* means 'night'; and though Nizami describes his heroine as exquisitely beautiful, some writers have referred to her sombre looks and questioned whether she possessed beauty only in the eyes of her lover. In one interpretation of the story she is asked, 'Are *you* the one for whom Qays lost his reason? I do not see that you are so beautiful', to which she replies, 'Silence! You are not Majnun!'[3] Does this imply that it is her inner beauty and strength that caused Majnun to fall in love? There is no doubt that Layla is a forceful woman. Though she is not able to ignore her family and marry the man she loves, she is not prepared to accept another, and rejects her chosen bridegroom unequivocally so that he 'shrinks and reels'[4] from her scorn. When he tries to approach her she strikes him such a blow that he falls to the ground, causing Nizami, who is mostly sympathetic to his heroines, to make a comment about women in general. In terms that will be familiar to those who have read the chapters on Cleopatra, Eve and Delilah (Chapters 10, 17 and 21), women are portrayed as the general cause of men's misfortune:

A dangerous friend, a fatal foe,
Prime breeder of a world of woe.[5]

As the story spread and was retold, it underwent numerous changes, acquiring new themes and motifs. Well-known poets including Amir Khusraw, Jami and others added their own elements to the plot. In some versions Majnun has conversations with various travellers and with a nightingale; in others he befriends a black dog that Layla finds wandering in the desert. Copies of the different versions were disseminated as far afield as Ottoman Turkey and India, and various editions were produced by scholars of Persian literature. The first English translation of Nizami's poem was made by James Atkinson 'of the Honourable East India Company's Bengal Medical Service' in 1836 (the quotations in this chapter are from Atkinson's somewhat archaic text). The plot involving tragic love and self-denial appealed equally to audiences in Europe, and in Britain it was adapted into an opera, *Kais, or Love in the Deserts*, performed at the Theatre Royal, Drury Lane. More recently the unattainable Layla became the subject of the 1970 love ballad by Eric Clapton. Since the first adaptation for Indian cinema in the 1920s there have been a number of Bollywood productions, the most recent being the 2018 *Laila Majnu* set in modern-day Kashmir.

Shirin

The tragic romance of Khusraw and Shirin, as told by Nizami, has been described as 'the story of the love and sorrow of a princess and a woman and a wife, in its sincerity unequalled by any other work in Persian literature'.[6] Though the plot includes numerous twists and a number of the standard ingredients of romance, the characters and events are based on historical figures. The reign of the Sasanian King Khusraw II of Iran (AD 590–628) is recorded in both Muslim and Byzantine sources and there is evidence for the existence of a wife or mistress named Shirin and of other characters and events in the story. Shirin, whose name means 'sweet' in Persian, is claimed by some to have been Syrian. In the tenth-century historical work the *Shahnamah* ('The Book of Kings') by Firdawsi, the deeds of Khusraw are treated extensively and the seventh-century Byzantine historian, Theophylact Simocatta, refers to an offering given by Khusraw to the church of St Sergius in Rosapha for prayers that Shirin might bear a child to him. In an Armenian historical work Shirin is described

5 Shirin is shown the portrait of Khusraw by one of her handmaidens, in Nizami, *Khamsah* (Herat, c.1495) Or 6810, f. 39v.

as a Christian from Khuzestan (a province of present-day Iran) and as one of Khusraw's most influential wives who protected Christians in his kingdom. In other sources it has been suggested that the Muslim Khusraw's reluctance to marry her could have been due to her religion.

Though Firdawsi first described Shirin as a humble woman of ill repute, according to Nizami she was the niece of the Armenian queen, Mahin Bahu. In his *Khamsah* she is revealed in a dream to the Persian Prince Khusraw as his future wife and he sends his friend, the painter Shapur, to find her. Arriving in Armenia, Shapur shows Shirin a portrait he has painted of Khusraw and she falls in love with the young man in the picture (Image 5). Unlike Layla (or Mah Ji and Humayun in Chapter 23) she is not prepared to wait for Mr Right to come looking for her; she sets off in secret on the queen's swiftest horse, Shabdiz, to find him.

In the meantime King Khusraw is forced to flee Persia after an uprising, and he heads to Armenia to find the woman of his dreams, but when he arrives

6 Khusraw spies Shirin bathing, in Nizami, *Khamsah* (Baghdad, 1465) IO Islamic 138, f. 75.

he is given the news that his father has died so he must return home to claim the throne. He rules justly but before long he is deposed by a wicked usurper and is exiled once again. This provides an opportunity for him to travel once more to Armenia to find his elusive Shirin, who – as luck would have it – is on her way back to Persia to find him! On his journey he stops at a pool where he spies a woman bathing naked, and he admires her beauty (Image 6). It is Shirin, but they do not recognise one another and continue in opposite directions. At last, after numerous mishaps the lovers finally meet up in Armenia, but the feisty Shirin refuses to marry Khusraw until he has reclaimed his throne. To do so he needs the help of the emperor of Constantinople, who agrees to provide assistance on condition that Khusraw marries his daughter Maryam (a character who has been associated with the Christian saint and martyr, Golinduch[7]) and takes no other wives until she dies.

While Khusraw is elsewhere, a sculptor named Farhad falls in love with

7 Farhad greets Shirin on her horse, in *Majalis al-Ushshaq* ('The Assemblies of the Lovers')
Kamal al Din Gazurghi (Shiraz, c.1600), IO Islamic MS 1138, f. 186v.

Shirin (Image 7), but Khusraw plans to dispose of him by giving him the near-impossible task of single-handedly carving a stairway through the mountain of Bisitun, a seemingly insurmountable rock face in the province of Kermanshah, Western Iran. When he has almost completed the pass, Khusraw sends him a message that Shirin is dead. Farhad, a model of strength and devotion, throws himself off the mountain and dies, so that Khusraw is filled with remorse and confesses all to Shirin. She is devastated and has an elaborate tomb built for Farhad as a place of pilgrimage for faithful lovers.

Not long afterwards Maryam too dies (in some accounts she is poisoned by Shirin) and so Shirin writes to Khusraw to remind him that he is now free

8 Khusraw and Shirin in bed together in Nizami, *Khamsah* (Isfahan, *c*.1666) Add MS 6613, f. 40r.

to marry. Having spent some time feasting and carousing at court, he sets off for Armenia, but on the way he falls for a woman in Isfahan and spends time in her arms, leaving Shirin fuming. When he at last arrives at Shirin's castle, she welcomes him with great ceremony but speaks to him from her roof, refusing his kisses and advances until he begs forgiveness and promises to marry her. After a number of false steps they finally exchange vows and are united in perfect love (Image 8).

For many years the couple reign happily until Shiruyah, Khusraw's son by Maryam, who is also in love with Shirin, imprisons his father in a dungeon. Shirin chooses to join her husband in captivity, comforting him with stories and words of love, and staying awake at night to keep him safe. When one night she finally succumbs to sleep, an assassin creeps into the cell and stabs Khusraw in the liver. Knowing how tired Shirin is, he bleeds to death without a sound and when she awakes her heart goes 'numb with sorrow and she [weeps] for hours on end'. A message from Shiruyah arrives, telling her that in one week she must marry him, so she gives away all their possessions to the poor and arranges an elaborate burial for Khusraw with a golden coffin. Dressed not in mourning but in 'robes of red and yellow', she follows his body into the burial vault, locks the door, covers him with kisses and stabs herself in the liver to share the same death (Image 9). Some say that her blood flowed over Khusraw's body, awakening him so that the lovers shared one last kiss, and others say that 'the stars paused in their celestial course in stark amazement at a love so fine… Thus were [Khusraw] and Shirin united for all eternity'.[8]

Nizami is believed to have written his poetic version of the story he described as the 'sweetest of all' as a tribute to his beloved first wife, Afaq, who may have inspired the character of Shirin. She has a strong sense of justice and uses her influence to guide Khusraw away from a life of pleasure and luxury, reminding him of his duty to his people and refusing to give in to him until he is prepared to make a real commitment to her. Scholar and translator Peter Chelkowski describes Shirin thus: 'She is well-educated, independent, fearless, resourceful, imaginative, erotic, and humorous. Her loyalty knows no bounds.'[9] Among the heroines of Persian romance she stands out as a woman who, though prey to jealousy and loneliness, does not allow her lover or any other man to influence her actions. It is she who controls her own story to its tragic end.

9 The suicide of Shirin at Khusraw's tomb, in Nizami, *Khamsah* (India, 1595) Or MS 12208, f. 102r.

مبارک باد وشیرین کشکرخواب | بابرزش سپادان ڈشای | یہ بنم پسروان کشع ہہاتآ
کہ چون انجار رسید کویدد عای

V bñ q̃ cheſt li vns de ches · ij ·
Enſi que lanc̃ · parole a le royne
et deus autres chr̃s parolent as
autres pucheles.

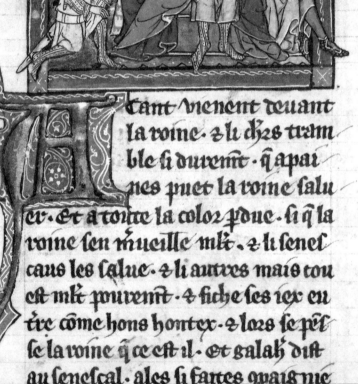

Tant vienent deuant
la roine · ⁊ li chr̃s trãm
ble ſi durem̃t · q̃ apai
nes puet la roine ſalu
er · Et a toute la color p̃duc · ſi q̃ la
roine ſen mueille mlt · ⁊ li ſeneſ
caus les ſalue · ⁊ li autres mais tou
eſt mlt pourem̃t · ⁊ fiche ſes iex eu
tre cõme hons hontex · ⁊ lors ſe p̃̃
ſe la roine q̃ ce eſt il · et galah dist
au ſeneſcal · ales ſi fartes avais nic

Lancelot kneels at Guinevere's feet in the *Lancelot-Grail*
(N. France, 1316) Add MS 10293, f. 76v.

Partners
and Lovers

Part Five

R dist li contes ke quan
la bataille fu finee bien
sorent cil dehongefort
ke Galides estoir con
quis z kil uenoir au castiel rendre

19.

Guinevere, Queen of Camelot

King Arthur's Britain is peopled by men of action – the invincible Lancelot and his fellow knights of the Round Table, the magician Merlin and a cast of kings and princes. Tales of their legendary courage and exploits fill many pages. But this magical world is also home to exceptional female characters, from the mysterious Lady of the Lake, who gives Arthur his charmed sword Excalibur, to Morgaine the fairy enchantress and mischief-maker, and not forgetting the Damsel of Hungerford, a *femme fatale* who shoots men from the ramparts of her castle with a siege weapon called a mangonel. These strong women have mysterious powers, holding many of the secrets of the realm, and at their centre is Guinevere, Camelot's beautiful but enigmatic queen; she personifies the romantic feminine ideal but in many ways remains a shadowy figure, her motives difficult to fathom.

From its origins in Celtic folklore, there have been as many versions of Guinevere's story as the names given to her – Ginevra, Gwenhwyfar, Gaynor, Guanhumara, Guennivar, Waynor and so on. In early Welsh legend, her name Gwenhwyfar meant 'white ghost'; she was described as the most faithless of the three faithless wives of the island of Britain,[1] daughter of the giant, Gogyrfan, and cause of the downfall of her husband. Geoffrey of Monmouth's twelfth-

---

1 Arthur and Guinevere greet a visitor to their court, in *Lancelot du Lac* (miniature added at Pleshey Castle, Kent, *c.*1375) Royal MS 20 D IV, f. 102v.

century chronicle, *History of the Kings of Britain,* which first popularised the Arthurian legends, told of Guanhumara's infidelity with the traitorous usurper Mordred, Arthur's bastard son. According to various Welsh tales, either Mordred abducted and beat Guinevere or she was carried off by one King Melwas so that St Gildas and the abbot of Glastonbury had to procure her release. The themes of infidelity and abduction in various forms became central to her story. In the German *Lanzelet* she was taken by 'King Valerin of the Tangled Wood' to his fortress, to be rescued by Arthur and Malduc the wizard, and in the French *Livre d'Artus* King Urien captured her during Arthur's wars with the rebellious kings of Britain. In these early tales she is portrayed as either a wicked adulteress or a precious possession to be stolen and recovered.

The theme of infidelity is explored in the courtly love affair between Guinevere and Lancelot, as first told by the French author Chrétien de Troyes. The love story is interwoven with the many chivalric exploits of Arthur's knights and the quasi-religious quest for the Holy Grail in two medieval epics: the hugely popular French prose *Lancelot-Grail* and the English Sir Thomas Malory's *Morte Darthur.* They became the point of departure for the modern adaptations that have proliferated, from the Victorian era (for example, Tennyson's *Idylls of the King*) to the present, where Camelot continues to inspire writers of fantasy.

The outline of Guinevere's story, summarised from the medieval romances, is as follows. Guinevere was the daughter of King Leodegrance of the kingdom of Cameliarde (which some say was near Sherwood Forest or may have been in today's Cornwall). She first met Arthur as a young girl, soon after his coronation, when he came to rescue her father from the invading Saxons. Guinevere served Arthur and his companions at the victory celebration feast (Image 2). This was Arthur's first impression:

Et li rois artus le regarde moult durement si li plot moult et enbelist che quil la vit devant li. Car ce estoit la plus bele feme qui fust en toute bretaigne au tans de lors...ele ot biaute en lui plus y ot bonte et larguece et courtoisie, sens et valour, douchour et deboinarete.[2]

Arthur could not take his eyes off her, as she made all around her seem beautiful. For this was the most lovely woman in all Britain at that time...and as beautiful as she was, this was surpassed by her goodness, generosity, courtly demeanour, good sense, worthiness, sweetness and nobility.[3]

Guinevere was impressed by this 'good and handsome knight',[4] and she thanked him with sweet sincerity for rescuing her father. Her eloquence and

2 Guinevere meets Arthur and mops his brow with a cloth after the battle, in the *Lancelot-Grail* (N. France, 1316) Add MS 10292, f. 122r.

charm held Arthur spellbound, so that he stopped eating and completely forgot where he was. Though Merlin, his magician and adviser, later warned him that she was too beautiful for her own good and would bring disaster for them both, he yearned to marry her. Guinevere's father granted permission and was so overjoyed at the advantageous match that he presented Arthur with the Round Table as a wedding gift, along with a hundred knights. A great celebration was held in the church of St Stephen at Camelot and Arthur assigned Guinevere her functions at court: she was to act as his treasurer and supervise the writing of their annals.

Not long after the wedding, Arthur set off with his troops to the continent, where he defeated the entire Roman army and was crowned emperor by the Pope in Rome. Returning triumphant he was met in London by Queen Guinevere and her ladies, and a great feast was held to celebrate these victories. Malory and the *Lancelot-Grail* give no details about the king and queen's marriage but there are brief glimpses of day-to-day life at Camelot in the romances of Chrétien de Troyes. On one occasion Arthur abruptly leaves a gathering of knights during an important feast and is 'detained' by the queen in her chamber: '*Si demoura tant deles li Qu'il s'oublia et endormi*' ('He stayed

3 Arthur and Guinevere at a banquet in Camelot, in *La Queste del Saint Graal* (N. France, 1315–25) Royal MS 14 E III, f. 89r.

with her so long that he forgot himself and fell asleep').[5] Guinevere is portrayed by Malory as the respected mistress of the knights and maidens of her court, dispensing advice and acting as an arbiter of fashion and model of courtesy.

Before long, with the arrival of the young Lancelot, the harmony at court is disrupted; at their first meeting Guinevere is struck by his extraordinary beauty. Guinevere is initially amused by the young man's adoration and enjoys flirting with him, presenting him with a sword as a token of her favour. Then she too falls in love and they kiss for the first time. In Malory's words: '*quene Gwenyvere had hym in grete favoure aboven all other knyghtis, and so he*

4 Lancelot and Guinevere kiss in the *Lancelot-Grail*, Add MS 10293, f. 76v.

loved the quene agayne aboven all other ladyes dayes of his lyff, and for hir he dud many dedys of armys'[6] ('Queen Guenever held him in great favour above all other knights, and certainly he loved the queen in return above all other ladies all his life, and for her he did many deeds of arms').

William Morris describes the Queen's recollection of their first kiss in his nineteenth-century poem, *The Defence of Guinevere*:

Came Launcelot walking; this is true, the kiss
Wherewith we kissed in meeting that spring day,
I scarce dare talk of the remember'd bliss.[7]

en vn lit en amble.

5 Lancelot and Guinevere embracing in bed, in the *Lancelot-Grail*, Add MS 10293, f. 312v.

Later they spend their first night together while Arthur is campaigning against the Saxons (Image 5). Lancelot is captivated, and on several occasions he carelessly risks his life to save the queen. To escape from his mounting feelings of guilt and shame at betraying his king and from Guinevere's possessive jealousy, the young hero rides out on a series of chivalrous adventures. He falls under the spell of other women, fathering a child (the future Galahad) with fair Elaine. When Guinevere finds out he has been with Elaine, even though he was tricked into it, she confronts him with these words:

'A, thou false traytoure knyght! Loke thou never abyde in my courte, and lyghtly that thou voyde my chambir!'	*'False traitor knight that you are, be sure never to abide in my court, and avoid my chamber!'*
'Alas!' seyde sir Lancelot...he lept oute at a bay-wyndow into a gardyne, and there wyth thornys he was all to-cracched of his vysage and hys body, and so he ranne furth he knew nat whothir, and was as wylde as ever was man. And so he ran two yere...[8]	*'Alas!' said sir Lancelot...he leapt out of a bay window into a garden, and there he was all scratched by thorns on his face and his body, and so he ran away not knowing where he went and was as wild as ever a man was; and he roamed about in this way for two years...*

6 Lancelot fights for Queen Guinevere's honour, watched by the queen and King Arthur, in the *Lancelot-Grail*, Add MS 10294, f. 68r.

To put on a brave face and show that she is able to enjoy life without Lancelot, Guinevere holds a great banquet in London for twenty-four knights, including Gawain and his brothers. The feast includes a dish of apples and pears. But one of the knights, who bears a grudge against Gawain, poisons some of the apples, knowing they are his favourite fruit. An apple is eaten by Patrise, who falls down dead on the spot, and Gawain immediately suspects Guinevere of trying to poison him. Mador, Patrise's relative, accuses the queen of murdering his cousin and nobody defends her. Arthur appeals to his young knights to prove Guinevere's innocence, asking, 'Where is Lancelot – he would do battle for you'. Then an unknown knight on a white horse appears and announces that he has come to prove her innocence by winning a jousting competition in her name. Of course it is Lancelot, and naturally he defeats Mador, earning the gratitude of King Arthur and promising always to be her knight and to protect her, whether in right or wrong (Image 6).

Meanwhile the devious Morgaine, Arthur's half-sister, who hates Guinevere, tries every means possible to convince the king that his wife is betraying him with Lancelot; however the high-minded Arthur refuses to accept what is obvious to those around him. He, too, is unfaithful on occasion, but this is always blamed on the women who trick or enchant him into being with them.

Then in the midst of these intrigues, Guinevere is abducted once again, this time by the wicked knight Meleagant, who takes her to his castle at Gorre. Lancelot, hearing that she is in danger, returns from his adventures and rides to the rescue. This episode is recounted in Chrétien de Troyes' *Le Chevalier de la Charrette* ('The Knight of the Cart'), where he describes how Lancelot almost falls off his horse when someone gives him an ivory comb belonging to Guinevere. The strands of her hair are *Si biax, si clers et si luisanz* ('so fair and light and radiant')[9] that he cannot take his eyes off them.

Et bien .c.m. foiz les toche,	*A hundred thousand times he touches them*
Et a ses ialz et a sa boche,	*To his eyes and mouth,*
Et a son front et a sa face.	*And to his forehead and face.*[10]

In a famous episode, Lancelot crawls across a sword-bridge to reach Guinevere. He spends a blissful night with her in the tower where she is held captive, and promises to return to rescue her. But his hands are wounded and bleeding from tearing apart the metal bars on her bedroom window and this causes suspicion among Meleagant and the other knights when they see the blood on her sheets, so he has to flee. After enduring many battles and ordeals, Lancelot finally beheads Meleagant in a tournament and Guinevere is free. However, she can only offer him a half-hearted kiss as Arthur is watching.

Before long, Guinevere is racked by guilt and again becomes jealous, believing Lancelot to be in love with the Maid of Escalot. The knight Bohort, Lancelot's kinsman and ally, reproaches her for banishing him from court once again. He bitterly claims that he never saw a great man who loved a woman without ultimately regretting it, and he cites the example of the biblical hero Samson, brought down by his lover Delilah (see Chapter 21). He also raises the subject of Tristan, who had died less than five years ago for the love of Iseult, when she rejected him though he did her no wrong. (Iseult, like Guinevere, was merely trying to remain faithful to her husband.) For Bohort, Guinevere is even worse than these other women because her lover, Lancelot, is the most heroic of all, combining all the good qualities of every worthy man in the pantheon, and he will surely die if she continues to reject him.

a Pres ce q̃ meſtre
gautier map ot
tretie des auentes

7 Lancelot and Bohort ride up to rescue Queen Guinevere from the fire, in *Lancelot du Lac* (Oxford, *c.*1300) Royal MS 20 C VI, f. 150r.

The love affair is now an open secret at court, and so Mordred hatches a plot to produce evidence that will convince Arthur. While the king is out hunting, Mordred's companions burst into Guinevere's chamber and find the couple together. Lancelot fights his way through his attackers and escapes, promising to return and rescue the queen. Now Arthur cannot avoid the truth. Guinevere must be tried for treason; her punishment is to be burned at the stake (Image 7). With minutes to spare, Lancelot rides to the rescue once again, escaping with Guinevere to his castle, Joyous Gard, leaving a trail of dead and wounded Camelot knights in his wake. Arthur, while relieved that the queen's life has been spared, is now forced to take revenge and sets off in pursuit of his beloved friend and his wife.

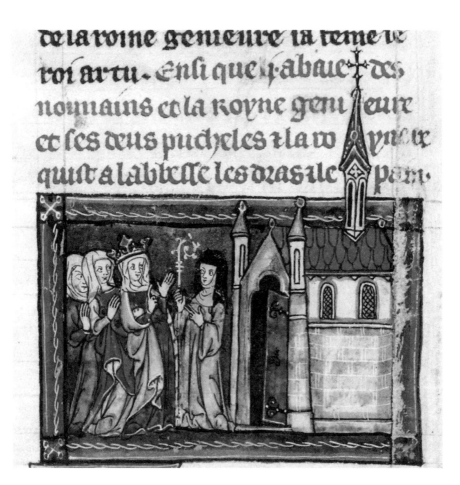

8 Guinevere and two attendants make vows before a nun as they enter the convent, in the *Lancelot-Grail*, Add MS 10294, f. 87v.

While Arthur is away pursuing Lancelot, Mordred seizes the throne, and Arthur returns to meet him in the final battle of Salisbury Plain. He is mortally wounded and carried away by ladies in an enchanted barge to the island of Avalon. Malory's Guinevere finally takes control of her own destiny at this point. She enters a convent at Amesbury where she remains until her death (Image 8), and though Lancelot returns to England to find her, she refuses to see him or kiss him one last time. After she dies, he has her body taken in a procession to Glastonbury, where she is buried beside Arthur. Their remains were supposedly discovered at Glastonbury in 1101 and later re-buried by King Edward I and Queen Eleanor in a marble tomb. Historians believe that this story was invented by the monks of Glastonbury Abbey to benefit from medieval tourism, but the location is marked by a plaque today in the midst of the romantic ruins of the abbey chapel. There are other versions of Guinevere's final days; in the gruesome ending of the French tale, *Genievre*, she dies and her body is placed in a prison cell with Mordred, who feeds on it before dying of hunger himself.

The medieval epics provide a varied and complex picture of Guinevere – was she a gracious and courageous queen, a victim of court intrigue or a manipulative seductress? In his poem about King Arthur, Alfred Lord Tennyson judged her harshly, blaming her for the destruction of the ideal of the Round Table; she did not comply with his Victorian ideal of submissive femininity.[11]

More recent authors of fantasy fiction have portrayed Guinevere in multiple guises, but have generally given her greater control over her own destiny. These are just a few examples:

- a woman of action who runs the kingdom while Arthur is away (Gillian Bradshaw, *In Winter's Shadow*, 1982), or one who complains that courtly pursuits are boring and is regarded as 'hormonal and irrational' by her husband (Geoffrey Turton, *The Emperor Arthur*, 1985);
- a feisty serving girl with whom Arthur falls in love; they ultimately marry despite the difference in social status, in the 2008 BBC series, *Merlin*;
- a young girl who disguises herself as a boy (Kiersten White, *The Guinevere Deception*), or a knight who becomes queen (2016 television series, *Legends of Tomorrow*);
- a feminist, Dark Age warrior-queen (for example, in Catherine Christian's *The Pendragon* and the 2020 TV series *Red Spear*).

Clearly, she is a female character who has adapted along with changing attitudes to women and sexual morality across the centuries and continues to fascinate storytellers.

Helayne

Parva

20.

Helen of Troy

The immortal Helen of Troy, or Helen of Sparta, was famous for her divine beauty, and worshipped as a goddess by some. She is blamed for the destruction of the city of Troy and the death of the Greek and Trojan heroes who went to war over her. Her story has been used from ancient times to explore questions of morality, desire and female agency, and has been adapted by successive generations to reflect attitudes to these questions. Should she be seen as a calculating temptress or a helpless pawn in events controlled by powerful gods and men? Storytellers have differed widely in their opinions of her, though almost all have agreed on her desirability: Homer described her as 'the shining among women',[1] while for Christopher Marlowe's Doctor Faustus she was 'the face that launch'd a thousand ships'.[2]

In classical mythology, Helen was the daughter of none other than the god Zeus (Roman Jupiter) who changed himself into a swan to impregnate a mortal woman named Leda. Their offspring was a daughter who emerged from an egg, growing into an exquisitely beautiful young woman. Because her father was the king of the gods, she was the half-sister of many of the most important divinities, including Aphrodite (Roman Venus) and had many famous suitors.

---

1 Helen's arrival in Troy, in *Chronique de la Bouquechardière* (Rouen, 15th century) Harley MS 4376, f. 90r.

When she was a mere 7 or 10 years old, depending on the source, she was snatched from the temple of Artemis (Diana) in the Greek city of Sparta, where she was dancing to honour the virgin goddess. Her abductor was none other than Theseus (of Minotaur fame), who was then 50 years old and recently widowed, and according to Plutarch he drew lots with his friend Pirithous to decide who should marry her. Theseus won, and he hid her in the home of a friend near Athens so that her brothers (the Dioscuri) had to wage war against the Athenians to rescue her. So even as a child she apparently caused a war, though many would blame her abduction and the subsequent battle on the men in this episode.

Finally, after a contest in which Odysseus took part, Helen's mortal father Tyndareus selected Menelaus as her husband and together they became rulers of Sparta. They had a daughter, Hermione, and three sons, according to some sources. But Helen was well known to all the gods and goddesses of Olympus and she became a pawn in one of the cruel games by which they manipulated the lives of mortals.

The fateful series of events leading to the Trojan War began at the wedding of Peleus and Thetis, future parents of Achilles (Image 2). When they did not include Eris (goddess of discord) on the guest list, she burst in on the celebrations, causing consternation by throwing a golden apple marked 'for the most beautiful' among the guests. Three goddesses claimed this honour – Athena (Roman Minerva), Hera (Juno) and Aphrodite (Venus) – and so it was decided that the young Paris should choose between them. Paris chose Aphrodite because she had bribed him by promising him the loveliest woman in all the world as his bride. True to her word she arranged for him to be sent to Sparta to meet Helen. For the reasons explored below, he abducted her and sailed with her to Troy, setting in motion the events leading up to the bloody war between the Greeks and Trojans. Some even say that Zeus wished to reduce the number of humans populating the Earth, as they were causing him too much trouble, and that Helen and Achilles were the two crucial elements in his plan – she as the main cause of the Trojan War and he as its fiercest killer.

In some accounts of the Troy story, Helen is portrayed as a pawn in the ongoing war games between the Greeks and Trojans. During a previous attack on Troy, the Greek prince Telamon had abducted Hesiona, King Priam's sister, and made her his concubine. Paris, son of Priam, was instructed to lead a small expedition to negotiate Hesiona's return, but when the Greeks refused this

2 The three goddesses Minerva, Juno and Venus at the wedding feast of Peleus and Thetis, in Christine de Pisan, *L'Épistre Othéa* ('Letter of Othea') (Paris, *c*.1412) Harley MS 4431, f. 122v.

Maidens or Monsters?

uis la ceste de discorde

tepte. cp

w an fp fout les dieux et deesse

3 King Priam sends Paris to Greece (left); Paris captures Helen in the Temple of Cythera (right), in *Grandes Chroniques de France* ('Chronicles of France') (Paris, c.1340) Royal MS 16 G VI, f. 4v.

4 Paris kneels before Priam and Hecuba with Helen, in *Des cas de nobles hommes et femmes*, a translation of Boccaccio's *De casibus virorum illustrium* ('On the Fates of Famous Men') (France, mid-15th century) Add MS 35321, f. 22r.

request, he abducted Helen, as she had been promised to him by Aphrodite. Image 3 (from a work of French chronicles that includes the Trojan story as an origin myth) shows Paris being sent to Greece by his father, then grasping the arms of the resisting Helen in the Temple of Cythera.

In the *Roman de Troie* the French author Benoît de Sainte Maure claimed that Helen, on hearing that the handsome young Paris had arrived in Greece, decided to display her seductive charms to him. She went with her attendants to the Temple of Cythera, where she had heard that Paris planned to sacrifice

et distrenrancum oceuls en lo:
confoil nous pons bien conoi
stre que li grec ne soufferront
me si gnr hotte come nous len:
auons faire se il la puecenr ame
cer. Et lendit-1est uenue qui est
garms si neit homs. pour æ noz
truons prendre guarre q sitost

wis 1our qui su aprelles
lemesius fier forr7lardis1prous
1 combitant qui ceminoi cogie
au roi prianr oller hu 1sacom
gme guarceri.sien chastel que
u auoir bel1forr su lermage de
La mer illucques pres auques
a cemie 1ournee. Et al cenoir

5 Paris places a ring on Helen's finger in a ceremony in the royal palace at Troy, conducted by a priest in elaborate vestments and surrounded by members of the royal family, while courtiers celebrate from the rooftops, in the *Histoire ancienne* (Naples, c.1330) Royal MS 20 D I, f. 53r.

to Artemis, and they fell in love at first sight. In the medieval Latin *Historia destructionis Troiae* ('History of the Destruction of Troy') we are told that as soon as Paris saw Helen 'he coveted her and...he seethed with intense desire' at her 'excessive loveliness', which is described by the author, Guido delle Colonne, in detail, including the perfection of her eyelashes, teeth, shoulders and fingernails.[3] Returning at night, Paris abducted Helen with her belongings and sailed for Troy.

On her arrival in Troy, Helen was met with great fanfare by King Priam (Image 4), who was certain the Trojans would now be able to exchange her for his sister, Hesiona. But, undoubtedly against his father's wishes, the next day Paris married Helen (Image 5), ignoring the warnings of Cassandra and others that his actions would bring about the destruction of Troy.

The Greek army under Agamemnon pursued Paris and Helen to Troy and – following one fruitless attempt at negotiation – they decided to attack. After many bloody battles and huge loss of life on both sides, the city of Troy was sacked and burned and the Trojan women were taken as slaves and concubines. Menelaus managed to rescue Helen from her chamber and, though some of the

fu quthes de son roiaume 1 es
toit remes en cypre ou il auo
 it fonde une ate q estoit appel
lee sallemine gnt abelle 1 do
se dehaus murs 1 illu ecestoit
tout asseur. Apres m dta com
met emopus somanmer. auo
it este aus du serpet droicala

as sa mere 1 commet li droicult
commandent q il en feist u l h
ce isun t tous retvus dontme
nestvus le prist 1 de ffendre co
tre tous ceuls qui dire noul
dront q il ne fust digne de gou
uerner lempire qui qui li vou
dra mette sus de loialte il lega

6 Menelaus and Helen sail home to Greece, where they are greeted in the palace by courtiers, in the *Histoire ancienne*, Royal MS 20 D I, f. 181r.

Greeks demanded that she pay the price for the terrible destruction she had caused, he was able to conduct her safely to his ship and they sailed home to Greece (Image 6), where they lived tranquilly into old age.

One of the questions explored in the different versions of Helen's story is, was she abducted by Paris or did she elope with him willingly? In Homer's *Iliad* she is portrayed as an innocent victim, cursed with godlike beauty, who suffers deeply at the destruction she has caused, weaving a tapestry to tell her story while lamenting, 'I wish bitter death had been what I wanted, when I came hither… forsaking my chamber, my kinsmen, my grown child, and the loveliness of girls my own age'.[4] Stesichorus, the sixth-century BC Greek lyric poet, apparently went blind after he slandered Helen in his poetry, and so in order to regain his sight he changed his story. He absolved Helen from any guilt by claiming that a substitute had been sent by the gods to Troy to cause the war. Apparently the real Helen had been concealed in a cloud by Zeus and taken by Hermes (Mercury) to Egypt to live in the palace of Proteus in Egypt

7 Paris writes a letter to Helen, in Ovid, *Heroides*, translated by Octavien de St-Gelais (Paris, c.1500) Harley MS 4867, f. 115r.

Salut ennoye atoy o dame
belame.
Le dieu puis qui ne peult
a grant peine
Salut auoir pour bien
quil face ouurez

for the duration of the war. And Proteus was an honourable man so Helen had remained untouched for ten years.

Meanwhile in Euripides' tragedy, *The Trojan Women*, Helen is portrayed as a vain and shallow beauty who causes terrible suffering by the use of her seductive charms. At the end of the war she is brought before her husband Menelaus to be killed. Hecuba, the queen of Troy, who has seen her husband and sons slaughtered and her city destroyed by the Greeks, lays the blame on Helen: 'I thank you, Menelaus, if you will slay that wife of yours. Yet shun the sight of her, lest she strike you with longing. For she ensnares the eyes of men, overthrows their towns, and burns their houses, so potent are her witcheries!'[5]

But Helen defends herself bravely, claiming that Hecuba herself is to blame for giving birth to Paris and ignoring the evil prophecy that he would be the cause of Troy's destruction. She criticises Menelaus, who should not have left her alone at home with a strange man while he went off to Crete, and finally she blames Aphrodite who helped Paris to seduce her. Naturally Menelaus, ignoring his own part in the slaughter, lays the blame squarely at his wife's door. He sentences her to death, dismissing her with these words: 'Away to those who shall stone you, and by your speedy death requite the weary toils of the Achaeans [Greeks], so that you may learn not to bring shame on me!'[6]

The Roman poet Ovid imagines letters between Helen and Paris (Image 7), in which Paris writes to her of his pre-ordained desire for her and she replies contemptuously that his letter has profaned her eyes and complains that her famous beauty is a burden to her.[7]

Medieval authors take different views on who is to blame for Helen's abduction. Boccaccio describes her as 'resplendent in celestial beauty, wanton in royal elegance and desirous of being admired'.[8] So although she could not help being beautiful, her flirtatious behaviour was to blame for what happened (Image 8). John Lydgate's Middle English *Troy Book* is unequivocal in its condemnation of both Paris for stealing another man's wife, and Helen for being the passive cause of the violence (though he claims he is merely reflecting the views of his source, Colonne's *Historia*, see above):

> Allas, allas! I seie to thee Eleyne,
> Unhappy woman, and causere of oure peyne.[9]

In *Troilus and Criseyde*, Chaucer compares Helen to Criseyde, judging the latter to be more beautiful, and reminds us that both women brought death and disaster on the men they loved (Paris and Troilus). Shakespeare's virtuous heroine in *The Rape of Lucrece* (see Chapter 16), contemplating an image of Troy's destruction, says in disgust, 'Show me the strumpet that began

8 Paris leads Helen towards his waiting fleet, in *Des cleres et nobles femmes*, an anonymous French translation of Boccaccio's *De mulieribus claris* ('On Famous Women') (Rouen, c.1440) Royal MS 16 G V, f. 39v.

this stir'.[10] More modern interpretations see Helen as a narrative construct, an elusive literary character on whom it would be pointless to pass judgement. Mark Haddon, author of the radio play *A Thousand Ships*, puts these words into the mouth of his Helen:

> *The truth is that no-one cares who I am. You read the stories. You read the poems. You haven't got a clue. Nothing fits. Nothing makes sense…I'm a sorceress, a victim, a whore, a wife. I'm a devil. I'm an angel. I'm every woman that ever lived. I'm nobody, a blank slate for you to write whatever you like on.*[11]

Helen has fascinated and inspired artists, from the medieval illuminators whose work is presented here to Dante Gabriel Rossetti, who depicted her as a Pre-Raphaelite beauty. And like Cleopatra (Chapter 10), her image has been adapted to conform to the contemporary ideals of beauty. Her origins, her story and her motivations remain a subject for debate among feminist critics, storytellers and scriptwriters. But perhaps the most bizarre Helen is one of the oldest of all, and the least well known. As described by Natalie Haynes in *Pandora's Jar*,[12] this Helen was the daughter of Musaeus, a poet from before the time of Homer, and she owned a *diglosson arnon* ('a bilingual goat'). A cause for fame indeed!

an quatre mil quarante q̃ta
apzes la creacion du monde
pour lors que aftanus fil
de Eneas fonda la cite dalbanne. San
son qui par vv ans gouuerna le peu
ple des Juifz fut auant sa natiute
denunce par lange de dieu. Sanson
filz dung Juifz appelle Manue eut

21.

Delilah

Delilah is the third of three women in the life of the Old Testament hero Samson, the strong man who fought a lion and brought down the Philistines, enemies of the Jews. Samson seems to have had trouble with women; his first wife was a Philistine herself, and she was burned to death by her own people. This was after Samson had burned all their ripe corn by lighting the tails of foxes and letting them loose in the fields. In retaliation he slaughtered a thousand Philistines with a donkey's jawbone. He then had a drink of water and went to the land of Gaza, where the Bible tells that he spent the night with his second woman, a harlot. The people of Gaza lay in wait for him, but in the morning when he saw this he tore out the gates and gate-posts of the city and threw them on top of a hill. The Bible then says 'And it came to pass afterward, that he loved a woman in the valley of Sorek, whose name was Delilah'.[1] Delilah is the only one of the three women whose name is given, but still she remains an enigma, as her status in society is not explained. Was she a widow, a rare example of an independent woman or – as most people have concluded – a prostitute? Was she a Philistine or an Israelite? The former is more likely as she ultimately betrayed Samson to the Philistines, but as she was offered a generous bribe she may even have betrayed her own people.

The Bible states that Samson loved Delilah but it does not say how she

[1] Delilah cuts Samson's hair and Samson destroys the temple, in Boccaccio, *Des cas des nobles hommes et femmes* ('On the Fates of Illustrious Men and Women') (France, mid-15th century) Add MS 35321, f. 28r.

2 (left) Samson carrying off the gate of Gaza, and Samson with his hands bound; (centre) Samson and the lion, and Samson and Delilah; (right) Samson pulling down the Philistines' temple, in the St Omer Psalter (Norfolk, c.1335) Yates Thompson MS 14, f. 57v.

felt about him, so were her motives were purely mercenary? Did she charm him in order to betray him? The Book of Judges states that several Philistine leaders each offered her 11,000 pieces of silver to reveal the secret of Samson's strength. So she went to her lover and asked him his secret; three times he gave her false leads, and she acted on them. First she tied him up with fresh bowstrings but he snapped them, then she tried binding him with new ropes and he broke them like threads, and then she wove his long braids in the loom and he tore them out. But she continued to nag and cajole him, accusing him of not loving her enough to confide in her. At last she wore him down so that 'his soul was vexed unto death'[2] and he gave in, revealing his true secret: if his long hair was shaved he would lose his strength. Satisfied at last that she had the truth, Delilah let him fall asleep in her lap and then called for someone to shave off his seven long braids. When Samson awoke his strength had left him and the Philistines seized him, bound him in shackles and gouged out his eyes. Delilah simply disappeared – from the scene and from the story altogether. The implication is that she cared nothing for Samson's fate and went off to enjoy spending the silver she had earned with her treachery. The events surrounding Samson's death are familiar to most of us; Samson's hair grew again and one day in the midst of a crowded festival attended by all the most important Philistines, he was able to tear down the two central pillars of the temple so that it collapsed on top of him, killing him and many of his enemies.

3 Samson is blinded, in the Smithfield Decretals (decorated London c.1340) Royal MS 10 E IV, f. 35v.

The story of Samson and Delilah was known and interpreted in many ways across medieval Europe. It raised questions about men and women, strength and love, mastery and victimhood. In a chivalric milieu where love was the overriding value, should a woman, given the choice, be loyal to her man or to her people? Multiple versions of the story in French and Latin verse and prose were adapted from the account in the Book of Judges. A Latin musical drama, *Samson dux fortissime* ('Samson the Strongest Leader'), survives from the thirteenth century, in which Samson is portrayed as a lover whose sufferings were likened to the knights of chivalric romance pining for unattainable ladies. In all of these Delilah is vilified, with details added to eliminate doubt as to her dubious character and motives, and sometimes these are introduced in images, perhaps mirroring the action in popular medieval drama. In one series of images in an English lawbook, it is Delilah herself who blinds Samson (Image 3).

The *Poeme anglo-normand sur l'ancien testament* ('Anglo-Norman poem on the Old Testament') includes the story, and in a prose version, the scene where she shaves Samson's hair is rendered in Anglo-Norman French as:

4 The blind Samson breaking the pillar supporting the temple, in a passage about the virtue of courage, in the Italian work, *Fiore de virtù e de costumi* (Padua, mid-15th century) Harley MS 3448, f. 30r.

Donc fist Dalida Sanson couchier sor ses escos et dormi et sur sa poitrine, puis a pris I rasor, si le rest li cheveaus, en quoy sa force estoit. Quant ce fu fait, si le geta fors de son escos et bien loins le bouta de sei, car tote sa force fu ja defallie et puis si la dit par grant felonie: Sanson, Phelistiens sont ja sur vos.

Then Delilah made Samson lie down upon her lap and sleep on her breast and she took a razor, and she sheared off his hair where his strength had been. When this was done, she threw him out of her lap and she pushed him away from her, because his strength had completely gone and then she said to him with great wickedness Samson, the Philistines are now upon you.[3]

Instead of calling on a barber, Delilah shaves Samson's hair herself, and this is how the scene is almost always portrayed in medieval manuscripts (Images 1, 5). In the *Dux fortissime* she hands Samson a glass of wine and gives him a kiss before putting him to sleep, then afterwards she turns to the Philistines in mocking triumph, 'Hurrah, hurrah, I have captured your enemy! Hurrah, hurrah, I am laughing at him, shaven'.[4] Delilah then callously pushes Samson away, leaving no doubt that this is a *femme fatale* who has been recruited to destroy the Israelite hero. Samson, naturally, blames Delilah, absolving himself

5a (left) Samson slaughtering the Philistines with the jawbone of a donkey; **5b** (right) Delilah cutting Samson's hair, in a *Bible historiale* (Netherlands, *c*.1415) Add MS 18856, ff. 118v, 119r.

from any blame, although he gave in to her because of his desire for her, when it was obvious she was going to betray him. Jacques de Vitry, a biblical commentator of the twelfth century, claimed, 'Samsons's hair was shorn by Delilah, just as the strength of his soul [was] robbed by the pleasures of the flesh'.[5] The Chorus in the *Dux fortissime* concludes that Samson's downfall was due to *fraus mulieris* ('a woman's deceit').

In a poem on the Old Testament in Anglo-Norman French, Samson uses the word *engin* (from Latin *ingenium*, meaning 'trickery', 'cunning', or 'artifice') to describe Delilah's actions:

Quant ot, dunc, sout il ben de fi;	When he heard it, he knew for sure
Que par engin sa femme fu il trai	That he had been betrayed by his wife's trickery[6]

The same word is used in this poem for Eve in Genesis (she uses her *engin* to persuade Adam to eat the forbidden fruit thereby causing the Fall of Man, see Chapter 17). In medieval chivalric romance, *engin* generally means the cunning methods used by clever women to subdue physically stronger men, so once again here themes are borrowed from literature.

Many of these themes are brought together in the *Bible historiale* ('History Bible'), a popular work in the fourteenth and fifteenth centuries judging by the number of copies to survive. It includes a commentary interpreting the biblical stories with reference to pagan history and mythology.

In the Queen Mary Psalter, an exceptional book owned by English royalty and containing a cycle of 223 scenes from the Old Testament, the story

Maidens or Monsters?

6a–6c Scenes from the life of Samson, in the Queen Mary Psalter (London, c. 1315), Royal MS 2 B VII, ff. 44r-46v:

6a (opposite top) Samson introduces Delilah to his father and their marriage is arranged;

6b (opposite bottom) Samson is enslaved and forced to labour for the Philistines;

6c During the Philistine's feast, Samson's young assistant blows a horn and he destroys the pillars of the temple.

of Samson and Delilah is told in a cycle of seventeen images with captions in Anglo-Norman French.

There are some additions to the story here that are not found in other versions. For example, in one image (6a) the fathers of the young Samson and Delilah are shown arranging their betrothal; in another (6b) Samson is depicted as a captive of the Philistines, whipped and forced to turn a mill wheel to grind corn. Then in the final image (6c) a boy is shown blowing a horn. This is apparently the young boy who guided the blind Samson to his position between the pillars of the Temple. Here, the caption clarifies that Samson protected his young companion from death even though he was a Philistine, telling him to flee and save himself. He then waited until the boy was safely outside before he brought down the temple and everyone inside was crushed, including Delilah, who was present among the Philistines in this version. The boy blows the horn in this image to announce that he has escaped to safety.

is noon so greuous

t is loeue

s pyllous

is pryde

mynyte

omynn varyable

ffreen other stable

Be Dalida dystoyued

atue forge and ffeyne

nthey hane conceyued

a myghty cheyne

nt out his eyen tweyne

w as I ffynde

made hym for to grynde

starh and solempne

this treson wrought

toune hym and condempne

was a ffoun hem brought

e/ tueyed hym in his thought

preuy mynde

so/ som made weye ffynde

edde/ thus be thought hym longe

in preuyly to ledde

we synar and strong/

y man took hede

/ with eure foer or drede

s ffomen alle

upon hem falles

uyyd on his ffoun

d ageyn hym struue

god wot ful many oon

w a ffoun his hede

Date to Dystryue

myn auctour

and gouernour

e/ yeveth an euydence

hal they counfayl out Dysturue

or lak of prouydence

Sampson

Dalida

Sampson

¶ The envoye of
this tragedye

So here Samson is shown as a tragic, vulnerable character, who acts to save an innocent child even as he takes awful vengeance on his enemies. Delilah is clearly identified with the villains of the story – the Philistines – and she receives her just punishment at the hands of the hero, Samson.

These themes are further explored by medieval authors including John Lydgate in his *Fall of Princes*, an English adaptation of Boccaccio's *De casibus virorum illustrium* ('On the Fates of Famous Men'). He uses his version of the story, *Samson and Dalida*, to comment on women's inability to keep a secret:

But women have this condicioun	*But women have this condition*
Off secre thynges whan thei have knowlchyng	*When they have knowledge of secret matters*
They bollyn inward, ther hertis ay fretyng;	*They boil inward, their hearts fretting:*
Outher they musten deien or discure	*Either they must die or disclose it,*
So brotil is off custum ther nature.	*So brittle is of custom their nature.*
...	...
Thus Samson was be Dalida deceyved,	*Thus Sampson was deceived by Dalida,*
She coude so weel flatre, forge and feyne.	*She was so good at flattery, forgery and pretence.*[7]

In the *Roman de la Rose* ('Romance of the Rose') the jealous husband cites examples of the greatest heroes of antiquity, Hercules and Samson, who feared no man but were deceived by the women who charmed them. He refers to the actions of Deianeira, who killed Hercules with a poisoned shirt, and Delilah who destroyed the mighty Samson (see Introduction, Image 7). It is tempting to note that both of these men may have gone on to kill and maim thousands more of their enemies had not two well-placed *femmes fatales* put a stop to this senseless slaughter.

7 Samson's downfall, in John Lydgate, *Fall of Princes* (Suffolk, c.1455) Harley MS 1766, f. 84r.

secondo ilpiu elmen dela uirtute
chessi destende ptucte loz parti
agioz bonta uuol magioz salute
magioz salute magioz corpo cape
selli a leparti igualmente compiute
unq: costui che tucto rape
laltro uniuerso secondo risponde
alcerchio che piu ama et che piu sape
erche setu alauirtu seconde
la tua misura nona laparuenza
delle substantie che tapagion tonde
u uedrai mirabil consequenza
di magio apiu et diminore ameno
in ciascum cielo asua intelligenza
ome rimane splendido et sereno
lemisperio dellaere quando soffia
borea daquella guancia onde piu leno
er che sipurga et risolue laroffia
che pria turbaua quel chel ciel neride
colle bellecze dogni sua parroffia
osi fecio poi chemi prouide
la dona mia del suo risponder chiaro
et come stella incielo iluer siuide
t poi chelle parole sue restaro
no altrimenti ferro dissauilla
che bolle come liochi sfauillaro
oncendio loro seguiua ogni scintilla
et eran tante chel numero loro
piu che doppiar delli scacchi simila
o sentia osannar dicoro uicoro
alpunto fisso chelitiene aluibi
et terra semp nequai sempre fuoro
t quella che uedea ipensier dubi
nella mia mente disse icerchi pmi
tanno mostrati yseraphi et cherubi

22.

Beatrice

The story of Beatrice, beloved muse of Dante, straddles fact and fiction in a unique way. Most of what we know about her is from the writings of Dante himself, in which she is a shadowy figure but a major influence on his life and literary oeuvre. After her death in her early twenties, Dante immersed himself in the study of philosophy and began to compose poems dedicated to her memory. His *Divina Commedia* ('The Divine Comedy') – considered one of the greatest works of European literature of the medieval, or indeed any, period – was, by his own admission, composed in her honour. She plays a leading role in this imaginative masterpiece, acting as Dante's rescuer, guide and inspiration.

From the few details provided by Dante about her and from historical records, scholars have assembled the facts about the 'real' Beatrice, if indeed she existed. It is believed that her full name was Beatrice di Folco Portinari and she was the daughter of a Florentine banker. Dante wrote that he met her only a few times, and he referred to her solely by her first name, giving no further details. The first meeting between the two took place when they were children, at a May Day party at the Portinari home in Florence when Dante was 9 years old and Beatrice a few months younger. Dante fell deeply in love with her, and although he only caught a glimpse of her once or twice over the next nine years, he later wrote about how he pined for her like a young knight for his lady in

1 Beatrice showing Dante the orders of angels and saints in Dante, *Paradiso,* Yates Thompson MS 36, f. 180r.

2 Dante and Beatrice meet two virtuous characters in Paradise; before them is Florence, which is shown as a corrupt city where the Devil pours florins into the hands of churchmen, in Dante, *Paradiso* (Tuscany, *c.*1445) Yates Thompson MS 36, f. 145r.

3 Beatrice in a mandorla carried by angels, in Dante, *Paradiso* (Naples, *c.*1370) Add MS 19587, f. 111v.

chivalric literature. Then when he was 18 years old, Dante saw Beatrice walking down the street in Florence with friends. Their eyes met briefly through the veil she was wearing, and although they did not have the chance to speak to each other, this meeting left an indelible impression on the young poet. However, few marriages in the thirteenth century were love matches, and both Beatrice and Dante were married into (separate) powerful families in Florence (the city is depicted in Image 2).

Though they may not have seen one another again, Dante was deeply affected by Beatrice's death and much of his poetry was inspired by his longing for her. His visionary work, *La Vita Nuova* ('The New Life') tells of how this passionate love for Beatrice drove the young poet to acquire sufficient knowledge to be able to do justice to her in his writing. He describes his goal in passionate terms:

> After writing this sonnet a marvellous vision appeared to me, in which I saw things that made me decide not to say anything more about this blessed lady until I was capable of writing about her more worthily. To achieve this I am doing all that I can, as surely she knows. So that...I hope to say things about her that have never been said about any woman.

> Then, if it be pleasing to Him who is the Lord of benevolence and grace, may my soul go to contemplate the glory of its lady – that blessed Beatrice, who gazes in glory into the face of Him qui est per omnia secula benedictus [who is blessed for ever and ever].[1]

He followed this with an encyclopaedic work known as *Il Convivio* ('The Banquet') in which he described how he was torn between the past and present after Beatrice's death, until he found a new love, Lady Philosophy. She taught him that the greatest goal was knowledge, and 'the love of her dispelled and destroyed every other thought'.[2] The stage was now set for Dante's greatest work, the *Divina Commedia*, in which he fulfilled his promise to himself and Beatrice. In it he imagined a spiritual journey through *Inferno* (Hell), *Purgatorio* (Purgatory) and *Paradiso* (Heaven), with Beatrice as his protector and guide, culminating in their joint experience of sublime love in the presence of God.

The story begins on Easter Thursday in 1300, when Dante has lost his way in a dark wood and is threatened by three beasts, a lion, a leopard and a she-wolf, who bar the way to salvation. He is rescued by the poet Virgil, who has been sent by Beatrice, 'a fair, saintly lady', who instructed him to find Dante and show him the path out of the wood. Virgil describes Beatrice's sparkling eyes, a sign of her inner beauty:

4 Dante and Virgil standing before the gates of Hell; Virgil points to Beatrice and her two companions floating on white clouds above, in Dante, *Inferno*, Yates Thompson MS 36, f. 4r.

Lucevan li occhi suoi piu che la stella;
e comniciommi a dir soave e piana;
con angelica voce.

Her eyes surpassed the splendor of the star's;
and she began to speak to me – so gently
and softly – with angelic voice.[3]

Virgil and Dante set off on the arduous journey (Image 4) to the cold depths of Hell where they witness the unspeakable torments of the damned, and finally reach the frozen centre where Satan is devouring the most hideous murderers and traitors. Then they face the arduous climb up the mountain of Purgatory, and all the while Dante is spurred on by Virgil's assurance that he is following Beatrice's instructions and that she will be waiting for him at the end of his journey. When he must walk through a wall of fire on the final ledge of Purgatory, he finds courage to do so when Virgil reminds him that he will see the 'glad and lovely eyes'[4] of Beatrice on the other side.

He bids goodbye to Virgil and enters the Earthly Paradise, where the River Lethe washes away the memory of sin. Here he has a vision of Revelation and Beatrice appears in a chariot pulled by griffins, surrounded by a cloud of flowers, to guide him through Paradise (Image 5). Dante is overwhelmed with the same feeling of love that he felt as a young man, but at first Beatrice

5 Dante is led to Beatrice who is seated in the chariot with two ladies, in Dante, *Purgatorio*, with Latin commentary in the left margin (N. Italy, 1300–50) Egerton MS 943, f. 121.

treats him like a child, scolding him for weeping over Virgil's departure. She addresses him: 'her stance still regal and disdainful, she continued, just as one who speaks but keeps until the end the fiercest parts of speech: "Look here! For I am Beatrice, I am!"'.[5] She accuses him of false imaginings and for straying from the path of devotion to her.

Only when he confesses his past errors to her does she absolve him and reveal her true beauty, then she instructs him to write down all that he has seen on his journey, saying, 'Take note; and even as I speak these words, do you transmit them in your turn to those who live...'[6]

Beatrice's goodness and beauty draw Dante upwards, and on their journey through the nine celestial spheres she reassures and encourages him with her beatific smile. She answers his questions on diverse subjects, from the nature of matter on the moon to the significance of holy vows. Meeting many souls along the way, from Charlemagne to St Francis of Assisi, they continue ever upwards. Ascending past angels and saints, through realms of dazzling light, they reach the tenth sphere or Empyrean. Here, in the presence of the Celestial Rose, Beatrice is transfigured, becoming so beautiful as to defy description. She takes her place in the Rose and Dante prays his thanks to her. He looks into the Eternal Light and his soul becomes one with God. This is Beatrice's gift to him (Image 6).

We do not know how much of the story of Dante and Beatrice is true, and how much is imaginary. Is Beatrice an allegory of goodness and beauty (her name means 'beautifier'), a symbol of divine wisdom, the female incarnation of God, as she appears in Dante's writings? Or is she Beatrice Portinari of Florence, as first identified by the writer, Boccaccio, who was still a child when Dante died and produced a 'biography' that is considered highly unreliable? It seems she is both. Pietro Alighieri, in a commentary to his father's work, wrote, 'after she died, to enhance the fame of her name, he wanted her to be taken as an allegory and type of theology in this poem'.[7] More recently, the eminent Dante critic Teodolinda Barolini has noted that in the *Commedia* Dante has removed Beatrice's earthly qualities, turning her into a divine symbol, a Virgin Mary-like character who exists within the context of the poetic work to meet the needs of the lover-poet.[8] Others have argued that although in the *Vita Nuova* she is a courtly heroine or object of love, in the *Commedia* she is given a powerful voice as Dante's mentor and guide and that she is portrayed as a complex and authoritative individual. In *Purgatorio* when she appears in person for the first time, she addresses Dante in direct speech. This is extremely rare for a female character in fourteenth-century literature.

Dante was nearly 40 years old and living in exile from his beloved Florence when he began work on the *Commedia*, and he completed it in 1321, the year he died. At a time when Latin was considered the language of learning and culture, he chose to write in his mother tongue, the language of Florence, enriching and inventing to create a new form of Italian that could express the magnificence of his vision, and creating an original rhyme scheme of three-line stanzas. The work gained popularity immediately, especially in Florence after the return of Dante's two sons to the city of his birth, and over 600 manuscripts survive from the fourteenth century alone.

The majority of images in this chapter are taken from the British Library manuscript, Yates Thompson MS 36, made in Tuscany for Alfonso V, king of Aragon, Naples and Sicily (reigned 1416–58). The luminous images of saints and angels, of the couple flying over Florence and of Beatrice touching the white rose (Images 2, 6) are by Giovanni di Paolo (d.1482), who illustrated the book of *Paradiso*. His scenes of the nine circles of Paradise range from heavenly visions to beautiful Tuscan landscapes with gentle hills (Image 2). Another Sienese artist, Priamo della Quercia (d.1467), painted the scenes of *Purgatorio* and *Inferno*. His depiction of the gates of Hell (Image 4) is notable for the vivid colours of the buildings and clothing and the expressive qualities of the characters. A graceful and elegant Beatrice, in a flowing pink robe, smiles serenely as she floats against a background in lustrous blue tones. She is the authority figure, instructing Dante and guiding him with her touch (Image 6) and is the perfect model of femininity.

6 Dante and Beatrice before the Celestial Rose, with the Holy Trinity and the orders of angels among the petals, in Dante, *Paradiso*, Yates Thompson MS 36, f. 185r.

Numerous artists from Botticelli to William Blake have been inspired by Dante's work and have produced likenesses of Beatrice. The Pre-Raphaelite poet and artist, Dante Gabriel Rossetti, painted *Beata Beatrix* (now in the Tate Britain) as a portrait of his muse and wife, Elizabeth Siddal, in an ecstatic pose as Dante's Beatrice. He translated the *Vita Nuova* into English and remained fascinated by the relationship between the pair throughout his career. Beatrice's ethereal properties combined with her sense of purpose make her one of the most enthralling female characters in medieval literature.

23.

Princesses Mah Ji and Humayun

The mystical romance of Princess Mah Ji and Prince Shah Ji is known as the *Pem Nem*, which translates as 'The Toils of Love'. It belongs to a genre of Sufi (Islamic mystical) literature called the *prem marg* ('Path of Love'), in which the love story symbolises the quest of a Sufi seeking union with God. Mah Ji the beloved represents God, the ultimate goal of the seeker, Shah Ji. She is both a symbol of perfection and a real woman who suffers the pangs of love. The action takes place in an aristocratic milieu that mirrors the Deccani court of southern India in the sixteenth century. The intimate and colourful illustrations (all taken from the unique manuscript of this text, now in the British Library) provide a link between the Sufi poetic tradition and the characters, who exist within a Hindu culture that would have been familiar to the book's intended audience. While the spiritual progression of the hero is conveyed through the varied landscapes, the interior scenes focus on women's life at court. Details of dress and furnishings are portrayed in exquisite detail, as are the elaborate wedding ceremonials; this is perhaps an indication that the book was intended for a woman of the court.[1]

The heroine Mah Ji is a beautiful young princess who lives on an island

---

1 Shah Ji, seated on a carpet with the king of Kuldip, faints at the sight of his beloved, in the *Pem Nem* (c.1600) Add MS 16880, f. 82v.

2 Detail of Shah Ji with an image of Mah Ji on his breast; he is resting in the wilderness while looking for her, in the *Pem Nem*, Add MS 16880, f. 47r.

called Sangaldip, where her father is king. The love story begins when an image of Mah Ji is brought to Prince Shah Ji by a tortoise. She in turn receives a picture of Shah Ji, delivered in the same way (sadly the tortoise does not appear in any illustrations). The two fall deeply in love and the face of the princess appears etched on Shah Ji's chest, representing an image of her that he carries around with him in his heart (Image 2).

Shah Ji leaves his home in the northern kingdom of Kuldip, setting off on a journey southwards to find his beloved. He travels through rocky landscapes, seeing only wild animals, and his isolation mirrors his feelings of longing for Mah Ji. Then he must cross the ocean to reach the island of Sangaldip where the princess lives. He is met by the king, who (fortuitously) is his uncle, and is taken to the palace where the beautiful Mah Ji and her female attendants are waiting. When she appears and walks through the garden towards him, he is so overcome at the sight of her that he faints, falling over backwards, to the astonishment of the king and courtiers. In the background a huge pink, blue and white plant with red blossoms reflects Mah Ji's beauty (Image 1); this is a

3a Shah Ji cries a river of tears (left); **3b** Shah Ji speaks to Mah Ji in the palace; a golden spray from his mouth represents his words of love (right), in the *Pem Nem*, Add MS 16880, f.90v, f. 119r.

sign that she is the beloved one. The two herons beside the ornamental lake in the background are a reminder of the joining together of male and female in the animal world.

But the path of love is not smooth. Shah Ji becomes convinced that the Mah Ji he has just met is merely a reflection of the image on his chest, which in fact is his real beloved. He experiences a great inner struggle, weeping a river of tears (Image 3a), but decides he must leave the flesh-and-blood princess and devote himself to contemplation that will lead him to the truth. He bids his Mah Ji a sad farewell and walks out of the palace, leaving her alone and desolate.

Mah Ji goes through a period of pining and lament lasting for the twelve months of the Hindu calendar, including the festivals of Holi and Diwali. As the year passes the seasons reflect her changing emotions, mirroring a Sufi poem of spiritual awakening. She spends her time with her ladies in the garden of the palace but keeps her distance, appearing sad and lonely with her eyes

4a (left) Mah Ji playing board games and tending to pet birds with her companions during her period of separation from Shah Ji, in the *Pem Nem*, Add MS 16880, f. 135r.

4b (above) Mah Ji is doused with water to cool the flames of love, in the *Pem Nem*, Add MS 16880, f. 138r.

downcast (Image 4a). At Holi she sits apart, resting her head on her hand while her maid pours water over the flames of love that surround her (Image 4b). She is portrayed as an elegant and dignified figure, fulfilling her duties at court, though her deep sadness cannot be disguised.

During a year of soul-searching and meditation, Shah Ji gradually comes to realise that he has been greatly mistaken. It is of course the real Mah Ji who is the object of his affection, not her image; his love for her is true and she is not an illusion. So he returns to the palace to find her, fainting again with emotion when they are reunited. Mah Ji is overjoyed and the couple spend many happy hours together in the palace, making plans for the future.

Before long a wedding is planned and an auspicious date is set. The marriage is celebrated with all the elaborate ritual befitting a royal couple at the court of Bijapur; a third of the thirty-four images in the manuscript illustrate the preparations and extended rituals of the wedding, including the adornment of the bride, the procession of the bridegroom and the wedding meal of the couple. Mah Ji is prepared beforehand by her women; her arms are decorated (Image 5) and she dons the traditional wedding garments and jewellery. Shah

5 Dancers entertain Mah Ji as her arms are beautified before her wedding, in the *Pem Nem*, Add MS 16880, f. 184r.

Ji arrives on a horse, accompanied by a procession of musicians, dancing girls and an elephant. He lifts his bride into the bridal palanquin and they are carried to a pavilion in the gardens where they are left alone at last. In one of the wedding rituals (Image 6) they wash hands together in a gold basin as a symbol of their union. This is the joyful ending to Shah Ji's long quest and Mah Ji's year of patient waiting. After many trials they have reached the pinnacle of fulfilment and true happiness, just as a mystic reaches the end of a spiritual journey by attaining true perfection and understanding.

The *Pem Nem* is a unique legend, though it is related to other Persianate romances and contains similar themes. It takes the form of a *masnavi* or narrative poem in rhyming couplets, a genre frequently employed in spiritual poetry. The text survives in only one manuscript, now part of the Urdu collections in the British Library, and believed to be an autograph copy by its author Hasan Manjhu Khalji. It has been dated to the city of Bijapur in the 1590s, during the reign of the cosmopolitan Sultan Ibrahim Adil Shah II, a mystic and an enlightened patron of the arts.

One of the most fascinating aspects of the *Pem Nem* legend is the language. While the text is clearly copied in elegant calligraphic script, the poem is difficult to decipher as it was composed in an obscure, early form of Deccani Urdu and contains some words from Marathi and other local dialects of the area. The British scholar David Matthews, who identified and studied the text, found that the unique dialect combined with what appeared to be wordplay (including strings of single-syllable words without discernible syntax) made a line-for-line translation almost impossible. With his extensive knowledge of Urdu language and literature, he managed to decipher enough of the text so that, with the help of the thirty-four illustrations, the story could be followed and understood.

The images are unusual in that they show visually the emotions of the leading characters. Shah Ji has a river of tears spouting from his eyes; Mah Ji is shown engulfed in the flames of passion (Images 3a, 4b). Their surroundings are often reflections of their heightened emotions or isolation (Images 2, 4a). The portrait of Mah Ji on the chest of Shah Ji is a powerful reminder of his feelings of love for her and shows his mistaken belief that the image is more real than the woman herself. The idea of the lover's heart being attached to an image of the beloved is a trope in Indian romance literature, but this is a rare example where it is clearly illustrated. Though the settings are real, the characters themselves have a sense of mystery and wonder. Mah Ji herself combines the roles of the ethereal goal of Shah Ji's quest and the real woman with strong emotions who is adorned in traditional costume for her wedding.

Humayun

Humayun is a Chinese princess, daughter of the Faghfur or emperor of China, and her lover Humay is a Syrian prince, but their story is similar in many ways to that of the Indian lovers, Mah Ji and Shah Ji (notably, both pairs of lovers have almost identical names). Again, their trials of love represent a journey of the soul towards perfection, told in the language of courtly love and in the form of a *masnavi*.

The young lovers' desire for one another begins, as it did for Mah Ji and Shah Ji, with the popular literary topos of a picture of the beloved. One day when out hunting Humay chases a magical onager (Asian wild ass) with ruby lips and golden hooves, following the creature through a desert and into a magical garden. There a fairy shows him a picture of the beautiful Humayun

---

6 Mah Ji and Shah Ji wash hands together as part of the wedding ceremony, in the *Pem Nem*, Add MS 16880, f. 224v.

and he falls deeply and irrevocably in love with her. The fairy encourages him to use the beautiful image to guide him towards the inner meaning it conceals, thereby attaining selflessness. Without a thought for home and family, Humay sets off on a long and treacherous journey to find Humayun, accompanied by his foster-brother Bihzad. They have many improbable adventures and are beset by temptations, to which Humay regularly succumbs. At one stage they are captured by evil cannibal pirates but their ship runs aground in a storm and miraculously all except the two heroes are drowned. Having barely recovered from their ordeal they are dismayed to see a group of horsemen galloping towards them. They cannot believe their luck when, rather than attacking them, the horsemen explain that their king has just died and according to custom they have set out to make the first person they meet their new ruler. Humay thus becomes king of the Empire of the East and for a time he is contented to rule his kingdom, forgetting all about his quest. Then one night Humayun appears in a dream and reproaches him, saying:

> If you are a true lover, forgo the throne
> Bear witness to your love with the blood of your heart![2]

So 'without any companion save the grief of his heart'[3] Humay sets out once more to find his beloved. He crosses a sea of fire, kills a malicious sorcerer and captures his castle, finds the treasure of Kai Khusraw, and frees a young maiden called Parizad, who turns out to be the cousin of Humayun. They journey onwards to China and there they are received at the Faghfur's court. Parizad rushes off to tell her cousin about her rescuer, praising Humay to the skies for his bravery and good looks. Humayun cannot wait to see for herself and when she enters the room, Humay is stunned, fainting at the wondrous apparition. When he awakes she has vanished and he is obliged to join a hunting party organised by the Faghfur. He manages to evade his companions and races back to court, arriving at nightfall to find Humayun on her balcony gazing out over the beautiful garden beneath. The scene is illustrated in Image 7, including a *bait* or verse describing her bright face and dark hair, which are compared to the moon and night sky:

> The prince spied the moon at the edge of the roof.
> Plaited round his moon he saw the evening.[4]

7 Humay arrives at the gate of Humayun's castle, in Khvaju Kirmani, *Humay and Humayun* (Baghdad, 1396) Add MS 18113, f. 18v.

Though the building is modelled on a real palace in Iran, a comparison with the balcony scene in Shakespeare's *Romeo and Juliet* immediately comes to mind. Having killed a guard who has challenged him, Humay climbs over the wall and onto the roof of the palace, singing a love song. Humayun and Parizad invite him in and the lovers are at last able to embrace, exchanging vows of love.

When he leaves, Humay kills a faithful old gardener who bars his way and so before long he is arrested and imprisoned by the Faghfur in the castle of Turan. Luckily the lord of the castle's daughter is besotted with the captive, and promises to set him free if he will spend a few nights with her, which he does. Once he is free he rides back to Humayun's castle, but she has heard about his compromise and dismisses him at once. Humay rides away dejectedly, but before long Humayun regrets her action and follows him, disguised as a man. They meet in a forest and without revealing her identity she challenges him to a duel. They fight long and hard until finally Humay knocks Humayun to the ground (Image 8). The scene is described in the following lines:

When the love-nourishing king took his dagger
The fairy-faced (one) drew her helmet from head.[5]

Humay recognises his beloved in time and faints (again), but before long the pair are blissfully in one another's arms.

Though the lovers are together once more, Humay's trials are not yet over. He writes to Humayun's father to ask for her hand in marriage and ostensibly permission is granted. However the perfidious Faghfur imprisons his daughter in a chamber beneath the vizier's palace and when Humay arrives to claim his bride he receives instead a letter of condolence from her father. He is so distressed that he loses his reason and wanders into the desert, where he lives for a time among the wild animals. Luckily, help is once more at hand in the form of cousin Parizad, who uses her charms to captivate Farinush, the son of the vizier who is Humayun's captor. Farinush joins forces with Humay's long-lost companion Bihzad, who has miraculously appeared from out of the steppes with an army, and they rush off into the desert to find Humay. When they tell him the good news that his beloved is alive and well, he is immediately restored to health and the final happy solution is now within reach. In quick succession Humayun is freed, Humay kills the Faghfur in battle and takes over as king of China and the pair are married with great ceremony. After some time, Humay becomes homesick, and so, leaving the throne to the faithful and

8 Humayun fights Humay incognito; just as he is about to cut off her head with his dagger she reveals that she is his beloved, in *Humay and Humayun*, Add MS 18113, f. 23r.

9 Humay and Humayun feasting in a garden and listening to musicians, in *Humay and Humayun*, Add MS 18113, f.40v.

Maidens or Monsters?

competent Farinush and Parizad (now married), he returns with Humayun to the Kingdom of the East. Here he arranges the marriages of two young couples at his court (their equally star-crossed relationships are among the many and diverse sub-plots 'of Shakespearian complexity'[6] interrupting the main thread of the narrative; they have been omitted here for the sake of brevity!). Humay and Humayun then continue their journey to his home in Syria and before long Humayun gives birth to a son. The couple rule justly and peacefully for many years until Humayun dies, and Humay retreats to live in a cave, leaving the throne to his son, Jahangir.

Humay u Humayun is one of five poems from the *Khamsah* of the Persian court poet Kvaju Kirmani, composed in the first half of the fourteenth century and influenced both by the earlier work of the famous Nizami (see Chapter 18) and traditional Persian folklore. The British Library manuscript featured here contains three of the poems in the *Khamsah* and was produced for Sultan Ahmad Jalayir in Baghdad. It is a rare copy of the text and is admired for its early calligraphy and exquisite illuminations.

In tandem with many Arabic and Persian works in the genre, as well as Western medieval romances (for example Guinevere, Chapter 19), the action centres on the hero Humay who rides off on a quest, conquers evil in many guises, succumbs to temptation in the form of other women, and finally attains his romantic and dynastic goals. Four happy marriages are contracted and future stability is implied for the three kingdoms of China, the Empire of the East and Syria. Motifs such as the portrait, music, the involvement of animals in the plot, the capture of a castle, fainting, imprisonment and madness are common themes.

However, even more so than for Princess Shah Ji, the reader is told very little of the character, thoughts and feelings of the heroine, Humayun, and the images, though exquisite, provide few clues. The atmosphere is romantic, with lyrical descriptions of gardens and natural scenes. Humay expresses his feelings in music and poetic speeches – one even addressed to a candle and another to a cloud. But Humayun, from the evidence available, is given few chances to speak. J. C. Bürgel, who provides the fullest accessible synopsis of the plot in English, has only this to say in his discussion of the portrait episode: 'Humayun is intended to be a symbol of God, or, at least, of God's beauty'.[7] In Image 8, the mystical union of the couple is echoed in the natural world, where the horses and trees form perfect pairs: a series of mirror images. Humayun, like Mah Ji, is both courtly heroine and spiritual goal, both strong-willed princess and mystical dream vision. Her emotions and motivations as a literary character are elusive, perhaps because it is of questionable value to view heroines of *masnavi* from a psychological perspective.

Three personifications: Fortune with her wheel, Raison (Reason) and Vertu (Virtue), in Martin de France, *Lestrif de Fortune et Vertu* (an allegorical debate between Fortune and Virtue) (S. Netherlands, late 15th century) Royal MS 16 F IV, f. 3r.

Mystical, Magical and Allegorical Women

Part Six

dames et damoiselles du pa
is et comment elle se parti
en fourme de serpente. C. iii.

24.

The Fairy Melusine

The medieval legend of Melusine had its origins in human-hybrid and fairy-lover folktales of the oral traditions of Britain and France. The protagonist is a fairy woman who is half-human, half-snake and is one of the most elusive, yet compelling, characters in medieval literature. As she is of fairy lineage, her union with a mortal man is transgressive, ending in tragedy and flight, but not before she builds a castle and founds a great dynasty.

Melusine's story begins before her birth, when her recently widowed father, King Elinas of Albany (Scotland), is out hunting in the forest and comes upon a lovely young woman singing beside a fountain. She is the fairy Presine, and her song is so beautiful that the king forgets all about hunting, follows her through the forest and asks her to marry him. She agrees on one condition (and this is a foretaste of the taboo on her daughter, Melusine): that he does not try to visit her when she is giving birth to one of their children.

Elinas gives his promise, they marry before long, and Presine gives birth to triplet daughters, Melusine, Melior and Palatina. But Elinas is so overjoyed when he hears the news that he rushes to her side too soon, forgetting his promise. As soon as she sees him, Presine gathers up her daughters and disappears with them to l'Isle-Perdue ('Hidden Island'). Later they move to Avalon, where the girls grow up hearing every day from their mother that had

1 Melusine transforms into a serpent and flies out of the window of the Chateau de Lusignan, watched by incredulous courtiers, in Jean d'Arras, *Roman de Melusine* (Amiens, *c*.1445) Harley MS 4418, f. 214v.

2a–c Female hybrids in the margins of:

2a The Gorleston Psalter (East Anglia, c.1315) Add MS 49622, f. 68v;

2b The St Omer Hours (N. France, c.1320) Add MS 36684, f. 96v;

2c The Luttrell Psalter (Lincolnshire, c. 1330) Add MS 42130, f. 175r.

their father kept his word they would all be living happily with him in Albany. Melusine persuades her two sisters that they should avenge their mother by imprisoning King Elinas in Mount Brumbelioys in Northumberland. But Presine is outraged at this betrayal of their father and punishes each of them with a fairy curse. Melusine's punishment is that every Saturday she will turn into a serpent from the waist down; if she hides this from the man she marries, she will prosper and so will her family, but if her husband discovers her secret the consequences will be disastrous. Her sister Melior is sent off to exile in a castle in Armenia and Palatine is imprisoned in the mountain of Guigo in Aragon. Later, Elinas dies and Presine buries him in a noble tomb guarded by a giant.

Meanwhile Melusine leaves Avalon and wanders in the forest of Coulombiers in Poitou where she is destined to meet her future husband, the Breton Prince Raymondin, nephew of the Count of Poitiers. This is how it happens. One evening while Raymondin is out hunting in the forest with his uncle the two set off in pursuit of a particularly ferocious wild boar, leaving their attendants far behind. Near a spring in the middle of the forest, they are confronted by the dangerous beast, and Raymondin, while dealing the final blow to the boar, fatally wounds his uncle by accident (Image 3).

Aghast at what has happened and overcome by deep remorse, Raymondin is wandering aimlessly on forest paths when he is seen by three fairy maidens who are dancing in a glade by the light of the moon. Melusine, one of the three,

3 Raymondin is distraught at the death of his uncle, who lies beside the wild boar he has just killed, in the *Roman de Melusine*, Harley MS 4418, f. 17r.

4 The marriage of Raymondin and Melusine, in the *Roman de Melusine*, Harley MS 4418, f. 36r.

takes him by the hand and wakes him from his reverie. As soon as he lays eyes on her, he is captivated.

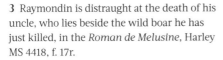

Et quant Raimondin l'oyt, si la regarda, et apperceut la grant beaulté qui estoit en elle, et s'en donna grant merveille; car il luy sembla que oncques mès si belle n'eut veue. Adoncques Raimondin sauta de dessus son chevau, et s'encline reveramment.

And when Raymondin heard her voice, he looked at her and found that she possessed great beauty, and he marvelled at it; for it seemed to him that he had never seen anyone so beautiful. Then Raymondin leapt down from his horse and bowed reverently.[1]

He is amazed that the beautiful maiden knows his name and seems to know all about him. Melusine promises that if he is faithful to God, she will help him to become the most powerful of his noble lineage. In return he asks her to marry him and she accepts, on condition that he promise never to question her about where she goes on Saturdays. On Melusine's advice, Raymondin returns to court at Poitiers, where everyone believes his story that his uncle was killed by the wild boar, and an elaborate funeral is held. Raymondin is granted land

5 Melusine at the building of the Chateau de Lusignan, *Roman de Melusine*, Harley MS 4418, f. 43v.

by his cousin, the new Count of Poitiers, and he brings Melusine to court. An elaborate wedding feast takes place, after which the couple are blessed in a chapel surrounded by the great and good of Poitiers (Image 4).

The Count of Poitiers and his courtiers wonder about Melusine's origins and ancestry, but Raymondin persuades them that she is of noble birth and she soon wins the admiration of all for her beauty and courtly demeanour. No sooner has everyone departed after the wedding celebrations, than Melusine assembles a great workforce to clear the ground and build a castle that is *grande et forte à merveilles* ('marvellously huge and strong'). She calls together all the nobility of Poitiers to admire her work and names it the Chateau de Lusignan. By now Melusine is pregnant and she gives birth to a boy, Urien, who has very large ears and one red and one blue eye. Meanwhile Raymondin, to whom Melusine has revealed that he is the son of Henry the Lion, goes to Brittany to

6 Urien and Guyon fight a sea battle near Rhodes, in the *Roman de Melusine*, Harley MS 4418, f. 80v.

claim his rightful inheritance. When he returns he finds that Melusine has built the town of Lusignan surrounded by huge defensive walls and battlements.

In the years that follow Melusine bears nine more sons to Raymondin, several of them marked with strange signs and deformities because of their supernatural origins. She is an exemplary mother, instructing them in the arts of chivalry, military strategy and good government, and when they ride out to win power and prestige, she supplies them with generous resources for their expeditions. Eight of her sons go on to occupy high positions in Europe and the East, establishing the illustrious Lusignan dynasty. Intertwining episodes in the central part of the legend give an exciting account of their respective sieges, naval battles, jousts, victories and marriages to heiresses.

Two of the Lusignan sons, Urien and Guyon, set off for Cyprus to relieve the king who has asked for help against Saracen invaders. Melusine provides them with a substantial force of men, ships, horses and provisions and they arrive in Cyprus, having won a decisive victory against Saracen enemies on the way (Image 6). The king has a daughter, Hermine, who is young and beautiful and who is entranced when she hears of Urien's strength and prowess, despite his strange appearance. The young heroes arrive in Cyprus, and the invaders are duly defeated but in the process Hermine's father is mortally wounded. Before he dies, Urien promises to marry his daughter, thereby inheriting the kingdom of Cyprus (though apparently he later regrets his promise as he would rather travel the world before settling down).

Two other brothers, Antoine and Renaud, marry the daughters of the rulers of Luxembourg and Bohemia and the eldest, Urien, befriends the Sultan of Damascus, travelling with him to Jerusalem and establishing a truce that will allow Christian pilgrims access to Jerusalem for 100 years, before returning to govern his inherited lands in Poitou.

Meanwhile back in Lusignan all is not well. Raymondin's brother has sown doubt in his mind about Melusine's absence every Saturday – is she being unfaithful to him or is she hiding something sinister? So Raymondin decides to spy on her in her bath one Saturday (Image 7); he uses his sword to make a small hole in the wall of her chamber and this is what he sees:

[Il] vit Melusine qui estoit en la cuve jusques au nombril en signe de femme, et peignoit ses cheveulx; et du nombril en bas en signe de la queue d'une serpente grosse comme ung quaque à harenc, et moult longuement debatoit sa queue en l'eaue, tellement qu'elle le faisoit bondir jusques à la voulte de la chambre.

[He] saw Melusine in the bath; down to her navel she looked like a woman, and was combing her hair; and from the navel down she had the tail of a serpent, as fat as a herring barrel, and she flapped her tail around in the water at length, and so vigorously that she made it bounce right up to the ceiling of the room.[2]

Raymondin is devastated and rushes away, lamenting that he has lost his lovely wife, 'the most loyal and best of women ever born, next to she who bore our Saviour' (i.e. the Virgin Mary). He berates his brother for causing him to doubt Melusine, and warns him to leave his castle immediately before he does something he will regret. Raymondin laments all night (and for a whole paragraph), but in the morning Melusine comes to lie beside him and so he imagines she did not notice him spying on her. However, some time later, when the news reaches Lusignan that their son Geuffroy has burned an abbey with all the monks inside it, the enraged Raymondin calls Melusine a

7 Melusine's husband secretly watches her bathing, in a woodcut from *Dis ouentürlich buch bewiset wie von einer frauwen genantt Melusina...* ('This Adventure Book Tells How a Woman Named Melusina...') (Strasbourg, *c.*1477).

'*tresfaulce serpente*' ('deceptive serpent') and blames her impure blood for the fact that none of their sons are good people. Melusine falls to the ground in a faint, realising that she can no longer stay with Raymondin. Having made her preparations, she climbs onto the windowsill, bids her lord and his companions adieu and flies away in the form of a dragon, circling above Lusignan, crying out and lamenting in a pitiful voice (Image 1).

Adieu mon amy, mon bien, mon cueur et ma joye...tu ne me verras jamais plus en forme de femme.	*Farewell my dearest friend, my heart, my joy...you will never again see me in woman's form.*[3]

The people of the city lament, as Melusine had brought them prosperity and good fortune, and in all the churches and abbeys prayers are offered up for her. But she is gone forever, returning only at night to watch over her younger sons and, later, to foretell with dire screams the death of each successive Count of Lusignan. Raymondin comes to bitterly regret his betrayal and makes a pilgrimage to Rome, retiring to a hermitage to die.

The *Roman de Melusine ou la Noble Histoire de Lusignan* ('Romance of Melusine or the Noble History of Lusignan') was composed by Jean d'Arras in 1393, with a poetic version by the Parisian author Couldrette following shortly afterwards, in the early 1400s. The story borrows from Arthurian and other legends such as *Henno aux grandes dents* ('Henno of the Big Teeth') in which Henno's mother is seen in the bath with a dragon's body, and *La Dame du chateau d'Esperver* ('The Lady of Esperver Castle') in which the lady (a diabolical spirit) escapes from Holy Mass by breaking out through the wall of the castle chapel and flying away.

Yet d'Arras's text is a strange mixture of fact and fiction; he uses fairy-tale characters and supernatural events to create mythical origins for the powerful Lusignan dynasty, in reality one of Europe's foremost families who famously participated in the Crusades. And because of this genealogical link, d'Arras is compelled to make Melusine into a Christian woman. When she first meets Raymondin in the forest she claims that she is '*de par Dieu et crois comme bon catholique doibt croire*' ('I am on the side of God and believe as a good Catholic should'). The combination of the supernatural and the religious may seem incongruous, but the two come together seamlessly in other legends such as the Holy Grail. In addition, the deeds of Melusine's sons (the Lusignan brothers) are presented as a historical narrative, though d'Arras invents and alters events to suit his purposes. For example, rather than winning a glorious battle against the Saracens (as Urien does in the romance) the real Guy de Lusignan bought the island of Cyprus in 1191 from the English king, Richard the Lionheart, who had captured it from the Byzantines during the Third Crusade.

Jean, Duc de Berry, who commissioned the *Roman de Melusine* from d'Arras, laid siege to the Chateau de Lusignan during the reconquest of Poitou from the English in 1373. (It was said that Melusine paid her last visit at this time.) The duke was an important patron of the arts and brother of the French king who became the new Lord of Lusignan. He also commissioned the famous illuminated Book of Hours known as *Les Très Riches Heures du Duc de Berry*, in which a dragon is shown flying over the castle (Image 8).

From the twelfth century onwards, noble families in Europe had developed a strong interest in genealogy, and this led to a proliferation of semi-historical works allying them with fictional forebears. Legendary ancestors

8 A dragon flying over the Chateau de Lusignan in the calendar page for March, in *Les Très Riches Heures du Duc de Berry* (Netherlands and France, 15th century) Chantilly, Musée Condé, MS 65, f. 3v.

from Charlemagne to the Trojan heroes were claimed by various powerful figures. Jean de Berry himself claimed ancestry from Melusine through his mother, Bonne of Luxembourg, said to be descended from Antione, one of Melusine's sons. Similarly, Jacquetta of Luxembourg, mother of Elizabeth Woodville (who married the English king Edward IV), was believed to have descended from Melusine, and so the English royal family was linked to this same fairy ancestor from the fifteenth century. The Chateau de Lusignan itself fell into disrepair and was demolished in the eighteenth century; today only some of the foundations remain.

conugio ſernoꝛ.
natus ex libero uentre.
cognacōne ſpūituali·
cognacōne legali·
eo qui cognouit coſanguineā uxis ſue.
conſanguinitate ⁊ affinitate
frigidis ⁊ maleficiatis. ac impotētia coeundi·
mitimo̅io cōt̅ iɴde̅m ecē contracto.

his qui filii ſunt legittimi
qui mitimo̅ium accuſare poſſunt ul̅ teſtificari·
diuoꝛcijs.
donacōib; int̅ uir̅ ⁊ uxrem. ac dote p̅r diuoꝛciu̅ reſtitu̅
ſecundis nupcijs.

Contverere dn̅e et eripe animam mean
ſaluum me fac propter miſericoꝛdiam ꜩtat

25

Mermaids and Sirens

Mermaids and Sirens have played a leading role in legend and folklore around the world from ancient times. Their images are found in the most unlikely places and in many different forms. In the medieval and Renaissance periods they were carved on tombs and statues, inside temples and churches, and on palaces and fountains. They appear regularly in the margins of medieval manuscripts, especially prayer books and psalters, but also law books, bibles and historical texts, where they are commonly shown coquettishly holding a comb or mirror (Images 1a, 1b) or suckling their young (1c).

These fascinating creatures are related to the fish-deities, both male and female, which are represented in art from earliest antiquity, and are found in carvings and statues from as far afield as Ireland, Serbia and Israel, and are in some cases related to the mother goddess of fertility. In the Chinese *Shan Hai Jing* ('Book of Mountains and Seas'), there are a variety of 'fish-women' characters including the *Diren* who is like our mermaid in appearance, and

1a A mermaid, with a mirror and comb, is approached by a traveller with a staff and a dog, in the Luttrell Psalter (N. England, c.1330) Add MS 42130, f. 70v.

1b A mermaid with a mirror (or is it an apple she is plucking from the branch above her?) and a (rare) merman are in the margins of the Smithfield Decretals, a law book (Toulouse, 1300; decorated London, c.1340) Royal MS 10 E IV, f. 3r.

1c A mermaid suckling her child, with an acrobatic monkey on her tail, in the Alphonso Psalter (Westminster, c.1300) Add MS 24686, f. 13r.

2 Two Sirens (one winged, with clawed feet, and the other with a fish's tail, holding a mirror), swim beside a ship with sailors who are under their spell, in the Queen Mary Psalter (London, c.1315) Royal MS 2 B VII, f. 96v.

the *Lingyu* who is described as having a human face, a fish tail and human feet. Examples from early Middle Eastern cultures include the Syrian Atargatis, as well as male fish-gods such as Dagan of Mesopotamia, and Oannes from Babylon. Atargatis is the Syrian goddess of love and fertility and partner of Hadad, god of thunderstorms. In one story she fell in love with a shepherd and they conceived a child, but as he was mortal her love was too strong and killed him. Heartbroken, she tried to drown herself in a lake, but because she was so beautiful the gods would not let her die and turned her into a half-fish.

In Slavic tradition, the *rusalka* was a pagan water spirit with long, flowing hair who provided life-giving moisture to forests and farms. She later developed into a young woman who was betrayed by her husband or lover and died a violent death, often by suicide, and thus became an unclean soul that lurked in the depths of a lake or river. The well-known Czech opera, *Rusalka*, by Dvořák, is based on this tale, and it may have provided the inspiration for Hans Christian Andersen's nineteenth-century fairy tale, *The Little Mermaid*, in which a young mermaid gives up her enchanting voice in exchange for a potion that will enable her to walk on earth. However, only if she wins the love of an earthly prince whom she saved from drowning will she become immortal, otherwise she will die. When the prince does not fall in love with her because she cannot speak to him and instead marries another woman, she throws herself into the sea and dissolves into foam, becoming a spirit of the air.

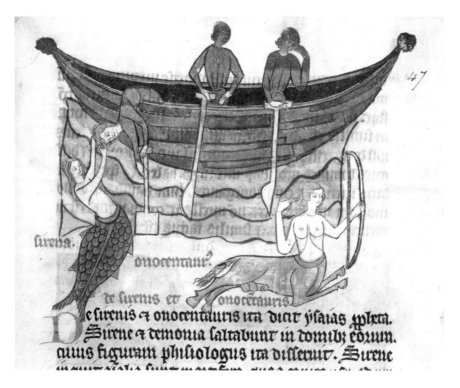

sirena.

onocentaur?

te sirenis et onocentauris.

De sirenis et onocentauris ita dicit ysaias propheta. Sirene et demonia saltabunt in domibus eorum. cuius figuram phisiologus ita disserit. Sirene in mari stabiles sunt...

3 A sailor plugs his ear to block out the sound of the Siren's charm; his shipmate is already being pulled by his hair into the sea, entranced by the Siren's beauty and her melody; below is a centaur holding a bow, in Hugh of Fouilloy, *Aviarium, Bestiary* (N. France, early 13th century) Sloane MS 278, f. 47r.

Sirens first appear in Greek mythology in Homer's *Odyssey* dated to the eighth century BC. Here the enchantress, Circe (who is herself a daughter of the ocean nymph Perse), warns Odysseus against the *femmes fatales* who will be lying in wait for him on his way home to Ithaca: 'Whoso in ignorance draws near to them and hears the Sirens' voice, he nevermore returns… the Sirens beguile him with their clear-toned song'.[1] She advises him to plug his sailors' ears with beeswax so that they will not be captivated by the Sirens' voices, revealing to him that there is a way he himself can hear them without being lured to his death. He should have his sailors bind his hands and feet to the mast of the ship but leave his ears unblocked; then even if he implores and commands them to let him free, they should ignore him or fasten the ropes even more tightly.

Following these instructions, the crew row their vessel as fast as they are able. When the Sirens call Odysseus by name, promising him access to their knowledge of all things, past and future, even he, the 'Glory of the Greeks', cannot resist their enticements and asks his men to free him from the ropes that tie him to the mast. But two of his comrades, Eurylochus and Perimedes, refuse to do so and in the end everyone escapes unharmed. Homer does not give a physical description of the Sirens, only of their beautiful voices, though as the Greek noun (Σειρήν, Seirên)) is feminine, we know that they are women. He locates their island near the rock of Scylla in a desolate territory littered with human remains: 'in a meadow, and about them is a great heap of bones of mouldering men and round the bones the skin is shrivelling'.[2]

The two Sirens in the Odyssey become three in later stories, named Aglaopheme, Thelxiepia and Pisonia, and they are described as having wings and playing musical instruments. They live on the island of Anthemoessa and are either the daughters of the river god Achelous or the sea god Phorcys. In the legend of Jason and the Argonauts, the *Argo* and its crew of Argonauts are almost lured to their death by them but their singing is drowned by the sweeter music of Orpheus and so they escape. Some say that the Sirens were so distressed at having failed to capture both Odysseus and Jason that they killed themselves. But what would have happened to Odysseus and Jason had they not managed to escape? It was said that those whom the Sirens captured with their songs either threw themselves into the sea and drowned, fell asleep for eternity or were torn apart as they slept.

However, some ancient writers, including Plutarch, had a more positive attitude towards Sirens; he described their songs as part of the music of the spheres that enticed souls towards the stars: 'delightfully charming, and detaining the souls which pass from hence thither and wander after death; working in them a love for divine and heavenly things, and a forgetfulness of everything on earth; and they extremely pleased follow and attend them'.[3]

Sirens first make an appearance in Christian texts in the Latin Vulgate, the translation of the Bible by St Jerome in the late fourth century. In a passage from the Old Testament Book of Isaiah, the city of Babylon is described after its destruction as filled with ghastly creatures – and here he renders the Hebrew *thennin* ('jackal') as the Latin *sirena*:

sed requiescent ibi bestiae et replebuntur domus eorum draconibus et habitabunt ibi strutiones et pilosi saltabunt ibi; et respondebunt ibi ululae in aedibus eius et sirenae in delubris voluptatis

but wild beasts shall rest there, and their houses shall be filled with serpents, and ostriches shall dwell there, and the hairy ones shall dance there: And owls shall answer one another there, in the houses thereof, and Sirens in the temples of pleasure.[4]

ex pli cit liber

jn

m1

uu

cel

eft

Ab

bei

peregr

moabi

fua a

uocab

uxor

duobu

all

ep

ui

gu

m

m

martul noemi.

4 Siren-like creatures
decorate the letter *I[n Diebus
unius judicis]* ('In the Days
when Judges Ruled') above
and below an image of Old
Testament characters at the
beginning of the Book of
Ruth in the Montpellier Bible
(Lyons, early 12th century)
Harley MS 4772, f. 120v.

So here Sirens are associated with snakes, and Jerome compares them to Satan, who seduced Eve in the garden of Eden with his Siren-like voice.

For Jerome and early theologians, Sirens were unequivocally cursed; they became entirely negative figures and were associated with Lilith, the night monster or female demon of Jewish folklore. In his *Commentariorum in Isaim prophetam* ('Commentary on Isaiah'), Jerome warns Christians against them in the strongest terms:

5 Mermaids (one with wings) play musical instruments, in Brunetto Latini, *Li Livres dou Trésor* ('The Book of Treasures') (Thérouane, early 14th century) Yates Thompson MS 19, f. 150v.

The hydra and the scorpion who are in poetic fables, burn them in a hot fire, crush them under your sandal: the hounds of Scylla and the deathly songs of the Sirens, pass them by with your ears blocked; so that we can listen and understand what the prophet Isaiah said.[5]

Jerome and Augustine considered them not fully human and therefore cursed; they were seen in the same light as monsters and demons. The Sirens' music was associated with worldly pleasures such as dancing, and they became a symbol of female vice and temptation. They represented wantonness and sexual enticement as well as pagan rites and the sinful practices that the Church was determined to quash in the early days of Christianity. Some writers compared Siren songs to the lure of classical, pre-Christian philosophy and literature, which they saw as dangerous; in their view it was preferable, indeed safer, for everyone to study only Christian texts.

And how exactly did people picture Sirens? In late antiquity and the early Middle Ages, images varied between bird-like and fish-like creatures, the latter being more like the mermaids we are familiar with (Image 5). The *Physiologus* (a moral Christian text of the third or fourth century that describes animals, birds and imaginary creatures) groups Sirens with onocentaurs, creatures with the torso of a man and the body of a donkey, and other half-human half-animal creatures. This type of classification is found in medieval encyclopaedic works.

Maidens or Monsters?

6 A twin-tailed Siren, representing the sin of flattery, with a sinking ship beside her, in *Fiore de virtù e de costumi* (Padua, mid-15th century) Harley MS 3448, f. 17v.

One illustration in a *Physiologus* manuscript from ninth-century Rheims (Bern, Burgerbibliothek MS 318) shows a Siren with a fish or salamander tail but the written description is of a bird-woman, so there seems to have been some confusion.

Sirens were viewed by some scholars as ancient prostitutes who used their wings and talons to wound and captivate men. For them, Christian heroes must ignore these threats and temptations in order to stay on the path to salvation, just as Odysseus and his men escaped the Sirens and Scylla to return to their home in Greece. Isidore of Seville, the seventh-century encyclopaedist, describes them as follows:

> *People imagine three Sirens who were part maidens, part birds, having wings and talons; one of them would make music with her voice, the second with a flute, and the third with a lyre. They would draw sailors, enticed by the song, into shipwreck. In truth, however, they were harlots, who, because they would seduce passers-by into destitution, were imagined as bringing shipwreck upon them. They were said to have had wings and talons because sexual desire both flies and wounds. They are said to have lived among the waves because the waves gave birth to Venus.*[6]

With time, artists and sculptors began portray Sirens with fish tails and human torsos, so that they became synonymous with mermaids. In the twelfth century twin-tailed Siren-mermaids began to appear, some with an uplifted tail in each hand (Image 6), which some have interpreted as the sign of a sexual predator. The comb and mirror which are often pictured as a mermaid's attributes (see Images 1a, 1b) are also associated with the wicked Whore of Babylon in the biblical Book of Revelations.

In the early histories and legends of Britain there is a tradition of sea monsters; the *Liber monstrorum,* a book of monsters of Anglo-Saxon origin, has one of the earliest descriptions of a Siren as a fish-like creature with a tail:

> *Sirens are sea-girls, who deceive sailors with the outstanding beauty*
> *of their appearance and the sweetness of their song, and are most like*
> *human beings from the head to the navel, with the body of a maiden, but*
> *have scaly fishes' tails, with which they always lurk in the sea.*[7]

In the Old English poem *Beowulf,* the evil mother-monster Grendel is from the same tradition; she is described as a *merewif* who lives in a foul cave under the sea. In the twelfth century, the Bestiary of Philippe de Thaon, dedicated to Queen Adeliza (wife of King Henry I of England) and written in the dialect of French spoken in England at the time, describes the Siren with both talons and a fish tail:

Sereine en mer hante,	*A Siren haunts the sea*
cuntre tempeste chante,	*She sings in a storm*
e plure en bel tens,	*And weeps in calm weather*
itel est sis talent;	*This is her way*
e de femme ad faiture	*She has the shape of a woman*
entresque a la ceinture,	*Up to the waist*
e les pez de faucun,	*And has falcons' feet*
e cue de peissun	*And the tail of a fish*[8]

Sirens and mermaids were part of both learned and popular tradition. In the *Historia regum Britanniae* ('History of the Kings of Britain'), the Welsh cleric, Geoffrey of Monmouth, tells how Brutus, who was sailing from Troy to found a new dynasty in Britain, had his ships attacked and almost overturned by Sirens in the waters around the British Isles. Collections of tales about King Arthur and his predecessors, including the popular *Roman de Brut* ('Romance of Brutus') included descriptions of these creatures who threatened sailors. In another twelfth-century French work, the popular account of the sea journey of an Irish monk, *Le Voyage de Saint Brendan,* includes encounters with a

7 Alexander and his army ride up to a river and the men are embraced by the women living in the water (S. Netherlands, c.1290–1300) Harley MS 4979, f. 68r.

huge serpent as well as a bird-like creature with huge claws who fought against a dragon while the terrified sailors watched from their boat. St Brendan was on a voyage to Paradise and the monsters he encountered at sea represent the evil forces he must overcome to get there.

The fantastic legends about Alexander the Great's life and deeds, as told in the medieval French *Roman d'Alexandre en Prose* ('Prose Alexander Romance') and related works, describe his encounters with strange mythical creatures including dragons, blemmyae (headless men with their faces in their chests) and talking trees at the edges of the known world. In one episode Alexander and his soldiers come upon a river filled with reeds, inhabited by beautiful naked women with hair down to their ankles. Some of the Macedonian soldiers cannot resist the call of these women and are dragged underwater, where they are held in a deathly embrace until they drown, while their companions watch, powerless (Image 7).

A popular legend told by the Greek geographer, Pausanias, was about a tragic mermaid named Thessaloniki who lived in sea off the coast of Greece in the second century AD. She was Alexander the Great's sister, whose hair he had washed with the waters of immortality; though he had found these waters at the Fountain of Youth in Asia, he did not drink them himself and so he died aged only 33. His sister was grief-stricken and haunted the Aegean Sea. It is said that to this day she hails passing ships and asks the sailors if her brother is alive or dead. If they tell her the truth – that he is long dead – she turns into a furious demon, pulling the ship and all its crew to the bottom of the ocean; if they say he still lives and reigns, she allows them to pass by unharmed.

8 On the left, Dante and Virgil meet the Slothful (Canto XVIII); on the right, Dante (in blue) kneels at the feet of a naked Siren, then he is saved by the good woman in pink with a halo. A miniature by Priamo della Quercia of Canto XIX of Dante's *Purgatorio* (Tuscany, c.1445) Yates Thompson MS 36, f. 98v.

In the *Divina Commedia* ('Divine Comedy') Dante meets a Siren in *Purgatorio* ('Purgatory'). She appears to him in a dream in the hour preceding dawn as a stammering, cross-eyed, sallow crone, but then under his gaze her complexion transforms and she begins to sing in an enticing manner. When she has him under her spell she tells him she is the Siren who seduced Ulysses (Odysseus): '*Io volsi Ulisse del suo cammin vago / Al canto mio*' ('I turned Ulysses from his path with my song').⁹ Then a saintly woman appears and reveals that the first woman is not the *dolce serena* ('sweet Siren') he imagined but 'rotten and stinking', and she rebukes Virgil for not taking better care of Dante, who has had a lucky escape. Virgil tears the Siren's clothes and reveals her belly so that the stench awakens Dante from his dream and he continues on his journey (Image 8).

The late fourteenth-century legend of Melusine, the fish-tailed fairy, is told in Chapter 24. Another character closely associated with Sirens in medieval literature was Circe, the female enchantress in Homer's *Odyssey* (see above), who also lured sailors to her island. Boccaccio, in *De mulieribus claris* ('On Famous Women'), claims that she was the daughter of the sea nymph Perse and that she used spells and incantations to change men into various types of wild beast. He describes her as a sinister woman who lived in Italy and used her caresses and sweet words to persuade men to abandon morality for a life of piracy and thieving, thus allowing their animal nature to dominate. In addition

Maidens or Monsters?

9 A cherubic mer-creature in the border of a page containing prayers for the Office of the Dead, in the Sforza Hours (Milan and Ghent/Brussels, c.1500) Add MS 34294, f. 270r.

Circe is accused of turning her husband into a woodpecker. On Sirens in general, Boccaccio goes as far as to claim that they are half-fish because like prostitutes they are slippery and have a habit of flipping about and babbling while they make love to men. They adorn themselves with luxurious clothes and entice foolish men to give them all their possessions so that they are drowned not in the sea but in the quagmire of lust.[10] So he blames women for enticing men into a life of criminality and comments that there are many temptresses about, including Circe and the Sirens, to lead men astray.

As medieval accounts of journeys to unknown lands were more widely circulated, mermaids and Sirens came to represent the exotic and alien. They were depicted at the edge of such maps as the fourteenth-century Hereford *Mappa Mundi* to represent the uncharted oceans and the lure of the unknown. Christopher Columbus believed he had seen a mermaid in the fifteenth century. In the late Middle Ages and the Renaissance images of sea nymphs and tritons were included in coats of arms and manuscript borders (Image 9) as part of the classical revival in art. To this day they are to be seen on figureheads, tattoos and in the logo of a well-known chain of coffee shops.

olubilis fortune zc
mance le vii. liuue
lequel selon mon ad
uis ie laque vn chap
pitres a translater en
estre le premier chappitre de se
licite pour bonne fortune z enuers
pour bien fortune non pas pour
estat parfait par la conueruacion
de tous biens sy comme lappelle
boece ne pour la diuision z faction
diuine sy comme nous crestiens
lentendons de se licite donc ques
quiest estre de fortune et biens
temporelz parle sy valeruns et
dit non pas aussi decelle qui est
en la speculacion de la premiere
verite et en la congnoissance des
choses diuines de laquelle a escrite
parle ou vi. liuue de ethiques
sy parler donc ques de ceste fortu
neuse mondaine felicite comme
valeruns ou vii. et dit ainsi
lacteur. Nous auons raconte
ou chapitre precedent plusieurs
exemples de fortune volable et
louable et muable mais nous
pouons pour raconter de fortune
constant et estable par sy ap ie
appert quelle a grant comnoissa

de laytement en moyen aduistez
et de bailler eschauscement prou
sperivez mais quant elle veult
oublier sa malerinte elle ne
baille point sans plus grant
plante de biens mais les bailles
tres srans et perpetuelz letra
la labeur valeruns entent peuie
tiel toute larme dun homme
sy comme vne vicaruee ou vnz
aultre office perpetuel lacteur
videamus ergo zc translateur
en ceste partie valeruns comme
amettre exemple de ceste mate
et en mect seulement deulx
lun dun riche romanvz lans
dun pour estreuse qui est mo
bel mais cellui qui est du rou
main est tout clev en la lettre
qui dit ainsi lacteur. Or veons
donc ques aquans de gruez de for
tune quintus metellus sut
estoure du premier iour de sa
naisance iusques alafin sluis
estoure / Elle le sist naistre prince
en ce monde elle lui donna tres
nobles parens elle lui adiousta
grant euue de couraige et
force de corps qui pou pour souffrir
a paines et labours elle lui
donna femme seconde de chaste

26.

Lady Fortune

An easily recognisable image in medieval manuscripts is the haughty female figure of Lady Fortune, turning her wheel to determine the fate of each and every one of her subjects. From rulers to lovers, and from the rich and powerful to the common man or woman, nobody could escape her tyrannical power. Kings and emperors are shown atop the wheel of fortune and then falling to its lowest point, a demonstration that pride comes before a fall, and Lady Fortune herself is often blindfolded, symbolising the randomness of human fate.

In a work of human history that extends from Creation in the biblical Book of Genesis to the reign of Julius Caesar, Lady Fortune is shown as a queen with a sceptre, turning a wheel holding four figures (Image 2). Two are dressed as kings; one is rising up the wheel, and is labelled *regnabo* ('I shall reign'), and the other at the height of power, is labelled *regno* ('I reign'). The other two figures wear plain white robes; one is tumbling head-first towards the ground, with the word *regnavi* ('I have reigned') and finally at the bottom, crushed by the wheel, lies the unfortunate fallen ruler, labelled *sum sine regno* ('I am without a kingdom'). The accompanying text charts the rise and fall of many famous figures including Alexander the Great and King Arthur.

So who was Fortuna, or the Lady Fortune, and what were her origins? Her antecedent among the ancient Greeks was probably a goddess named Tyche

1 Lady Fortune with her wheel, surrounded by supplicants, in *Les Fais et les dis des Romains*, a French translation of Valerius, *Facta et dicta memorabilia* ('Memorable Deeds and Sayings') (Paris, c.1475) Harley MS 4373, f. 14r.

2 Lady Fortune turns her wheel, in the *Histoire ancienne* ('Ancient History') (France, early 15th century) Stowe MS 54, f. 197r.

who appears on coins in the Hellenistic period, blindfolded and balancing on a ball. The Roman goddess Fortuna, who succeeded her, became a very important member of the pantheon of gods in the early years of the Roman empire, with numerous temples dedicated to her. For Virgil she was '*Fortuna omnipotens et ineluctabile fatum*'[1] ('all-powerful Fortune and inescapable fate'), governing the lives of all men and women, both rich and poor, as ordered by the divine will of Jupiter (Greek Zeus). The Roman historian Pliny later claimed:

> *Fortune is the only god whom everyone invokes; she alone is spoken of, she alone is accused and is supposed to be guilty... To her are referred all our losses and all our gains. and in casting up the accounts of mortals she alone balances the two pages of our sheet.*[2]

Belief in Lady Fortune as the mistress of human destiny was outlawed by the early Church, alongside the tradition of oracles and fortune-telling, as it was in conflict with the Christian concept of free will. For the fourth-century Church leader Jerome, all pagan gods were viewed as demons, only worshipped by Saracens and sinners. Nevertheless, the Roman beliefs persisted in popular culture, and Fortuna appears as part of the pantheon of gods in Martianus Capella's fifth-century work, *De nuptiis Philologiae et Mercurii* ('The Marriage of Philology and Mercury'), a commentary on the arts. Here she is portrayed

Maidens or Monsters?

3 Boethius and Philosophy discuss Fortune, who is half black and half white, her robe patterned with the letter F in gold; a rich family is on her right and a poor family on her left, in *Le Livre de Boece de Consolacion*, a French translation of Boethius, *De consolatione philosophiae* (Bourges, 1477) Harley MS 4336, f. 1v.

4 Virgil explains the role of Fortuna to Dante as they watch the torments in the fourth circle of Hell, in *Inferno*, Canto VII (Tuscany, *c*.1445) Yates Thompson MS 36, f. 12v.

as an immature, capricious 'chatterbox among women' ('*omnium garrula puellarum*')[3] who does not respect authority and is the last to arrive at the council of the gods, keeping Jupiter and the other gods waiting.

The concept that the fate of humankind was subject to the fickle mistress Fortuna remained popular in the Middle Ages but it had to be reconciled with Christian doctrine, in which an all-powerful God was believed to take care of humanity. Writers and philosophers looked for a solution to this problem. Some viewed Lady Fortune as a convenient explanation for 'hidden causes', or phenomena in the universe that were otherwise impossible to explain. In other words she was retained, but made subject to a supreme God. Boethius, the late Roman scholar and Christian philosopher, introduced Lady Fortune in his work, the *De consolatione philosophiae* ('The Consolation of Philosophy'), in which he attempted to reconcile the unreasonableness of fortune with the Christian message of salvation. In this work, the writer, imprisoned and awaiting death at the hands of the Ostrogothic king Theodoric, is visited in his cell by Lady Philosophy who comes to help him to accept his fate. She brings with her Lady Fortune, who is given the opportunity to defend herself; the two allegorical characters help Boethius to realise that both good and bad fortune are necessary for the world and advantageous to humanity, in that we are strengthened by our fortitude when we withstand adversity. Here Lady Fortune assumes the role of mediator between Divine Providence and humankind (Image 3).

It was perhaps Dante who achieved the most satisfactory reconciliation of Christian and pagan views. In the *Divina Commedia* ('Divine Comedy'), Virgil

5a–b Lady Fortune in Boccaccio, *De casibus virorum illustrium* ('On the Fates of Famous Men'):

5a Lady Fortune lectures Boccaccio in his study, in *Des Cas des nobles hommes et femmes* (a French translation by Laurent de Premierfait) (Bruges, *c*.1480) Royal MS 14 E V, f. 291r.

5b Poverty overcoming Fortune and, in the background, Andalo del Negro delivering a lecture, in *Des Cas des nobles hommes et femmes* (France, mid-15th century) Harley MS 621, f. 71r.

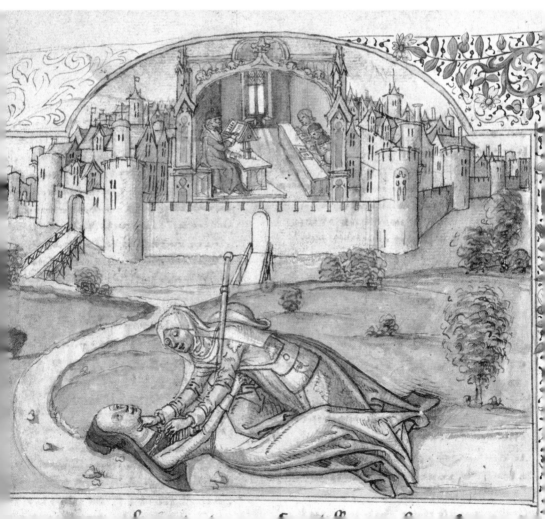

6 Blindfolded Lady Fortune and her wheel, in the *Roman de la Rose* (Paris, late 14th century) Add MS 42133, f. 42v.

(a Roman who lived before the Christian era and is therefore not admitted to Paradise) shows Dante the awful punishments that await those who have sinned, and the rewards awaiting the just and the good in Heaven. As Virgil is guiding him through the fourth circle of Hell, inhabited by the Avaricious, the Prodigals and the Wrathful, he mentions the goddess Fortuna and Dante asks for an explanation: '*Questa Fortuna de che tu mi tocche, che è?*' ('this Fortune whom you've touched upon just now – what's she?').[4] Virgil explains that, although she appears capricious, Fortuna is subordinate to the all-powerful will of God, punishing the wicked and rewarding the virtuous and thereby helping God to fulfil his unfathomable plan for humankind (Image 4).

Boccaccio refers to Lady Fortune many times in his *De casibus virorum illustrium* ('On Famous Men'), a collection of tales of the lives, loves and ultimate fall of illustrious male characters from history and mythology. For him she is an ambivalent figure (note the multiple arms in Image 5a), on the one hand punishing vice in a Christianised role, while on the other seeming wilful and malignant in her dealings with the wretches under her control. However, she claims that men have depicted her as cruel, foolish and blind simply because they do not understand the secrets of the heavens and they are blinded by their desires.[5]

Earlier in the same work, Boccaccio refers to the teaching of his tutor, Andalo del Negro, quoting his words, 'One should not blame the stars if those who suffer brought their misery on themselves'.[6] A contest between Fortune and her adversary, Poverty (both represented by women), ends with Poverty taming Fortune, forcing her to tie up half of her kingdom to a pole, and thus leaving good fortune free to roam. The implication is that humans themselves are responsible for their success or failure (Image 5b).

Negative attitudes to Lady Fortune persisted, and it remained convenient to blame her for human failures. In the *Roman de la Rose* ('Romance of the Rose'), a work that was attacked by Christine de Pisan and others for its misogyny, Lady Fortune is portrayed as a malicious woman who takes grim satisfaction in destroying the lives of successful men. A blindfolded figure, she turns her wheel so that men fall in the mud; she then applies a *douleureux emplastre* ('a painful poultice') impregnated with miserable poverty instead of vinegar to their hearts (Image 6).

Lady Fortune remained a powerful figure in the lives of men in the Renaissance, despite the ambivalent attitude of the Church, and in a treatise by the priest and provost Martin le Franc, she and Lady Virtue debate before Lady Reason; their topic is how the world should be governed. In the sixteenth and seventeenth centuries, she was evoked briefly in works by Machiavelli (*The Prince*) and Shakespeare (Sonnet 29) and she was painted by Rubens. But the motif of the wheel had faded by that time and she tended to be replaced by a fairly similar allegorical figure named Natura in debates over the relationship between the celestial and the earthly worlds. The word 'fortune' took on the meaning of 'material wealth' and became linked to the world of economics rather than philosophy.

27.

The Sibyls

Sibyls were wise, ancient and somewhat unpredictable prophetesses who lived in isolated settings near springs or caves in the ancient world. When consulted they would typically enter a fevered state, inspired by divine knowledge to predict future world events and the fates of kings. The earliest known Greek description of these women is in the writings of Plutarch, the philosopher, biographer and priest at the Temple of Apollo in Delphi (d.AD 119), where he quotes lines from Heraclitus (c.500 BC): 'The Sibyl with frenzied lips, uttering words mirthless, unembellished, unperfumed, penetrates through a thousand years with her voice by the god'.[1]

The word 'Sibyl' is thought to come a from Doric Greek expression meaning 'the will of God'. Their revelations were not usually concerned with personal circumstances, but rather with the fate of nations, religions and dynasties. In the Middle Ages the Sybils became one of the most potent female images in Western Christianity by prophesying the birth of Christ. St Augustine included them among the pre-Christian inhabitants of his *City of God* and they were painted by Van Eyck and Raphael, and included by Michelangelo in the Sistine Chapel frescoes, before falling out of favour in the Age of Enlightenment.

1 Twelve Sibyls foretelling the coming of Christ at the beginning of the prayers for the first Sunday in Advent; each one holds a garland containing part of the prophecy of Christ's birth and mission of salvation (on the opposite page is an image of King David on his deathbed, a link to the Old Testament prophecies); in the Breviary of Queen Isabella of Castille (Bruges, c.1490) Add. MS 18851, ff. 8v.

Most historians agree that the tradition of Sibyls originated in the Near East and from there entered Greek culture, though their true origins are unknown. The original *Libri Sibyllini* ('Sibylline Books') were supposedly written in Greek hexameters in the seventh century BC by a Sibyl of the Hellespont, and were later translated into Latin and kept closely guarded in a vault in the temple of Jupiter on the Capitoline Hill in Rome. They contained oracular texts that could only be consulted on the orders of the senate during a crisis or natural disaster. Dionysius of Halicarnassus wrote of one such occurrence in 459 BC when there were 'flashes shooting through the sky...the rumblings of the earth...[and a] storm of falling pieces of flesh'.[2] The advice from the *Libri* was a warning for the populace to stop their violent behaviour and make the appropriate sacrifices to the gods. Centuries later, in 125 BC, the births of several androgynes in the same year caused anxiety, triggering a further consultation of these texts. The *Libri* were destroyed by the western Roman ruler Stilicho in the early fifth century, but were soon replaced by another set of texts known as the *Sibylline Oracles*, believed to have been the work of Jewish and Christian authors based on ancient prophetic traditions.

The names of twelve Sibyls have come down to us; they are identified by their locations, though some of them are recorded as having moved at one time or another, and there is confusion around some of the identities. Their numbers increased over the centuries. In the earliest Greek sources only the Erythraean Sibyl is mentioned, but by the time the great Roman scholar Marcus Terentius Varro (d.27 BC) provides a list there are ten. In Image 1, from a prayer book owned by the Spanish queen, twelve Sibyls are depicted, along with their traditional attributes and prophecies. They are:
- the Libyan Sibyl (wearing a garland);
- the Delphic Sibyl (holding an inkpot/pipe?);
- the Cimmerian Sibyl;
- the Erythraean Sibyl (an old woman in a veil holding a sword);
- the Samian Sibyl (with headdress and veil);
- the Egyptian Sibyl (wearing a wimple);
- the Cumaean Sibyl (holding two books);
- the Sibyl of Hellespont (wearing an orange headdress);
- the Phrygian Sibyl (with a haggard face, holding a disc with stars);
- the Tiburtine Sibyl (holding rolled scrolls);
- the European Sibyl (veiled, holding a scroll).

Very little is known about some of these women, and several are only mentioned in one source, but there are three in particular who are the subjects of strange and ancient legends and were therefore favourites of medieval authors.

2 The Roman emperor Augustus kneeling down with his crown fallen beside him and the Sibyl prophesying and showing him a vision of the Virgin Mary with Christ, in a prayer book (N. Netherlands, 1486) Harley MS 2943, f. 18r.

The Erythraean Sibyl

The Erythraean Sibyl is believed to be the one referred to in the earliest Greek sources. Heraclitus, writing in the sixth century BC, claims that this Sibyl is 1,000 years old and she is later described by Apollodorus as coming from Erythrae, near Troy, in Asia Minor. She is thought to have been one of the early contributors to the *Libri Sibyllini* and, according to Varro, she 'foretold to the Greeks as they set out for Ilium, both the fall of Troy and Homer's fictions about it'.[3] As Homer's works are thought to have been composed in the eighth century BC, this would make her over 10,000 years old. Stories about the Erythraean and Cumaean Sibyls have been conflated in some of the sources and they may have been one and the same.

Both the emperor Constantine and St Augustine of Hippo alluded to prophetic verses uttered by the Erythraean Sibyl, 'plainly indicating the advent of Jesus by the initial letters of these verses, forming an acrostic in these words: IESUS CHRIST, SON OF GOD, SAVIOUR, CROSS',[4] and she thus became accepted as a divinely inspired prophetess of the Christian God for centuries. Boccaccio features the Erythraean Sibyl in his book on famous women, *De mulieribus claris,* where

3 The Erythraean Sibyl writing at a desk, from Boccaccio, 'De Erytrea seu Eriphila sibilla', in *Des Cleres et nobles femmes,* an anonymous French translation of Boccacio's *De mulieribus claris* (Rouen, c.1440) Royal MS 16 G V, f. 23.

he states that she was born in Babylon, that her name was Herophile but that she was named for the island of Erythaea where she lived. From a medieval perspective, he praises her for her eloquence and piety, for her eternal virginity, and for being much loved by God even though she was a pagan.

The Cumaean Sibyl (sometimes called Amalthea, Herophile or Demophile)

The most famous tale recorded about this Sibyl is in Ovid's *Metamorphoses,* a work that remained popular in the Middle Ages. When the god Apollo offered to grant the Cumaean Sibyl any wish if she would accept his advances, she picked up a handful of sand and asked to live as many years as the grains of sand she held in her hand. Apollo granted this wish but when she rejected his advances he turned her wish against her by refusing her eternal youth. So though she was

4 Aeneas with the Sibyl at the entrance to the Underworld, with Charon in his boat and Cerberus at the gate, at the beginning of Book VI of Virgil's *Aeneid* (Rome, c.1484) Kings MS 24, f. 131v.

fabled to have lived for over 1,000 years, many of those were spent wandering the earth as a melancholy, withering old hag. She predicted that eventually she would shrivel to almost nothing and only her voice would be left.

The Cumaean Sibyl's extreme longevity placed her between this world and the next, and so she was able to act as guide to the Roman hero Aeneas into the Underworld so that he could speak to his dead father one more time. As recounted in Virgil's *Aeneid*, she led the young hero, golden bough in hand, to a cave through which they passed into the realm of the dead. There they were confronted by Charon the boatman, the famous three-headed hound, Cerberus, and young compatriots of Aeneas who had lost their lives in the Trojan War (Image 4). But when they encountered Apollo, the Sibyl underwent a startling transformation, making wild gestures and behaving erratically:

non voltus non color unus/non comptaei mansere comae, sed pectus anhelum/et rabie fera corda tument, maiorque videri/nec mortale sonans

Nor countenance nor color was the same, nor stayed her tresses braided: but her bosom heaves, her heart swells with wild frenzy and she is taller to behold, nor has her voice a mortal ring.[5]

Varro, whose writings contain much of what we know about the Sibyls, told the story of how the Cumaean Sibyl brought the *Libri Sibyllini* to Rome, appearing before King Tarquinius Priscus and offering him her nine books of prophesies for the price of 300 gold coins. He laughed at her and called her mad for demanding such a ridiculous price, so she started burning the books three at a time – until finally he bought the last three books for the sum she had originally asked for all nine. These prophesies were translated into Latin to be kept at the Capitol in Rome, and further Sibylline Books were gathered from across the empire to add to the collection. In the age of Augustus the Sibylline prophecies were used as imperial propaganda. Horace was commissioned in 17 BC to write his *Carmen Saeculare* ('Hymn for a New Age') to celebrate Augustus's achievements and the promise of prosperity, in which the Sibyl is said to have prophesied the return of a new golden age: 'Life-giving Sun, who with your shining car bring forth the day and hide it away, who are born anew and yet the same, may you never be able to behold anything greater than the city of Rome'.[6]

The medieval author, Christine de Pisan, in her dream-allegorical work, *Le Livre du chemin de long estude* ('The Book of the Path of Long Study'), is visited in a dream by the Cumaean Sibyl (Image 5b). Here she is described as modestly dressed, prudent and moderate in her demeanour. She talks about herself and her fellow Sibyls and offers sensible advice, promising to guide Christine on the right path through the pitfalls of this world and the next.

Tiburtine Sibyl

The Tiburtine Sibyl does not feature until Roman times and may have been Etruscan in origin; her location was the town of Tibur (modern Tivoli) on the banks of the River Anio, and Varro claims that an image of her was found in the river, holding a book in her hand.[7] She became the most famous of the Sibyls in the Middle Ages as she was believed to have shown the first Roman emperor, Augustus, a vision of a young woman with a baby boy, accompanied by a voice from the heavens saying, 'This is the virgin who shall conceive the saviour of the world'. The episode was regarded as a prefiguration of the coming of Christ and was depicted in numerous medieval manuscripts (Images 2, 6).

A text known as the *Prophecy of the Tenth (or Tiburtine) Sibyl* was widely copied (Image 7) and tells how the Roman emperor summoned the Tibertine after 100 senators had experienced the same dream on the same night. In this dream, nine different suns had appeared in the sky. Asked to interpret the dream, the Sibyl explained that the suns represented nine future eras. She prophesied that one sun, described as having a blood-red colour, signified an era in which

5a Christine asleep (left); **5b** Christine de Pisan meets the Sibyl in a dream (right), in Christine de Pisan in *Le Livre du chemin de long estude* (Paris, *c.*1410) Bibliothèque nationale de France, fr. 836, ff. 3v, 12r.

a virgin named Mary would bear a child named Jesus, the Son of God, who would begin the Christian era leading up to a great emperor named Constans. He would vanquish the foes of Christianity including Gog and Magog, ushering in a golden age of prosperity and peace, but the era of the Antichrist would follow and at the end of time the Son of God would return for a final judgement over humankind. Although this text was composed by a Christian writer in the fourth century and expanded in around AD 1000, medieval authors believed the contents to be authentic and it was incorporated into chronicles and religious works. Over 130 copies survive in Latin, and there are known versions in Greek and Ethiopic; an Anglo-Norman French translation was produced in England in the twelfth century.

In the sixteenth century, earlier claims about the Sibylline Books were being seriously questioned and the Tiburtine's prophecy was recognised as a later construct. The Elizabethan explorer and writer, Sir Walter Raleigh, described the Sibyls' prophecies as 'no better than counterfeit pieces',[8] though in around 1600 the courtier, Jane Segar, composed a work on the 'Divine Prophecies of the Ten Sibylls' in English and dedicated it to Queen Elizabeth I. Although not much is known about her, Jane explains that her gift to the queen is her own work, 'the handyworke of a maiden your majesty's most faithful servant...graced with my pen and pencell', so not only was she the scribe of this book but she probably embroidered the beautiful cover of red velvet and

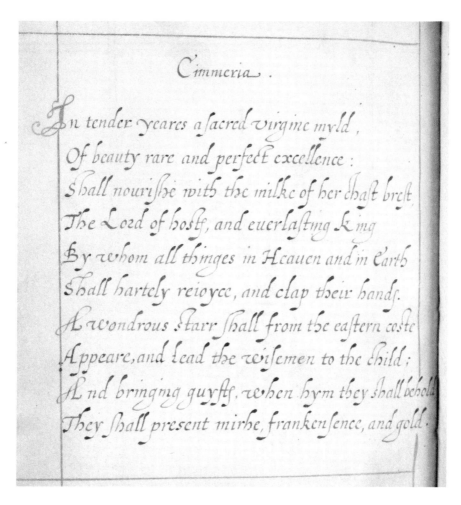

Cimmeria .

In tender yeares a sacred virgine myld ,
Of beauty rare and perfect excellence :
Shall nourishe with the milke of her chast brest
The Lord of hoste, and euerlasting King
By whom all thinges in Heauen and in earth
Shall hartely reioyce, and clap their handes.
A wondrous Starr shall from the eastern coste
Appeare, and lead the wisemen to the child;
And bringing guyftes, when hym they shall behold
They shall present mirhe, frankensence, and gold .

7 Jane Segar, the prophecy of the Sibyl 'Cimmeria' in English (England, c.1600) Add MS 10037, ff. 4v–5r.

painted the illuminations on the enamelled and gilt glass panels.[9] It seems that although the authenticity of the Sibylline prophecies was being questioned at this time, they must have been familiar to the literati in court circles. Today only the Christian name Sibyl is a reminder of these elusive prophetesses, though even that is currently rather unfashionable.

6 The Tiburtine Sibyl prophesying to Augustus about the birth of Christ, in the Book of Hours of Joanna of Castille (Ghent, c.1500) Add MS 35313, f. 90r.

28.

The Muses and Personifications

The Muses

The nine Muses, daughters of Jupiter (Greek Zeus), appear in a variety of guises in medieval and Renaissance art and literature. They feature in the works of Christine de Pisan and Chaucer and are pictured in manuscripts on a wide range of subjects. Debates raged about their number, attributes and identities, leading to inconsistencies in both textual and visual depictions. In the same way as other pagan figures, they were rejected by some Christian writers but others such as Dante gave them a role in the Christian cosmos.

According to early accounts by the Greeks Homer and Hesiod there were nine muses who lived on Mount Olympus – though in some classical sources only three were listed – and they were generally believed to be the daughters of Jupiter and Mnemosyne (the Titan goddess of Memory). Hesiod describes them thus: 'all of one mind, their hearts are set upon song and their spirit is free from care. He is happy whom the Muses love'.[1]

Ovid refers to the Muses as *doctae sorores* (learned sisters), and in late antiquity they came to be seen as personifications of learning, representing the liberal arts, namely poetry, literature, dance and music. They were associated

[1] Homer surrounded by the nine Muses at the beginning of the *Iliad*, (Florence, 15th century) Harley MS 5600, f. 15v.

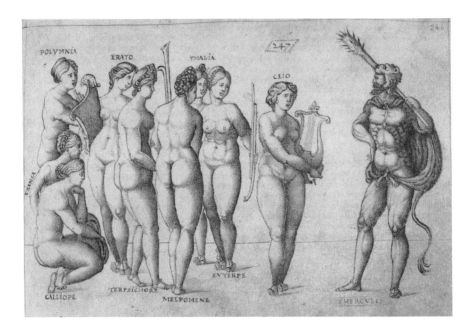

2 Hercules and the Greek Muses followed by a description by Lilio Gregorio Giraldi in the *Historia animalium* (Italy, 1595) Add MS 82955, f. 245v.

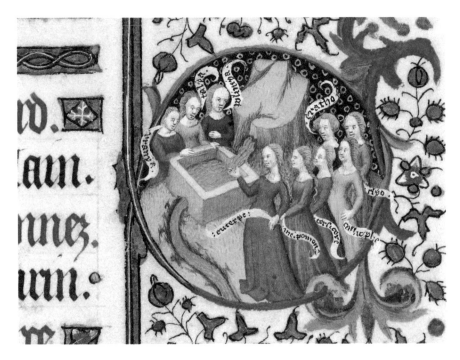

3 A marginal roundel of the nine Muses grouped around a fountain, from the calendar page for November (*Novem* = nine), in the Bedford Hours (Paris, *c.* 1420) Add MS 18850, f. 11r.

4 Clio, Melpomene, Euterpe and Thalia (left-hand page); Polyhymnia, Erato, Terpsichore and Urania (right-hand page), in Convenevole da Prato, *Regia Carmina* (Tuscany, *c*.1340) Royal MS 6 E IX, ff. 29v, 30r.

with the god Apollo and with springs or fountains (Images 3–5); after the fifth-century AD when Servius mistakenly claimed they lived on Mount Parnassus[2], they were often pictured among the laurel groves and springs of its slopes, dancing to Apollo's lyre.

Examples of the varied manuscript context in which images of the Muses can be found are the *Historia animalium* (a collection of annotated drawings of the world's fauna), the Bedford Hours (a highly illuminated prayerbook owned by the kings of England) and the *Regia Carmina* (a work in praise of Robert of Anjou, King of Naples, beseeching him to protect the town of Prato and unite Italy) (Images 2–5).

In the huge visually impressive manuscript of the *Regia Carmina*, illuminated by the fourteenth-century Italian artist Pacino de Buonagida, the nine Muses are pictured individually across three consecutive pages of almost half a metre in height (much reduced in Images 4 and 5), each with attributes or gestures suggesting their area of influence:

5 Calliope in the *Regia Carmina*, Royal MS 6 E IX, f. 30v.

Clio	*Muse of History*	emerging from a vessel with water, gesturing
Melpomene	*Muse of Tragedy*	emerging from a vessel with water, her chin in hand
Euterpe	*Muse of the Flute*	holding a jar with plants
Thalia	*Muse of Comedy*	smiling, holding out her orange robe
Polyhymnia	*Muse of mime*	emerging from a tall vessel, holding books and a chest
Erato	*Muse of Lyric poetry*	emerging from a vessel, gesturing
Terpsichore	*Muse of Verse and dance*	?conducting from a book on a lectern
Urania	*Muse of Astronomy or Christian poetry*	blue wings and crown-like hat decorated with stars, hands in praying position
Calliope	*Muse of Epic poetry*	playing a horn beside a vase-shaped fountain

An entire page is devoted to Calliope (her name means 'beautiful-voiced' in Greek), the oldest and usually considered the chief of the Muses (Image 5). She was the mother of Orpheus, whom she taught to sing so beautifully that he was able to charm the gods of the Underworld and ease the torments of the damned. When he was torn apart by *Maenads* (wild women) the other Muses helped her to gather his limbs and bury them at the foot of Mount Olympus.

6 The Muses with Sappho beside a river, in *De Stede der Vrouwen*, a Flemish translation of Christine de Pisan's *Livre de la Cité des Dames* (Bruges, 1475) Add MS 20698, f. 73r.

Dante, adhering to a long tradition of invoking muses in epic poetry, addresses Calliope at the beginning of his *Purgatorio*, the second part of the *Divina Commedia* ('Divine Comedy').

Ma qui la morta poesì resurga,	*But here, since I am yours, o holy Muses,*
o sante Muse, poi che vostro sono;	*may this poem rise again from Hell's dead realm;*
e qui Caliope alquanto surga,	*and may Calliope rise somewhat here,*
seguitando il mio canto con quel suono	*accompanying my singing with that music*[3]

He then refers to the story told by Ovid about the singing contest between the Muses and the Pierides, nine daughters of the king of Macedon. Calliope was chosen to represent the former, and Ovid describes how she 'rose, with her loose hair bound with ivy, tried out the plaintive strings with her fingers, then accompanied the wandering notes with this song'[4]. Her song was so beautiful that she won the contest and the Pierides were turned into magpies.

Chaucer, too, includes the Muses in his *Canterbury Tales* and *House of Fame*, where he presents himself in a humorous light, struggling to start composing his poem, while invoking Clio, Calliope and Polyhymnia in an attempt to gain Fame, Memory and Eloquence. Boccaccio is dismissive of the 'naked Muses', denying that they have inspired him in his writing, and claiming, 'Ladies have already been the reason for my composing thousands of verses, while the Muses were in no way the cause of my writing them'[5].

In her chapter on the Greek poet Sappho in the *Livre de la Cité des Dames* ('Book of the City of Ladies') Christine de Pisan has Sappho join the muses in 'perfect study' on Mount Parnassus (Image 6). Her dream allegory, the *Chemin de long estude* ('Path of Long Study') begins at the Fountain of Wisdom, where the narrator (Christine) sees nine ladies bathing nude in the beautiful, clear water. The Cumaean Sibyl who is her guide tells her that these are the nine Muses and '*Si tiennent la l'escole sainte / Qui de grant science est encainte*' ('There they hold their holy school which is a place of great learning')[6].

Statues of the Muses and carvings on tombs survive from classical times and in the eighteenth century, scholars and artists of the Enlightenment briefly revived their popularity. Thus they featured in the Baroque garden statuary and fountains that were produced for decorated stately homes and public buildings. In modern culture the word 'muse' has come to refer to a (usually female) artist's inspiration and the Muses' fame survives in the word 'museum' (the scholars of Alexandria worked at a *mouseion* or shrine of the muses, and it came to mean a place of learning and study).

The Graces

In Classical mythology, the Graces were the daughters of Jupiter (Greek Zeus) and Juno (Greek Hera) and in the *Odyssey* they were described as the handmaidens of Venus (Aphrodite). They resided with the Muses and one of their roles was to organise dances and adorn both gods and mortals at festivals. They also bestowed gifts such as fertility, youth, mirth and beauty on humans. The female figures of the three (or sometimes seven) Graces were depicted in mostly secular late medieval and Renaissance illuminations.

A Tudor manuscript commemorating a pageant at the marriage of Mary, sister of Henry VIII to Louis XII of France (who was thirty years her senior) shows the three Graces beside a fountain with lilies and roses. The accompanying verse tells that they have been sent from the above to bestow prosperity virtue and

7 The pageant at the Fontaine du Ponceau, with the three Graces; in the fountain are the lilies of France and the red roses of England, in a manuscript commemorating the marriage of Mary Tudor to Louis XII of France (Paris, 1514) Cotton MS Vespasian B.II, f. 6r.

happiness on the bridal couple. In contrast to their nudity in classical and neo-classical statuary, these Graces wear fashionable Tudor garments (Image 7).

The Virtues

The seven Heavenly Virtues, consisting of the Cardinal Virtues of Prudence, Justice, Temperance and Fortitude and the Theological Virtues of Faith, Hope and Charity, were adapted from Greek philosophical writings into early Christian tradition, and were portrayed as women in both liturgical and allegorical works. An early example is the opening page of the Book of Job in a

8 The Virtues on the opening page of the Book of Job (Namur, *c.* 1170) Floreffe Bible Add. MS 17738, f.3v.

large Romanesque Bible made at the Abbey of Floreffe in present-day Belgium in around 1170 (Image 8), where the three Theological Virtues are represented as women wearing robes and with silver halos. They are encircled by seven roundels with the Seven Gifts of the Holy Spirit, represented by busts of women and doves. All form part of an elaborate and complex image, where a scene from the Old Testament (Job's sacrifice to God during a feast with his sons and daughters at the top) shares the page with allegorical and New Testament figures. Below the Virtues are images of the apostles and Christ, and at the bottom of the page are depictions of the seven Corporal Acts of Mercy from the Gospels (feeding the hungry, clothing the naked, etc.). So here the Virtues are at the heart of Christian iconography.

Chastity, Humility and other virtues particularly recommended to women were represented by female characters in medieval allegorical texts,

9a Raison (Reason) advising the Lover in the *Roman de la Rose*, (Bruges, c.1500) Harley MS 4425, f. 43v.

9b Nature appears to the author in a dream and shows him Lady Vaillance, who is in a pavilion with other female allegorical figures in the *Chemin de Vaillance* (Path of Valour), (Bruges, c. 1480) Royal MS 14 E II, f. 1r.

but so were qualities that were associated more with men at the time, such as Reason and Wisdom. This was the case even in the *Roman de la Rose* ('Romance of the Rose') where women were seldom viewed in a positive light. In Image 9a, Reason, a modestly dressed woman, addresses a lengthy discourse on the various forms of love and on linguistic meaning to the Lover. She appears at first to represent rational thought, while rejecting passionate love. However some critics have seen this passage as intentionally comedic, in that the Lover ignores her attempt at intellectual debate and the sound advice she offers. She is wasting her words on one who is entirely focused on evading the guardians of the tower and capturing his beloved, the Rose, as represented by the bower of roses in the background.

The *Chemin de Vaillance* (Path of Valour), on the other hand, is a somewhat derivative late-medieval allegory with a less complex message. The narrator falls asleep in a field and embarks on a dream-journey in the service of Lady Vaillance, as instructed by Nature (Image 9b). He is accompanied by Prudence and Courage and avoids Cowardice and Laziness. On the journey he will meet a host of allegorical characters who will guide him; they include Lady Humility who will help him to conquer the Castle of Pride. His journey ends when he has learned the chivalric virtues of piety, courtesy and generosity.

Notes

All biblical quotations are taken from the King James Bible.

Introduction

1 Natalie Haynes, *Pandora's Jar: Women in the Greek Myths* (London: Picador, 2020), p. 2.
2 Elizabeth Carney, *Olympias, Mother of Alexander the Great* (New York and London: Routledge, 2006), pp. 1, 2.
3 Mary Hammer, *Signs of Cleopatra* (New York: Routledge, 1993), p. xvii.
4 Geoffrey Chaucer, *The Canterbury Tales*, Wife of Bath's Prologue, lines 788–93 (author's translation), Harvard's Geoffrey Chaucer Website: 'Text and Translations: Canterbury Tales' (Harvard University, 2024), online at https://chaucer.fas.harvard.edu/pages/wife-baths-prologue-and-tale-0
5 Walter Map, *Letter of Valerius to Ruffinus Against Marriage* (1180), quoted in Rachel Moss, 'Becoming a Woman in the Middle Ages', online at historyatnorthampton.com/2023/03/23/becoming-a-woman-in-the-middle-ages/
6 Christine de Pizan, *The Book of the City of Ladies*, trans. Earl Jeffrey Richards (New York: Persea Books, 1982), pp. 3–4.
7 Christine de Pizan, *The Treasure of the City of Ladies*, ed. Sarah Lawson (London: Penguin, 2003), p. 147.
8 Giovanni Boccaccio, Preface to *Concerning Famous Women*, trans. Guido A. Guarino (London: George Allen & Unwin, 1964), p. xxxvii.

1. The Amazon Women

1 Edith Hall, 'Hippolyta and the Amazons' (Bridge Theatre, 2019), online at https://bridgetheatre.co.uk/hippolyta-and-the-amazons/
2 A. Mayor, *The Amazons, Lives and Legends of Warrior Women across the Ancient World* (Princeton: University Press, 2014), p. 85.
3 Aeschylus, *Suppliant Women*, lines 288–9, trans. Ian Johnston from the edition by Herbert Weir Smith (1922), online at https://johnstoniatexts.x10host.com/aeschylus/suppliantwomenhtml.html
4 Diodorus Siculus, *The Library of History* (Loeb Classical Library, 1935), online at https://penelope.uchicago.edu/Thayer/E/Roman/Texts/Diodorus_Siculus/3D*.html

5 Natalie Haynes, *Pandora's Jar: Women in the Greek Myths* (London: Picador, 2020), p. 118.
6 Elizabeth Baynham, 'Alexander and the Amazons', *The Classical Quarterly*, vol. 51, no. 1 (2001), pp. 115–26, online at https://www.jstor.org/stable/3556333?read-now=1&seq=1#page_scan_tab_contents
7 *Livre de la Cité des Dames*, Harley MS 4431, f. 302v; author's transcription and translation.
8 Giovanni Boccaccio, *De mulieribus claris, XI, XII*, ed. Vittorio Zaccaria, trans. Jean-Yves Boriaud (Milan: Mondadori Classics, 1967), online at Biblioteca Italiana, http://www.bibliotecaitaliana.it/testo/bibit000947
9 Haynes, *Pandora's Jar* (see note 5), p. 125.

2. Medea

1 Apollonius Rhodius, *The Argonautica*, Book III, online at https://www.gutenberg.org/files/830/830-h/830-h.htm
2 ibid.
3 *Metamorphoses* 292, cited in K. Lind, *Seeking a Voice: Maternal Discourse in the Medea Legend* (undergraduate honours thesis, University of Redlands, 1997), online at: https://core.ac.uk/download/pdf/217141628.pdf, pp. 35–6.
4 Boccaccio, *Concerning Famous Women*, trans. Guido A. Guarino (New Brunswick: Rutgers University Press, 1963), online at: https://archive.org/details/boccaccio-concerning-famous-women/page/35/mode/2up?q=medea
5 John Lydgate, *The Fall of Princes*, ed. Henry Bergen (Oxford: Early English Text Society, 1967), Book 1, pp. 63, 65, online at https://xtf.lib.virginia.edu/xtf/view?docId=chadwyck_ep/uvaGenText/tei/chep_1.0297.xml;chunk.id=d3;toc.depth=1;toc.id=d3;brand=default
6 Geoffrey Chaucer, *The Legend of Good Women*, ed. Walter Skeat (Oxford: Clarendon Press, 1889), ll. 1365–7, 1381–2, online at https://www.gutenberg.org/cache/epub/45027/pg45027-images.html#hypsipyle
7 *Roman de la Rose*, ed. Pierre Marteau (Orléans: H. Herluison, 1878–80), l. 13994, online at https://

archive.org/details/leromandelarosep02guiluoft/
page/366/mode/2up?q=medee

8   Christine de Pisan, *Livre de la Cité des Dames*,
Harley MS 4431; author's transcription and
translation.

3. Salome, Daughter of Herod

1   Holkham Bible Picture Book, f. 21r; author's
transcription and translation.
2   ibid., f. 21v.
3   Gospel of Mark, 6:26.
4   Taymouth Hours, f. 108r; author's transcription
and translation.
5   Eurippus, *Life of John* and Niephorus Callistus,
Ecclesiastic History, quoted in Rosina Neginsky,
Salome: The Image of a Woman Who Never Was
(Cambridge: Scholars Publishing, 2013), p. 25.

4. The Goddess Minerva

1   Ovid, *Fasti*, Book 3, trans. James G. Frazer
(Theoi Classical Texts Library), l.834, online at
https://www.theoi.com/Text/OvidFasti3.html
2   Hugh G. Evelyn-White, *The Homeric Hymns
and Homerica with an English Translation*
(London: Heinemann, 1914), 28: 'To Athena', ll. 1–4,
online at Perseus Digital Library: https://www.
perseus.tufts.edu/hopper/text?doc=Perseus%3
Atext%3A1999.01.0138%3Ahymn%3D28
3   Christine de Pisan, *The Book of the City of
Ladies*, I.39, trans. Earl Jeffrey Richards (New York:
Persea Books, 1982), p. 81.
4   ibid., pp. 79–80.
5   ibid., p. 75.
6   Dante, *Paradiso*, 1.113, online at Columbia
University Digital Dante: https://digitaldante.
columbia.edu/dante/divine-comedy/paradiso
7   ibid., 2.7–9.
8   John Lydgate, *Reson and Sensuallyte*, 1044,
ed. Ernst Sieper, 2 vols (London: Early English
Text Society, 1901), Vol. I, l. 1044, online at https://
archive.org/details/lydgatesresonan00furngoog/
page/n63/mode/2up; author's translations.
9   ibid., ll. 1087–91; author's translation.

5. The Virgin Mary

1   Bible, Book of Isaiah 7:14.
2   Ambrose, *Expositio evangelii secundum Lucam,*
ed. M. Adriaen (Turnhout: Brepols, 1957), p. 55.
3   Hildegard of Bingen, *Ave generosa*, v. 5, text
and translation online at International Society

of Hildegard von Bingen Studies: http://www.
hildegard-society.org/2014/09/ave-generosa-hymn.
html

6. St Margaret of Antioch

1   *The Golden Legend of Jacobus de Voragine*,
trans. and adapted by Granger Ryan and Helmut
Ripperger (London: Longmans, Green & Co., 1941),
pp. 351–4.
2   *The Golden Legend*, trans. William Caxton
(1483), online at https://www.christianiconography.
info/goldenLegend/margaret.htm
3   *The Liflade ant te Passiun of Seinte Margarete*,
in Bodley MS 34, ff. 18v–19r, ed. and trans. E. R.
Huber and E. Robertson, TEAMS University of
Rochester Middle English Texts series, online at
https://d.lib.rochester.edu/teams/text/liflade-ant-
passiun-of-seinte-margarete
4   *The Golden Legend*, trans. Ryan (see note 1),
1.369.
5   David Farmer, *The Oxford Dictionary of Saints*
(Oxford University Press, 2011), p. 260.

7. Hairy Saints and Harlots

1   Maureen Boulton, *Sacred Fictions of Medieval
France: Narrative Theology in the Lives of Christ
and the Virgin, 1150–1500* (Cambridge: Brewer,
2015) p. 84.
2   *The Golden Legende or Lives of Saints,
compiled by Jacobus de Voragine, englished by
William Caxton* [Westminster, 1483–1484], ed.
F. S. Ellis (Temple Classics, 1900), Vol. 5, 'Thais',
online at https://sourcebooks.fordham.edu/basis/
goldenlegend/goldenlegend-volume5.asp#Thais
3   'St Thais', in *Saints' Lives in Middle English
Collections,* ed. E. Gordon Whatley, Anne B.
Thompson and Robert K. Upchurch (Kalamazoo:
Medieval Institute Publications, 2004), pp. 155–68.
4   'Pelagia, Beauty Riding By', trans. Sr. Benedicta
Ward, S.L.G., in *Harlots of the Desert, a Study of
Repentance in Early Monastic Sources* (Kalamazoo:
Cistercian Publications, 1986); Latin text in
Patrologia Latina, 73, 663–72), online at https://
web.archive.org/web/20201202181006/https://
facultystaff.richmond.edu/~wstevens/FYStexts/
biospelagias.pdf
5   Author's transcription and translation from
Add MS 22283.

8. St Helena of Constantinople

1   Ambrosius, *De obitu Theodosii*, in *Political Letters and Speeches*, trans. J. Liebeschuetz and C. Hill (Liverpool University Press, 2005), Chapter 42, online at https://cmuntz.hosted.uark.edu/classes/late-antiquity/ambrose_theodosius.pdf

2   Eusebius Pamphilus of Caesarea, *Vita Constantini: The Life of the Blessed Emperor Constantine*, trans. S. Bagster (1845), revised by E. Cushing, online at https://sourcebooks.fordham.edu/basis/vita-constantine.asp

3   ibid., Chapter XLII.

4   Ambrosius, *De obitu Theodosii* (see note 1), Chapter 44.

5   ibid.

6   Almann of Hautvillers, *Vita seu potius homilia de S. Helena*, in Julia Hillner, *Helena Augusta, Mother of the Empire* (Oxford University Press, 2023), p. 7.

7   Jean Wavrin, *Anciennes et nouvelles chroniques de la Grant Bretaigne,* Book 1, Chapter 44, in Royal MS 15 E IV, f. 73v, author's translation.

9. Mary Magdalene

1   Gospel of Luke 8:1–3.

2   Pope Gregory I, Homily XXXIII, translation online at Patristic Bible Commentary: https://sites.google.com/site/aquinasstudybible/home/luke-commentary/gregory-the-great-homily-33-on-the-gospels

3   'Le Blasme des Fames', in *Three Medieval Views of Women,* ed. and trans. G. K. Fiero, W. Pfeiffer and M. Allain (New Haven: Yale University Press, 2009), pp. 119–34.

4   Gospel of Luke 10:42.

5   St John Chrysostom, *On Virginity* (*De Virginitate*), quoted in *Not in God's Image*, ed. Julia O'Faolain and Lauro Martines (London: HarperCollins, 1979), pp. 150–1.

6   Letter of Louis IX, quoted in Victor Saxer, *Le Dossier Vézelien de Marie Madeleine: Invention et translation des reliques en 1265–1267* (Brussels: Society of Bollandists, 1975), online at https://archive.org/stream/sh-19-halkin-sancti-pachomii-vitae-grecae/SH-57-Saxer-Le-dossier-Vezelien-de-Marie-Madeleine-Invention-et-translation-des-reliques-en-1265-1267_djvu.txt

7   St Anselm of Canterbury, Oratio LXXIV, 'Ad Sanctam Mariam Magdalenam', *Patrologia Latina*, L CLVIII, cols 1010 and 1011.

8   Holy See Bulletin, 10 June 2016, online at https://press.vatican.va/content/salastampa/en/bollettino/pubblico/2016/06/10/160610b.html

10. Cleopatra, Queen of Egypt

1   Shakespeare, *Antony and Cleopatra* Act II, Scene 2, line 244 (Folger Shakespeare Library), online at https://www.folger.edu/explore/shakespeares-works/antony-and-cleopatra/read/

2   Plutarch, *Life of Anthony,* 27, in *Plutarch's Lives: With an English Translation* by Bernadotte Perrin (London: William Heinemann, 1919), online at http://www.perseus.tufts.edu/hopper/text?doc=Perseus%3Atext%3A2008.01.0007%3Achapter%3D27%3Asection%3D2

3   Plutarch, *Life of Caesar,* 49, in *Plutarch's Lives* (see note 2), online at http://www.perseus.tufts.edu/hopper/text?doc=Perseus%3Atext%3A1999.01.0244%3Achapter%3D49

4   Shakespeare, *Antony and Cleopatra* Act II, Scene 2, line 226 (see note 1).

5   Giovanni Boccaccio, *Concerning Famous Women*, trans. with an introduction and notes by Guido A. Guarino (New Brunswick, NJ: Rutgers Univesrity Press, 1963), Chapter LXXXVI, p. 197.

6   ibid., p. 192.

7   ibid.

8   *The Legend of Good Women, I. Cleopatra*, Online Medieval and Classical Library, at http://mcllibrary.org/GoodWomen/, lines 603–4.

9   ibid., lines 692–5.

10   Shakespeare, *Antony and Cleopatra* Act IV, Scene 15, line 63 (see note 1).

11   Pliny, *Natural History*, 9.119–21.

12   *The Art Journal*, N.S. X (1871), p. 174, quoted in George W. Whiting, 'The Cleopatra Rug Scene: Another Source', *The Shaw Review* 3, no. 1 (1960), pp. 15–17.

11. Olympias, Empress of Macedon

1   Marcus Junianus Justinus, *Epitome of the Philippic History of Pompeius Trogus*, trans. John Selby Watson (London: Henry G. Bohn, 1853) IX.5, online at http://www.forumromanum.org/literature/justin/english/trans9.html

2   *Greek Alexander Romance* 1.6, ed. and trans. Richard Stoneman (London: Penguin Books, 1991).

3   Peter Toth, 'The Indian Television Series *Porus*', in *Alexander the Great: The Making of a*

Myth, ed. Richard Stoneman (London: British Library, 2022), no. 13.

4   Kyng Alisaunder II. 161–6, quoted in Christine Chism, 'Winning Women in Two Middle English Alexander Poems', in Women and Medieval Epic, ed. Sara Poor and Jana Schulman (New York: Palgrave, 2007), p. 24; author's translation.

5   Aulus Gellius, Noctes Atticae, 13.iv, online at https://sententiaeantiquae.com/2016/08/29/awkward-letters-home-alexander-and-olympias/

6   Sarah B. Pomeroy, Women in Hellenistic Egypt: From Alexander to Cleopatra (New York, Schocken Books, 1984), p. 8.

12. Venus, Goddess of Love

1   The Epistle of Othea to Hector or the Book of Knyghthode, translated from the French of Christine de Pisan with a dedication to Sir John Fastolf by Stephen Scrope Esquire, ed. George F. Warner (London: J. P. Nichols, 1904), VII.

2   Yves Bonnefoy, Roman and European Mythologies, trans. Gerald Honigsblum et al. under the direction of Wendy Doniger (Chicago and London: UCP, 1992), p. 146, online at https://archive.org/details/romaneuropeanmyt00yves/mode/1up?view=theater

3   Macrobius, Saturnalia, ed. and trans. Robert A. Kaster (Cambridge, MA: Harvard University Press, 2011), Vol. 2, p. 58.

4   Ovid, Metamorphoses, Book 10:503–59, online at https://ovid.lib.virginia.edu/trans/Metamorph10.htm#484521427

5   Guillaume de Lorris, Roman de la Rose, ed. Franisque Michel and Dominique Martin (Paris: Didot, 1814–64), lines 3430–41, online at https://archive.org/details/leromandelarosep01guiluoft/page/n5/mode/2up; and translation based on A. S. Kline, Poetry in Translation, online at https://www.poetryintranslation.com/PITBR/French/LeRomanDeLaRosePartIV.php#anchor_Toc10457244

6   Guillaume de Lorris, Roman de la Rose (see note 5), lines 3477–81.

7   Jean de Meun, Roman de la Rose, final lines (22,006–7).

13. The Queen of Sheba

1   Bible, Gospels of Matthew 12.42 and Luke 11.31.

2   Flavius Josephus, Antiquities of the Jews 8.6, trans. Elliott Green in 'The Queen of Sheba: A Queen of Egypt and Ethiopia?', Jewish Bible Quarterly 29, no. 3 (2001), online at https://jbqnew.jewishbible.org/assets/Uploads/293/293_Sheba2.pdf

3   Bettina L. Knapp, 'Gerard de Nerval, the Queen of Sheba and the Occult', Nineteenth-Century French Studies 4, no. 3 (1976), pp. 244–57.

4   Bible, 1 Kings 10:1–13; 2 Chronicles 9.1–12.

5   ibid.

6   Quran, Sura 27.

7   Quran, Sura 34.

8   Abd-al-Wahhāb Najjār, Qeṣaṣ al-anbīā', 3rd ed. (Beirut, 1934), p. 308; quoted in Encyclopaedia Iranica: 'Belqīs', online at https://www.iranicaonline.org/articles/belqis-the-queen-of-sheba-saba-whose-meetings-with-solomon-solayman-are-a-favorite-theme-in-persian-and-arabic-literat

9   Cambridge Tafsīr I, Cambridge MS Mm.4.15, pp. 361–62, quoted in Enclopaedia Iranica: 'Belqīs' (see note 8).

10 Boccaccio, 'Nicaula Queen of Ethiopia' in Concerning Famous Women, trans. Guido A. Guarino (New Brunswick, NJ: Rutgers University Press, 1963), pp. 93–4.

11 Christine de Pizan, Le Livre de la Cité des Dames, II.4.2–3, ed. Miranda Remnek and Mary Skemp, online at https://web.archive.org/web/20050929022747/http://erc.lib.umn.edu/dynaweb/french/pizalaci/@Generic__BookTextView/3668#X

12 H. St John Philby, The Queen of Sheba (London: Quartet Books, 1981).

13 Bible, Matthew 12:42.

14. Candace of Ethiopia

1   The Greek Alexander Romance, Book III.18, online at https://www.attalus.org/translate/alexander3b.html, from The Life of Alexander the Great of Macedon by Pseudo-Callisthenes, trans. E. H. Haight (New York, 1955).

2   Bible, Acts 8:27–39.

3   Ernest A. Wallis Budge, The Alexander Book in Ethiopia (New York: AMS Press, 1976), p. 112.

4   ibid., p. 119.

5   Jacqueline de Weever, 'Candace in the Alexander Romances: Variations on the Portrait Theme', Romance Philology 43.4 (1990), pp. 529–46 (see p. 537, n. 12), online at https://www.jstor.org/stable/44942928?read-now=1&seq=1; Budge, The Alexander Book (see note 3), pp. 125–6.

6   Nizami Ganjavi, Sharafnamah, pp. 277–8,

279–80, in Haila Manteghi, 'Alexander the Great in the Persian Tradition: Its Influence on Persian History, Epic and Storytelling', unpublished PhD thesis (University of Exeter, 2016), p. 143.

7   Nizami Ganjavi, *Sharafnamah*, 306:254/2, cited in Julia Rubanovich, 'Re-Writing the Episode of Alexander and Candace in Medieval Persian Literature: Patterns, Sources and Motif Transformation', in *Alexander the Great in the Middle Ages,* ed. Markus Stock (Toronto: University of Toronto Press, 2016), pp. 123–52 (see p. 133).

8   ibid., 308:278, p. 134.

9   Maybudi, *Kashf al-asrar*, 4.371, in Rubanovich, 'Re-writing Alexander and Candace' (see note 7), p. 135.

10 *Eskandar-nāma*, trans. H. Wilberforce Clarke (1881), lines 97, 100–4, 124–7, online at https://bibliotecaparticular.casafernandopessoa.pt/9-1/2/9-1_master/9-1_PDF/9-1_0007_503-590_t24-C-R0100.pdf

11 Thomas of Kent, *Le Roman de toute chevalerie*, ed. Brian Foster (London: Early English Text Society, 1976), p. 217.

12 *Kyng Alisaunder,* ed. G. V. Smithers (Oxford: Early English Text Society, 1957), 1:13–15, 1:357, cited in de Weever, 'Candace in the Alexander Romances' (see note 5), p. 542.

13 'Nicaula, Queen of Ethiopia', in Giovanni Boccaccio, *Concerning Famous Women*, trans. Guido A. Guarino (New Brunswick, NJ: Rutgers University Press, 1963), pp. 93–4.

15. Elvide

1   H. P. Clive, *Floridan et Elvide: A Critical Edition of the 15th Century Text with an Introduction* (Oxford: Blackwell, 1959), ll. 53–4.

2   *Les Cent nouvelles Nouvelles*, ed. F. P. Sweetser (Geneva: Droz, 1966), ll. 209–12; author's translation.

3   *Floridan et Elvide*, ll. 57–8, in Yasmina Foehr-Janssens, 'Thisbe travestie: *Floridan et Elvide* ou l'idylle trafiquée', *Cahiers de Recherches Médiévales et Humanistes* 20 (2010), pp. 71–87, online at journals.openedition.org/crmh/12210?lang=it#ftn34

4   ibid., l. 491.

5   ibid., ll. 390–94.

6   ibid., ll. 508–18.

7   ibid., l. 168–9.

16. Lucretia

1   Livy, *Ab urbe condita*, Vol. I: Books 1–2, trans.

B. O. Foster, Loeb Classical Library 114 (Cambridge, MA: Harvard University Press; London: William Heinemann, 1919), 1.59, online at Perseus Digital Library: www.perseus.tufts.edu/hopper/text?doc=Perseus%3Atext%3A1999.02.0151%3Abook%3D1%3Achapter%3D59

2   *Le Roman de la Rose,* Harley MS 4425, f. 79r (author's translation).

3   Shakespeare, *The Rape of Lucrece*, ll. 736–7, online at shakespeare.mit.edu/Poetry/RapeOfLucrece.html

17. Eve, the First Woman

1   Vulgate Latin Bible, Book of Genesis, 2:21–3. English translation from King James version.

2   Bible, Douai-Rheims version, Genesis, 2:8.

3   Bible, Book of Genesis, 3:13,17.

4   Paul Studer, *Le Mystere d'Adam, an Anglo-Norman Drama of the Twelfth Century* (Manchester University Press, 1928), lines 357–58, online at https://archive.org/stream/lemystredadama00stud#page/n25/mode/2up.

5   *Vitae Adae et Evae* 24.2, in Keith Glaeske, 'The Children of Adam and Eve in Medieval Irish Literature', *Ériu* 56 (2006), pp. 1–11, online at https://www.jstor.org/stable/30007049

6   ibid., p. 6, n. 21.

7   *Le Blasme des Femmes,* Harley MS 2253, ff. 111r-v, in *Three Medieval Views of Women,* ed. G. Fieron, W. Pfeffer and M. Allain (London: Yale University Press, 1989), pp. 120–2.

8   *Le Livre de la Cité des Dames*, Harley MS 4431, f. 297r; author's transcription and translation.

18. Nizami's Layla and Shirin

1   James Atkinson, *Lailí and Majnún: A Poem from the Original Persian of Nazámi* (London: Valpy, 1836), p. 4.

2   ibid., p. 7.

3   ibid., p. 120.

4   ibid., p. 55.

5   ibid., p. 58.

6   J. Rypka, *History of Iranian Literature* (Dordrecht: D. Reidel, 1968), p. 211.

7   Gianroberto Scarcia, 'La "sposa bizantina" di Khosrow Parviz', in 'Kosrow o Sirin', *Encyclopedia Iranica*, online at www.iranicaonline.org/articles/kosrow-o-sirin

8   All quotations in this paragraph are from 'Khosrow and Shirin', in *Mirror of the Invisible World: Tales from the 'Khamseh' of Nizami*, trans.

and adapted by Peter Chelkowski (New York: Metropolitan Museum of Art, 1975), pp. 21–48 (p. 45).

9   Chelkowski, 'Commentary' on 'Khosrow and Shirin' (see note 8), p. 47.

19. Guinevere, Queen of Camelot

1   *Welsh Triad 80*, ed. and trans. Rachel Bromwich (Cardiff: University of Wales Press, 1978).

2   H. Oskar Sommer, *The Vulgate Version of the Arthurian Romances*, 8 vols (London: 1909–16), Vol. I, pp. 157–8.

3   R. Pickens, *Lancelot-Grail: The Old French Arthurian Vulgate and Post-Vulgate in Translation* (Brewer, 2010) pp.169–70.

4   ibid., p. 171.

5   *Le chevalier au lion ou Le roman d'Yvain*, ed. David F. Hult, Lettres gothiques (Paris: Librairie général française, 1994), p. 52.

6   Sir Thomas Malory, *Le Morte Darthur*, ed. E. Vinaver (Oxford University Press, 1977), p. 149.; author's translation.

7   William Morris, *The Defence of Guinevere* (London: Longmans, Green & Co., 1908), p. 9, online at www.gutenberg.org/files/22650/22650-h/22650-h.htm

8   Malory, *Le Morte Darthur* (see note 6), Bk XI, ll. 27–38, p. 487; author's translation.

9   *Le Chevalier de la Charrette (Lancelot)*, ed. K. D. Utti (Paris: Bordas, 1989), p. 1427.

10   ibid., pp. 1475–81.

11   Alfred, Lord Tennyson, *Idylls of the King* (London: Henry Frowde, 1904), online at www.telelib.com/authors/T/TennysonAlfred/verse/idyllsking/guinevere.html

20. Helen of Troy

1   Homer, *Iliad*, trans. Richmond Lattimore (London: Routledge, 1957), 3.171, online at The Chicago Homer, homer.library.northwestern.edu/

2   Christopher Marlowe, *The Tragical History of Dr Faustus*, ed. Alexander Dyce, 162, online at www.gutenberg.org/files/779/779-h/779-h.htm

3   Guido delle Colonne, *Historia destructionis Troiae*, ed. N. E. Griffin (Cambridge, MA: Medieval Academy Books, 1936), 7.173–230.

4   Homer, *Iliad*, 3.173–5.

5   Euripides, *The Trojan Women*, ed. E. P. Coleridge (London: George Bell, 1891), ll. 890–4, online at Tufts University, Perseus Digital Library:

www.perseus.tufts.edu/hopper/text?doc=Perseus%3Atext%3A1999.01.0124%3Acard%3D1033

6   ibid., 1040–1.

7   Ovid, *Heroides*, Epistles, trans. Grant Showerman, XVI–XVII, online at www.theoi.com/Text/OvidHeroides4.html

8   Giovanni Boccaccio, *Concerning Famous Women*, trans. Guido A. Guarino (New Brunswick, NJ: Rutgers University Press, 1963)', p. 74.

9   *Lydgate's Troy Book, A.D. 1412–20*, ed. Henry Bergen, 3 vols (Oxford University Press for the Early English Text Society, 1906–10), 2.4231–2.

10   William Shakespeare, *The Rape of Lucrece*, ed. W. G. Clark and W. Aldis Wright, 1471, online at Tufts University, Perseus Digital Library www.perseus.tufts.edu/hopper/text?doc=Perseus%3Atext%3A1999.03.0062%3Asection%3DThe+Rape+of+Lucrece

11   *A Thousand Ships* (BBC Radio Broadcast, 28 January 2002).

12   Natalie Haynes, *Pandora's Jar: Women in the Greek Myths* (London: Picador, 2020), p. 82.

21. Delilah

1   Old Testament, Book of Judges, 16:4.

2   ibid., 16:16.

3   *The Anglo-Norman Bible's Book of Judges, a Critical Edition (BL Royal 1 C III)*, ed. Brent A. Pitts and Huw Grange (Turnhout: Brepols, 2022) p. 54; online at https://munin.uit.no/bitstream/handle/10037/26970/article.pdf?sequence=2

4   Catherine Léglu, *Samson and Delilah in Medieval Insular French: Translation and Adaptation* (Palgrave: Macmillan, 2018), p. 200.

5   ibid., p. 91.

6   ibid., p. 178.

7   John Lydgate, *Fall of Princes*, ed. Henry Bergen, Early English Text Society (Oxford University Press, 1927), lines 6352–6, 6462–3; author's translation.

22. Beatrice

1   Dante Alighieri, *La Vita Nuova*, trans. Andrew Frisardi (Evanston: Northwestern University Press, 2012), 31, online at digitaldante.columbia.edu/text/library/la-vita-nuova-frisardi/

2   Dante Alighieri, *Il Convivio*, Book 2, trans. Richard Lansing (Garland, TX: Garland Library, 1990), Ch. 12, online at digitaldante.columbia.edu/text/library/the-convivio/book-02/

3 Dante Alighieri, *Inferno,* canto 2, trans. Mandelbaum (New York: Columbia University Libraries, 2014), online at: digitaldante.columbia. edu/dante/divine-comedy/inferno/inferno-2/ ('Texts and Translations: Mandelbaum').

4 Dante Alighieri, *Purgatorio,* canto 27, trans. Mandelbaum, online at digitaldante.columbia.edu/ dante/divine-comedy/purgatorio/purgatorio-27/ (see note 3).

5 ibid., canto 30.

6 ibid., canto 33.

7 Pietro Alighieri, Commentary on *Inferno,* 2.70–2, in *The Dante Encyclopedia,* ed. Richard Lansing (Abingdon: Routledge, 2000), p. 91.

8 Teodolinda Barolini, 'Commento Baroliniano', *Purgatorio,* canto 2, online at digitaldante.columbia. edu/dante/divine-comedy/inferno/inferno-2/

23. Princesses Mah Ji and Humayun

1 Deborah Hutton, 'The Pem Nem: A Sixteenth-Century Illustrated Romance from Bijapur', in *Sultans of the South: Arts of India''s Deccan Courts, 1323–1687,* ed. Navina Najat Haidar and Marika Sardar (Metropolitan Museum of Art and Yale University Press, 2011), pp. 44–63 (p. 51).

2 J. C. Bürgel, 'Humāy and Humayūn: A Medieval Persian Romance', in *Proceedings of the First European Conference of Iranian Studies, Turin 1987,* Vol. 2 (Rome, 1990): pp. 347–57 (p. 349).

3 ibid.

4 *Epic Iran: 5000 Years of Culture,* ed. John Curtis, Ina Sandmann and Tim Stanley (London: V&A Publishing, 2021), p. 208.

5 Teresa Fitzherbert, 'Khwājū Kirmānī (689–753/1290–1352): An Éminence Grise of Fourteenth Century Persian Painting', *Iran* 29 (1991), pp. 137–51 (p. 143); translations based on K. Aini's preface to, and edited text of, *The Masnavi Humay u Humayun, Compiled from the Oldest Manuscripts* (Tehran, [1348]).

6 ibid., p. 142.

7 Bürgel, 'Humāy and Humayūn', p. 352 (see note 2).

24. The Fairy Melusine

1 *Melusine par Jehan d'Arras,* ed. C. Brunet (Paris: Jannet, 1854), Ch. 4, online at www. gutenberg.org/files/65457/65457-h/65457-h.htm; author's translation.

2 ibid., Ch. 37.

3 ibid., Ch. 46.

25. Mermaids and Sirens

1 Homer, *Odyssey,* trans. A. T. Murray, 2 vols (Cambridge, MA: Harvard University Press, 1919), XII.39ff, online at Perseus Digital Library, www.perseus.tufts.edu/hopper/ text?doc=Perseus%3Atext%3A1999.01.0136 %3Abook%3D12%3Acard%3D36

2 ibid.

3 Plutarch, *Moralia. Quaestiones Conviviales,* trans. and revised by William G. Goodwin, Book 9, ch. 14.6, online at www.perseus.tufts.edu/hopper/ text?doc=Perseus%3Atext%3A2008.01.0312%3A-book%3D9%3Achapter%3D14%3Asection%3D6

4 Isaiah 13:21–2, Vulgate Latin version; Douai-Reims English Translation.

5 Jerome, 'Commentary on Isaiah', in Jacqueline Leclerq Marx, *La Sirene dans la pensée et dans l'art de l'Antiquité et du Moyen Age* (Brussels: Académie royale de Belgique, 1997), p. 59.

6 Isidore, *Etymologiae,* trans. Stephen A. Barney et al. (Cambridge University Press, 2009), Book XI, Ch. 3.30–31.

7 *Liber monstrorum,* trans. Andy Orchard, online at web.archive.org/web/20050118082548/http:// members.shaw.ca/sylviavolk/Beowulf3.htm

8 Philippe de Thaon, *Bestiaire,* a transcription from Oxford, Merton College Library MS 249, by Sebastian Dows-Miller, online at editions.mml. ox.ac.uk/editions/bestiary/; author's translation.

9 Dante, *Purgatorio* 19.22–3, online at Columbia University Digital Dante, digitaldante.columbia. edu/dante/divine-comedy/purgatorio/purgatorio-19/

10 Boccaccio, *Genealogy of the Pagan Gods,* quoted in Siegfried de Rachewiltz, *De sirenibus: An Inquiry into Sirens from Homer to Shakespeare* (published PhD thesis, Harvard University, 1983), pp. 164–8.

26. Lady Fortune

1 Virgil, *Aeneid,* 8.333–36, in Calypso Nash, '*Fatum/a* and *F/fortuna:* Religion and philosophy in Virgil's *Aeneid',* Paper given to the Virgil Society (2015), revised version online at digitalvirgil.co.uk/ pvs/2017/part7.pdf

2 Pliny the Elder, *The Natural History,* ed. John Bostock (London: Taylor & Francis, 1855), 5.32; online at Perseus Digital Library, www.perseus.

tufts.edu/hopper/text?doc=Perseus%3Atext%
3A1999.02.0137%3Abook%3D2&force=y

3 Martianus Capella, *De nuptiis Philologiae et Mercurii*, ed. F. Eyssenhardt, in Howard Patch, 'The Tradition of the Goddess Fortuna in Roman Literature and in the Transitional Period', *Smith College Studies in Modern Languages* III, no. 3 (1922), pp. 131–77 (see pp. 164–5, n. 16).

4 Dante Alighieri, *Inferno*, canto 7.68, trans. Mandelbaum (New York: Columbia University Libraries, 2014), online at digitaldante.columbia. edu/dante/divine-comedy/inferno/inferno-7/ ('Texts and Translations: Mandelbaum').

5 Giovanni Boccaccio, *De casibus virorum illustrium*, ed. P. G. Ricci and V. Zaccaria (Milan: Mondadori, 1983), 6.1, cited in Francesco Ciabattoni, '"Decameron" 2: Filomena's Rule between Fortune and Human Agency', *Annali d'Italianistica* 13 (2013), pp. 172–96 (see p. 178).

6 ibid., 3.1.

27. The Sibyls

1 Heraclitus, Fragment 39, preserved in Plutarch, *The Pythian Oracle* 397a, in Plutarch, *Moralia*, trans. F. C. Babbitt, Loeb Classical Library (Cambridge, MA: Harvard University Press, 1956) p. 273.

2 H. W. Parke, *Sibyls and Sibylline Prophesy in Classical Antiquity* (London: Routledge, 1988), p. 24.

3 From Varro's list of ten Sibyls, quoted in Lactantius, *Institutiones divinae*, ed. and trans. A Bowen and P. Garnsley (Liverpool: Liverpool University Press, 2003), 70–71:1:6.

4 Augustine of Hippo, *The City of God Against the Pagans*, ed. and trans. R. W. Dyson (Cambridge University Press, 1998), 849: 18.23.

5 Virgil, *Aeneid* (6.47–50), ed. and trans. H. R. Fairclough, revised by G. P. Gould, *Virgil*, Loeb Classical Library 63 (Cambridge, MA: Harvard University Press, 1999), p. 265.

6 Horace, 'Hymn for a New Age', in *Horace Odes and Epodes*, trans. Niall Rudd, Loeb Classical Library (Cambridge, MA: Harvard University Press, 2004), 263: 1–11.

7 Varro, quoted in Lactantius, *Institutiones divinae* (see note 3), 70–71:1:6.

8 Sir Walter Raleigh, *History of the World* (London, 1617), p. 705.

9 Calum Cockburn, 'Jane Segar, an Artist at the Elizabethan Court', British Library Medieval Manuscripts blogpost (10 January 2023), at blogs. bl.uk/digitisedmanuscripts/2023/01/jane-segar.html

28. The Muses and Personifications

1 Hesiod, 'Theogony', in *Homeric Hymns, Epic Cycle, Homerica*, trans. H. G. Evelyn-White, Loeb Classical Library, 57 (London: William Heinemann, 1914), online at https://www.theoi.com/Text/ HesiodTheogony.html

2 Maurus Servius Honoratus, *Commentary on the Aeneid of Vergil*, ed. by Georgius Thilo, 10.163, online at Perseus https://www.perseus.tufts.edu/ hopper/text.jsp?doc=Serv.+A.+6.78&fromdoc=Per- seus%3Atext%3A1999.02.0053

3 Dante, *Purgatorio*, I:7–10, online at Digital Dante, https://digitaldante.columbia.edu/dante/ divine-comedy/purgatorio/purgatorio-1/

4 Ovid, *Metamorphosis*, V, ed. A.S. Kline, online at https://ovid.lib.virginia.edu/trans/Metamorph5. htm#479128838

5 Giovanni Boccaccio, *The corbaccio, or, The labyrinth of love*, trans. A. K. Cassell, Anthony K. (New York: Medieval & Renaissance Texts & Studies, 1993); online at https://www.brown. edu/Departments/Italian_Studies/dweb/texts/ CorShowText.php?myID=C04&lang=it

6 Christine de Pisan, *Le Livre Du Chemin De Long Estude*, ed. Robert Püschel (Geneva: Slatkine reprints, 1974), ll. pp. 995–96.

Further Reading

General

Boccaccio, Giovanni, *De Mulieribus Claris/Les Femmes Illustres;* ed. Vittorio Zaccaria, trans. by Jean-Yves Boriaud (Paris: Les Belles Lettres, 2013).

Boccaccio, Giovanni, *Concerning Famous Women*, trans. with an introduction and notes by Guido A. Guarino (New Brunswick, NJ: Rutgers University Press, 1963).

Boccaccio, Giovanni, *Des Cas des Nobles Hommes et Femmes,* ed. Patricia May Gathercole (North Carolina: Chapel Hill, 1968).

Boccaccio Giovanni, *De casibus virorum illustrium,* ed. P. G. Ricci and V. Zaccaria, (Milan: Mondadori, 1983).

de Pisan, Christine, *Épistre Othea,* ed. Gabriella Parussa (Geneva: Droz, 1999).

de Pisan, Christine, *La Cité des Dames*, trans. Thérèse Moreau and Eric Hicks (Editions Stock, 1986).

Encyclopedia Iranica, ed. Ehsan Yarshater et al. (New York, 1996–), https://www.iranicaonline.org/

Franklin, Margaret, *Boccaccio's Heroines: Power and Virtue in Renaissance Society* (London: Routledge, 2008).

Haynes, Natalie, *Pandora's Jar: Women in the Greek Myths* (London: Picador, 2020).

Lindahl, Carl, *Medieval Folklore* (Oxford: University Press, 2002).

Salisbury, Joyce E., *Encyclopedia of Women in the Ancient World* (California: ABC_CLIO, 2001).

Smith, Susan L. *The Power of Women: a 'Topos' in Medieval Art and Literature'* (Philadelphia: University of Pennsylvania Press, 1995).

'The Shalvi/Hyman Encyclopedia of Jewish Women', online at the Jewish Women's Archive https://jwa.org/encyclopedia

1. The Amazon Women

Haynes, Natalie, 'The Amazons', in *Pandora's Jar: Women in the Greek Myths* (London: Picador, 2020).

Mayor, A., *The Amazons, Lives and Legends of Warrior Women across the Ancient World* (Princeton University Press, 2014).

2. Medea

Colavito, Jason, *Jason and the Argonauts through the ages* (Jefferson, NC: McFarland, 2014).

Graves, Robert, *Greek Myths*, revised edn.,
2 vols (London: Penguin, 1960, repr. 1990), II, pp. 153–157.

Jung, Marc-René, *La Légende de Troie en France au moyen age* (Basel & Tubingen: Francke Verlag, 1996), pp. 40, 565.

Wood, Michael, *In search of Myths and Heroes* (Berkeley: University of California Press, 2005), pp. 78–139.

3. Salome, Daughter of Herod

Jordan, W. C., 'Salome in the Middle Ages' in *Jewish History*, 26 (2012), pp. 5–15.

Neginsky, Rosina, 'Salome: The Image of a Woman Who Never Was' (Newcastle: Cambridge Scholars Publishing, 2013), online at https://www.cambridgescholars.com/resources/pdfs/978-1-4438-4621-9-sample.pdf

4. The Goddess Minerva

Hodapp, William, *The Figure of Minerva in Medieval Literature* (Cambridge: Brewer, 2019).

Wittkower, Rudolf, 'Transformations of Minerva in Renaissance Imagery', *Journal of the Warburg Institute*, 2.3 (1939), pp. 194–205.

5. The Virgin Mary

Rubin, Miri, *A History of the Virgin Mary* (London: Allen Lane, 2009).

Martin, John, *Roses, Fountains and Gold: The Virgin Mary in History, Art and Apparition* (San Francisco: Ignatius Press, 1998).

6. St Margaret of Antioch

Dresvina, Juliana, *A Maid with a Dragon: The Cult of St Margaret of Antioch in Medieval England* (Oxford University Press, 2016).

Wace, *La vie de Sainte Marguerite*, ed. Hans-Erich Keller (Tübingen: Niemeyer, 1990).

7. Hairy Saints and Harlots

Coon, Lynda, *Sacred fictions: holy women and hagiography in late antiquity* (Philadelphia: University of Pennsylvania Press, 1997).

Tracy, Larissa, *Women of the Gilte Legende: A Selection of Middle English Saints* (Cambridge: D. S. Brewer, 2003).

Ward, Benedicta, *Harlots of the Desert, a Study of Repentance in Early Monastic Sources* (Kalamazoo: Cistercian Publications, 1986).

8. St Helena of Constantinople

Coon, Lynda, *Sacred fictions: holy women and hagiography in late antiquity* (Philadelphia: University of Pennsylvania Press, 1997).

Loomis, Laura Hibbard, 'The Athelstan Gift Story: Its Influence on English Chronicles and Carolingian Romances', *PMLA*, 67.4 (1952), pp. 521–537.

9. Mary Magdalene

Haskins, Susan, *Mary Magdalene Myth and Metaphor* (London: Harper Collins, 1993).

Saxer, Victor, *Le Culte de Marie Madeleine en Occident: des origines a al fin du moyen age* (Paris: Librairie Clavreuil, 1959).

10. Cleopatra, Queen of Egypt

Hamer, Mary, *Signs of Cleopatra: history, politics, representation* (New York: Routledge, 1993).

Pomeroy, Sarah B., *Women in Hellenistic Egypt: from Alexander to Cleopatra* (New York: Schocken Books, 1984).

11. Olympias, Empress of Macedon

Carney, Elizabeth, *Olympias, Mother of Alexander the Great* (New York: Routledge, 2009).

Pomeroy, Sarah B., *Women in Hellenistic Egypt: from Alexander to Cleopatra* (New York: Schocken Books, 1984).

12. Venus, Goddess of Love

Bonnefoy, Yves, *Roman and European Mythologies*, trans. Gerald Honigsblum et al. (University Chicago Press, 1992).

Schreiber, Earl G., 'Venus in the Medieval Mythographic Tradition', *The Journal of English and Germanic Philology*, 74. 4 (1975), pp. 519–35.

Stephens, Wade C., 'Cupid and Venus in Ovid's Metamorphoses', *Transactions and Proceedings of the American Philological Association*, 89 (1958), pp. 286–300.

13. The Queen of Sheba

Abbott, Nabia, 'Pre-Islamic Arab Queens', *American Journal of Semitic Languages and Literature*, 58 (1941), pp. 1–22.

Philby, H. St John, *The Queen of Sheba* (London: Quartet Books, 1981).

Pritchard, James B., ed., *Solomon and Sheba* (London: Phaidon, 1974).

Sands, Sarah, *In search of the Queen of Sheba* (London: Austin Macauley Publishers, 2022).

Yūsofī, Ḡolām-Ḥosayn, 'BELQĪS', *Encyclopædia Iranica*, online edition, 2014, at https://www.iranicaonline.org/articles/belqis

14. Candace of Ethiopia

Amin, Haila Manteghi, 'The *Alexander Romance* in the Persian Tradition: Its Influence on Persian History, Epic and Story Telling' (unpublished PhD thesis, University of Exeter, 2016).

de Weever, Jacqueline, 'Candace in the Alexander Romances: Variations on the Portrait Theme, *Romance Philology*, 43.4 (1990), pp. 529–46.

Rubanovich, Julia, 'QAYDĀFA', *Encyclopædia Iranica*, online edition, 2014, http://www.iranicaonline.org/articles/qaydafa

Rubanovich, Julia, 'Re-Writing the Episode of Alexander and Candace in Medieval Persian Literature: Patterns, Sources and Motif Transformation' in *Alexander the Great in the Middle Ages*, ed. Markus Stock, (University of Toronto Press, 2015), pp. 123–152.

15. Elvide

Clive, H. P., *Floridan et Elvide: A Critical Edition of the 15th Century Text with an Introduction* (Oxford: Blackwell, 1959).

Foehr-Janssens, Yasmina, 'Thisbe travestie: *Floridan et Elvide* ou l'idylle trafiquée in *Cahiers de Recherches Médiévales et Humanistes*, 20 (2010), pp. 71–87.

Sweetser, F. P., ed., *Les Cent nouvelles Nouvelles*, (Geneva: Droz, 1966).

16. Lucretia

Franklin, Margaret, *Boccaccio's heroines : power and virtue in Renaissance society* (London: Routledge, 2017).

Glendinning, Eleanor, 'Reinventing Lucretia: Rape, Suicide and Redemption from Classical Antiquity to the Medieval Era', *International Journal of the Classical Tradition*, 20 (2013), pp. 61–82.

17. Eve, the First Woman

Fries, Maureen, 'The Evolution of Eve in Medieval French and English Religious Drama', *Studies in Philology* 99.1 (2002), pp. 1–16.

Murdoch, Brian, *The Apocryphal Adam and Eve in Medieval Europe: Vernacular Translations and Adaptations of the Vita Adae et Evae* (Oxford University Press, 2009).

18. Nizami's Layla and Shirin

Chelkowski, Peter, *Mirror of the Invisible World: Tales from the 'Khamseh' of Nizami*, (New York:

Metropolitan Museum of Art, 1975).

Pinder-Wilson, H., 'Three Illustrated Manuscripts of the Mughal Period', *Ars Orientalis*, Vol. 2 (1957), pp. 413–422.

Talatoff, Kamran, 'Nizami's Unlikely Heroines: A Study of the Characterizations of Women in Classical Persian Literature' in *The Poetry of Nizami Ganjavi: Knowledge, Love, and Rhetoric*, ed. Kamran Talatoff and Jerome Clinton (New York: Palgrave, 2000), pp. 51–81.

Turner, Colin, *Layla and Majnun by Nizami: A prose adaptation* (London: John Blake Publishing, 1997), online at https://sufi.co.za/wp-content/uploads/2021/06/Layla-and-Majnun-The-Classic-Love-Story-of-Persian-Literature.pdf

19. Guinevere, Queen of Camelot

Hopkins, Andrea, *The Book of Guinevere: Legendary Queen of Camelot* (Newark, NJ: Sarabande, 2011).

Lupack, Alan, 'Guinevere' in the Robbins Library Digital Project https://d.lib.rochester.edu/camelot/theme/guinevere

Walters, Lori, *Lancelot and Guinevere: A Casebook* (Oxfordshire: Taylor and Francis, 1996).

20. Helen of Troy

Benoit de Sainte-Maure, *Roman de Troie* (Cambridge: Boydell and Brewer, 2017).

Buchtal, Hugo, *Historia Troiana: studies in the history of medieval secular illustration* (London: Brill, 1971).

'Helen of Troy' in *World History Encyclopedia*, online at https://www.worldhistory.org/Helen_of_Troy/

21. Delilah

Eynikel, M. and Nicklas, Tobias, eds, *Samson Hero or Fool: The many faces of Samson* (Leiden: Brill, 2014).

Léglu, Catherine, *Samson and Delilah in Medieval Insular French: Translation and Adaptation* (London: Palgrave Macmillan, 2018).

22. Beatrice

Alexander, J. J. G., *Italian Renaissance illuminations* (London: Chatto and Windus, 1977).

Digital edition of the Divine Comedy with Mandelbaum Translation, ed. Teodolinda Barolini (Columbian University, 2019), online at https://digitaldante.columbia.edu/

Lansing, Richard, ed., *The Dante Encyclopedia* (London: Routledge, 2010).

Pope-Hennessy, John W., *Paradiso: the illuminations*

to Dante's Divine comedy by Giovanni di Paolo (New York: Random House 1993).

Stuber, Sophie, 'Reading Dante as a feminist', The Stanford Daily blogpost, online at https://stanforddaily.com/2018/06/04/reading-dante-as-a-feminist/

23. Princesses Mah Ji and Humayun

Bürgel, J. C., 'Humāy and Humayūn: a Medieval Persian Romance', in *Proceedings of the First European Conference of Iranian Studies, Turin 1987*, 2 vols (Turin, 1990), II. pp. 347–57.

Fitzherbert, Teresa, 'Khwājū Kirmānī (689-753/1290-1352): An Éminence Grise of Fourteenth Century Persian Painting', *Iran*, 29 (1991), pp. 137–151.

Hutton, Deborah, 'The *Pem Nem*: A Sixteenth-Century Illustrated romance from Bijapur' in *Sultans of the South: Arts of India's Deccan Courts, 1323-1687*, ed. Navina Najat Haidar and Marika Sardar (Metropolitan Museum of Art and Yale University Press, 2011), pp. 44–63. https://www.google.co.uk/books/edition/_/iWNHYID4WqAC?hl=en&gbpv=1&pg=PP1

Matthews, David, 'Pem Nem: A 16th Century Dakani Manuscript' in *From Cairo to Kabul: Afghan and Islamic Studies presented to Ralph Pinder-Wilson*, ed Warwick Ball and Leonard Harrow (London: Melisende, 2002), pp. 170–175.

Sims-Williams, Ursula, 'An illustrated 14th century Khamsah by Khvaju Kirmani' (British Library Asian and African Studies Blog, August 2013).

24. The Fairy Melusine

Baumgartner, Emmanuele, 'Fiction and History: The Cypriot Episode in Jean d'Arras's *Melusine*' in *Melusine of Lusignan, Founding Fiction in Late Medieval France*, ed. Donald Maddox and Sara Sturm-Maddox (Georgia: University of Georgia Press, 1996), pp. 185–200.

Jean d'Arras, *Melusine, or The Noble History of Lusignan*, trans. Donald Maddox and Sara Sturm-Maddox (Philadelphia: Penn State University Press, 2012).

Jenkins, Jeremy, 'The Tale of Melusine' (British Library European Studies Blog, October 2015).

25. Mermaids and Sirens

Dorofeeva, Anna, 'The siren: a medieval identity crisis', *Mittelalter* (2014), online at https://mittelalter.hypotheses.org/3612

Leclercq-Marx, Jacqueline, *La sirène dans la pensée et dans l'art de l'Antiquité et du moyen âge. Du mythe païen au symbole chrétien* (Brussels:

Académie royale de Belgique, 1997).

Urban, M. D. Kemis and Elmes, M.R., eds,
*Melusine's Footprint: Tracing the Legacy of a
Medieval Myth*, ed. by (Leiden: Brill 2017).

26. Lady Fortune

Frakes, Jerold C., *The Fate of Fortune in the Early
Middle Ages* (Leiden: Brill, 1988).

Patch, Howard, 'The Tradition of the Goddess
Fortuna in Roman Literature and in the
Transitional Period' and 'The Tradition of the
Goddess Fortuna in Medieval Philosophy and
Literature', *Smith College Studies in Modern
Languages* III (1921-1922), nos 3 and 4,
pp. 131-235.

27. The Sibyls

Drieshen, Clarck, 'New Prophecies of the Ancient
Sibyls' (British Library Medieval Manuscripts
Blog, December 2020).

Holdenried, Anke, *The Sibyl and her scribes:
manuscripts and interpretation of the Latin Sibylla
Tiburtina c. 1050-1500* (London: Routledge,
2006).

Malay Jessica L., *Prophecy and sibylline imagery in
the Renaissance: Shakespeare's Sibyls* (London:
Routledge, 2010).

McGinn, Bernard, '*Teste David cum Sibylla:* The
significance of the Sibylline Tradition in the
Middle Ages' in *Apocalypticism in the Western
tradition*, ed. Bernard McGinn (Farnham:
Aldershot, 1994), pp. 7-35.

28. The Muses and Personifications

Christian, Kathleen, 'The Multiplicity of the Muses:
The Reception of Antique Images of the Muses
in Italy, 1400-1600' in *Muses and their Afterlife in
Post-Classical Europe* (Conference Proceedings),
ed. C. Wedepohl et al. (London: Warburg
Institute, 2009), pp. 103-54.

Hardman, Phillipa, 'Chaucer's Muses and
His Art Poetical', *The Review of English Studies*,
New Series, 37.148 (1986), pp. 478-94.

Mojsik, Tomasz, 'Ovid, Metamorphoses 5,
254-6,2, and the Terms for the Muses in
Greek and Roman Culture', in *Symbolae
philologorum posnaniensium Graecae et
Latinae*, 33.1 (2023), 2720-2305, at
https://www.academia.edu/95352385/Ovid_
Metamorphoses_5_254_6_2_and_the_terms_
for_the_Muses_in_Greek_and_Roman_culture_
Symbolae_Philologorum_Posnaniensium_
Graecae_et_Latinae_?auto=download

Seznec, Jean, *The survival of the pagan gods:
the mythological tradition and its place in
Renaissance humanism and art* (Princeton
University Press, 1995).

List of Manuscripts

British Library

Other libraries:

Early Printed Books

Index

Page references in italic reflect images on which illustrations appear.

Shan Hai Jing 295–6
Shawqi, Ahmed, *Death of Cleopatra* (1927) 135
Sheba, Queen of *126*, 161–71, *160, 163, 165, 166, 168, 170, 171*
Shirin (Nizami's *Khamsah*) 7, 12, *184*, 219–24, *220, 221, 222, 223, 225*
Sibylline Oracles 316
Sibyls, the 171, *314*, 315–23, *317, 318, 319, 321, 322*
Siddal, Elizabeth 267
Silvestris, Bernardus 59, 153
Simeon manuscript, the 103, *103*
Simocatta, Theophylact 219
sin/sinners 96, 103, 118, 120, 204, 300, *301*, 312
sirens 295, *296*, 297–302, *297, 299, 301*, 304–5, *304*
Smithfield Decretals, the *77*, 78, *95, 97, 189*, 253, *253, 294*
snakes 10, 134, *135*, 140, 141, 298–9
Sol 151; *see also* Helios
Solomon, King *126*, 162, 163, *163*, 164–7, *165, 166*, 168, *168*, 169–70, *170*, 171, *171*
Sophronius 94, 96
Sparta 242
Speculum humanae salvationis 8, *166, 208*
spinning *19*, 53, *82*, 207, *208*
Stesichorus 246
Strabo 25, 175
Stratonice *see* Olympias, Empress of Macedon
Sudan *see* Kush, Kingdom of
Sufi literature 269, 271; *see also* Khalji, Hasan Manjhu, *Pem Nem*
suicide 134, *135*, 188, 191, 192, *194*, 195, 196, *197*, 198, *199*, 224, *225*, 296
supernatural beings/powers 82, 285–6, 289, 292; *see also* magic/magical powers
Surat al-Naml 164
Surat Saba 164

Talbot Shrewsbury Book: *Roman d'Alexandre en prose* 29, *140, 147, 174*
Tarquinius Priscus, King of Rome 320
Tarquinius Superbus ('Tarquin the Proud') *194*, 195, 196
Temperance (Virtue) 331
Tennyson, Alfred Lord 230, 239
Terpsichore (Muse) *327*, 328
Thais of Egypt (saint) 96–8, *97, 98*
Thalestris 27, *31*
Thalia (Muse) *327*, 328
Theotimus 84, 85, *86*

Theseus 242
Tiburtine Sibyl 316, 320–3, *322*
Titans 54, 325
Titus Livius *see* Livy
Tomyris, Queen of Scythia 61
transvestism *see* cross-dressing
Trier Cathedral 111
Tristan and Isolde 154
'Triumph of an Academic' *60*
Trojan Wars 8, 36, 56, 157, 242, 245–8, 317
Troy 26, 42, 53, 57, *240*, 241, 245, *245*, 248; *see also* Trojan Wars
True Cross, the 105, *105, 106, 107*, 108–11, *109*
Tyche 307–8

Udri 213
Ulysses *see* Odysseus
Urania (Muse) *327*, 328
Urdu language 274
Urien 288, 289–90, *289*

Valerius Maximus, *Facta et dicta memorabilia* *194*, 196, *306*
Valour/Lady Vaillance (allegorical figure) 333, *333*
Varro, Marcus Terentius 316, 317, 320
Veneto, Paolino, *Abbreviamen de las Estorias* 137
Venice *54, 60*
Venjance Alixandre 182
Venus (planet) 159, *159*
Venus 59, *148*, 149–59, *151, 152, 156, 158, 159, 243*, 330; *see also* Aphrodite
Vertu/Lady Virtue (allegorical figure) *282*, 313
Vézelay, abbey of 124
Vidin Miscellany 98
violence 9–10, 14, 29–30, 37–41, 43; *see also* murder
Virgil 133, 308
  Aeneid 155–7, 319, *319*
  in Dante's *Divinia Commedia* 263–4, *264*, 265, 304, *304, 310*, 310–12
Virgin Mary, the 10, 61, 65–78, *67, 68, 69*, 71, *72, 75, 76, 77*, 88, 108, *116*, 122, 211
  and the Annunciation 8, *64*, 66
  and birth of Christ 66–8, *66, 314*, 315, 317, 320–1, *322*
  Madonna and Child, representations of 72–4, *73, 88*
  Pietà, the 74–6, *74*
virginity 61, 78, 87, 191, 198, 318
virtue 15, 56, 59, 61, 72, 78
Virtues, the *282*, 331–3, *332*

Vitae Adae et Evae 205, 207
Vulcan 54, 58, 151–3, *151*, 157

Wace, *Vie de sainte Marguerite* 87
wantonness 96, 103, 120, 300
warfare 53, 57; *see also* Trojan War
water spirits 295–6; *see also* mermaids; sirens
Wauchier de Denain, *La Vie des Saints* 100
Wavrin, Jean de, *Anciennes et nouvelles chroniques de la Grant Bretaigne* 111–13, *112*
weaving 53, *55*, 56, 59
weddings 272–3, *273, 275*, 287, 288
wheel of fortune *306*, 307, *308, 312*
Wilde, Oscar, *Salome* 51
wisdom 53, 57, 59, *60*, 61, 171
Wisdom (allegorical figure) 333
witchcraft 34; *see also* magic/magical powers

Xantippe 14

Yetshak, *Kebra Negast* 167

Zena Eskender 175–6
Zeus 39, 54, 141, 142, 241, 242, 246
  children of *see* Helen of Troy
  see also Jupiter
Zeus Ammon 180
Zosima (saint) *92*, 94–6, *95*